GCSE Music
Study Guide

Paul Terry

Rhinegold Education

239–241 Shaftesbury Avenue
London WC2H 8TF
Telephone: 020 7333 1720
Fax: 020 7333 1765

www.rhinegold.co.uk

Music Study Guides

GCSE, AS and A2 Music Study Guides (AQA, Edexcel and OCR)
GCSE, AS and A2 Music Listening Tests (AQA, Edexcel and OCR)
GCSE Music Study Guide (WJEC)
GCSE Music Listening Tests (WJEC)
AS/A2 Music Technology Study Guide (Edexcel)
AS/A2 Music Technology Listening Tests (Edexcel)
Revision Guides for GCSE (AQA, Edexcel and OCR), AS and A2 Music (AQA and Edexcel)

Also available from Rhinegold Education

Key Stage 3 Elements
Key Stage 3 Listening Tests: Book 1 and Book 2
AS and A2 Music Harmony Workbooks
GCSE and AS Music Composition Workbooks
GCSE and AS Music Literacy Workbooks
Romanticism in Focus, Baroque Music in Focus, Film Music in Focus, Modernism in Focus,
The Immaculate Collection in Focus, *Who's Next* in Focus, *Batman* in Focus, *Goldfinger* in Focus,
Musicals in Focus

Rhinegold also publishes Choir & Organ, Classical Music, Classroom Music, Early Music Today,
International Piano, Music Teacher, Opera Now, Piano, The Singer, Teaching Drama,
British and International Music Yearbook, British Performing Arts Yearbook, British Music Education Yearbook,
Rhinegold Dictionary of Music in Sound

Other Rhinegold Study Guides

Rhinegold publishes resources for candidates studying Drama and Theatre Studies.

First published 2009 in Great Britain by
Rhinegold Publishing Limited
239–241 Shaftesbury Avenue
London WC2H 8TF
Telephone: 020 7333 1720
Fax: 020 7333 1765
www.rhinegold.co.uk

You should always check the current requirements of the examination, since these may change.
Copies of the Edexcel specification can be downloaded from the Edexcel website at www.edexcel.com.
Edexcel Publications telephone: 01623 467467, fax: 01623 450481, email: publications@linneydirect.com.

Edexcel GCSE Music Study Guide
British Library Cataloguing in Publication Data.
A catalogue record for this book is available from the British Library.
ISBN 978-1-906178-78-9
Printed in Great Britain by Headley Brothers Ltd.

CONTENTS

THE AUTHOR

Paul Terry has taught from primary to postgraduate level, including 15 years spent as director of music at the City of London Freemen's School. He was an examiner for ABRSM for nearly 30 years, and has been chief examiner in music for both OCSEB (now part of OCR) and Edexcel (for whom he pioneered the introduction of Music Technology as an A-level subject). He has also served as a member of the Secondary Examinations Council and its successor the Schools Examinations and Assessment Council, and has been employed as a music consultant for several examining boards.

Paul's many publications include *Musicals in Focus* and a number of music study guides for Rhinegold Publishing, three books on A-level music aural published by Schott, books on music technology and group music-making for Musonix Publishing, and various articles on music education for *Music Teacher*, *Classroom Music* and other periodicals.

ACKNOWLEDGEMENTS

The author would like to thank Nicola Eatherington and Dr Julia Winterson for their invaluable help in the preparation of this book, as well as Harriet Power, Katherine Smith, Clare Stevens, Lucien Jenkins, Jason Mitchell and Silvia Schreiber of the Rhinegold editorial and design team.

Rhinegold Publishing is grateful to the following for permission to use printed excerpts from their publications:

Electric Counterpoint by Steve Reich © Copyright 1989 by Hendon Music, Inc., a Boosey & Hawkes company.

King Jesus Will Roll All Burdens Away. Words and music by Kenneth Morris © 1947 Unichappell Music Inc. Carlin Music Corp. Reproduced by permission of Faber Music Ltd. All Rights Reserved.

Skye Waulking Song. Translation taken from *Edexcel GCSE Anthology of Music* (ISBN 978-1-846904-05-9) published by Pearson Education Limited. © Copyright 2009 Hinrichsen Edition, Peters Edition Limited, London. Reproduced by permission.

'Something's Coming' from *West Side Story* © Copyright 1956, 1957, 1958, 1959 by Amberson Holdings LLC and Stephen Sondheim. Copyright renewed. Leonard Bernstein Music Publishing Company LLC, Publisher. International copyright secured.

Why Does my Heart Feel so Bad? by Richard Hall (Moby) © 1999 Warner-Tamerlane Publishing Corp. (BMI) & the Little Idiot Music (BMI). All rights on behalf of the Little Idiot Music (BMI). Administered by Warner-Tamerlane Publishing Corp. (BMI). All rights reserved.

Yiri. Arrangement taken from *Edexcel GCSE Anthology of Music* (ISBN 978-1-846904-05-9) published by Pearson Education Limited. © Copyright 2009 Hinrichsen Edition, Peters Edition Limited, London. Reproduced by permission.

Yiri, composed by Madou Knone. Produced and published by Editions Sunset-France (1992).

Cover photograph of Anoushka Shankar © Frank Micelotta/Getty Images.

Photos licensed under http://creativecommons.org/licenses/by-sa/3.0/: Schoenberg's grave © Daderot; Hungarian National Theatre © Újfalusi Németh Jenö; Snare drum © Viames Marino; Balafon © Redmedea. Photos licensed under http://creativecommons.org/licenses/by-sa/2.5/: Capercaillie © Richard Bartz; Bouzouki © Arent; Talking drum © ϽΊ. Photo licensed under http://creativecommons.org/licenses/by-sa/2.0/: Miles Davis © Tom Palumbo.

This book has been written to support your work for Edexcel GCSE music and includes many tips on how to do well in the exam. The first two chapters offer advice on performing and composing, after which we look at how to study the set works for the written paper. The final chapter gives advice on how to answer the extended questions in the written paper, and also acts as a reference section that explains various points about melody, harmony and other matters – dip into it whenever you need.

Edexcel is the organisation that decides what you have to do in each part of this exam. It supervises marking, and awards grades and certificates. The details of the exam are printed in a long document called the specification, which can be downloaded from their website at www.edexcel.com.

Important technical terms are printed in **blue type**. Some are explained in a small box next to their appearance in the main text, and all are in the glossary on page 178. Make sure that you understand exactly what each of these means as they are likely to appear in exam questions. To get a good grade in the written paper, you also need to show that you can correctly use musical terms in your answers.

We hope that you will find this book enjoyable and useful, but remember that the entire exam is about your understanding of *music*. Words can provide explanations, but your best resource is your ears. Always focus in detail on the *sound* of the music you perform, compose and listen to.

Books can only offer general guidance. If there's something you find puzzling, don't give up and leave it – ask your teacher, who will be impressed that you care enough to ask for help.

COURSE OUTLINE

Your music GCSE consists of three units:

Unit 1: Performing music	One solo performance and one ensemble performance	30% of the total mark
Unit 2: Composing music	Two compositions, or two arrangements, or one composition and one arrangement	30% of the total mark
Unit 3: Music – listening and appraising	A 1½ hour written paper on the set works that you will study during the course	40% of the total mark

Although the subject is divided into three units for the exam, the skills involved (performing, composing, listening and appraising) are closely related and they all form an essential part of a musician's training. Your work for Unit 2 has to be related to the music you have studied for Unit 3. You can, if you wish, perform your own compositions for Unit 1, and what you learn in Unit 3 will help you improve your skills in performing and composing of all kinds. It is therefore likely that you will work on all three units in parallel throughout most of the course.

Your performances and compositions can be completed at any time before the final deadline, which is likely to be by the end of April in the year in which you submit your work for assessment. However, it is very unwise to leave completing these tasks until that late in the course. If you should have an accident which prevents you performing, or you are ill, or you lose vital parts of your coursework – or even if you find you are not as ready as you'd have hoped – there will be little time to put things right.

In any case, by the start of the summer term you are likely to be revising hard for Unit 3, and for all your other GCSE subjects, so any last-minute problems over music coursework could be the final straw! This brings us to our first (and most important) tip:

Top Tips

With your teacher, plan a coursework timetable for performing and composing that gives you several spare weeks to repeat work if anything should go wrong. Then be sure to keep to that timetable.

We all find it easy to start with good intentions, but it becomes hard to stick to our plans as work builds up. It really is up to you to show your maturity by keeping to a scheme that will spread your workload and maximise your results. Remember that a sensible plan can include some 'self time' for relaxation and a little partying. No plan will mean no fun if it turns out that you spend the final weeks leading up to your deadlines panicking about what you haven't done! Keep up to date with your work and you will deserve to do well. Good luck with your studies!

An **ensemble** (pronounced *on-som-b'l*) is a group of performers.

For this unit you have to give two performances – one as a soloist and the other as a member of an **ensemble**. You can sing, play an instrument, or create a performance using music technology. The performances will be recorded and marked by your teacher, who will then send samples of the marked work to Edexcel for checking.

You have a totally free choice in the music you perform, although we shall see later how a sensible choice of pieces can help to maximise your marks.

The recordings can be made at any time during the course. Your teacher will decide on suitable dates, which are likely to be well before the main examination period begins. Remember that whatever date is chosen, it needs to be early enough to allow time for you to have another go if things don't go to plan on the day. This is especially important for ensemble performances, which might have to be postponed if any members of your group are absent for final rehearsals or for the recording.

You must choose any one of the options in the left-hand column for solo performing, and any one of those in the right-hand column for ensemble performing (we'll look at what each option means in the next section):

Solo performing	Ensemble performing
■ Traditional solo performance ■ Solo improvisation ■ Sequenced performance ■ Realisation	■ Traditional ensemble performance ■ Ensemble improvisation ■ Multi-track recording ■ Rehearsing and directing

SOLO PERFORMING OPTIONS

Traditional solo performance

This is the type of performance that you might give in a concert, in which you present a solo (with or without accompaniment) that you have learned. The music can be in any style – the word traditional does not imply that it has to be a classical piece.

If two or more musicians perform the same notes for any length of time, we say that their parts are **doubled**.

If you choose music designed to have an accompaniment, you should rehearse and record it with an accompanist or a backing track. Although your own part may occasionally be **doubled** by the accompaniment, it is essential that you are not doubled throughout most of the piece. For example, a song in which most of the vocal line is also played on the piano should be avoided. Similarly, you must not perform to a backing track that includes your own part – which means that singing along with the soloist on your favourite CD is not allowed.

If you play an instrument that does not normally perform solo, such as drum kit or bass guitar, you can choose to be accompanied by a small group. However, you must take a lead in the performance and you should try to include sections in which you have a clearly defined solo role.

Solo improvisation

In an improvisation, much of the music is created on the spot, as the performance takes place, rather than being fully prepared in advance – although there is almost always some degree of pre-planning. This option might suit those who enjoy playing jazz or who perform music in which improvisation plays an important role (such as Indian classical music, African drumming or traditional Irish flute music).

If you choose this option, you will start from some basic material that Edexcel call a stimulus. This could be a chord pattern, rhythm, melody, an Indian **rag**, or perhaps a picture or a poem to suggest creative ideas. This stimulus can be provided by you or by anyone else.

Sequenced performance

If you are keen on music technology, this could be the option for you. Instead of performing live, you have to prepare a MIDI sequence of a piece of music that consists of at least three simultaneous and independent parts (such as melody, bass and at least one other part). You have to input all the parts yourself, and the sequence needs to be musically shaped as well as being accurate, so skill in detailed note-editing will be needed.

If you want to sequence your own composition, or if you want to include loops or audio **samples** that you haven't produced yourself, your work will be treated as a realisation (as explained in the next section).

Realisation

This option includes performances that don't fall into any of the first three categories, such as:

- A sequence of your own composition, or a sequence that includes loops or samples that you haven't produced yourself
- A live performance of your own composition for which there is no detailed score
- A creative DJ-style performance (using decks)
- A sound diffusion (a performance based on pre-recorded sounds that were produced either live or electronically).

ENSEMBLE PERFORMING OPTIONS

The choice you make for ensemble performance doesn't have to relate to your solo option. For example, you could choose traditional solo performance for your solo, and multi-track recording for your ensemble option. Or, if you play two instruments, you could choose to perform on one for the solo and on the other for the ensemble. However …

Traditional ensemble performance

The minimum size of an ensemble is two people – yourself and one other. However, if the piece is simply an accompanied solo, it cannot be counted as an ensemble by the soloist (although it can be by the accompanist), so in most cases an ensemble will need to consist of at least three people.

The parts in an ensemble must be independent, with little or no doubling. This means that you cannot count singing the same part as other people in a choir, or playing as one of several first clarinettists in a wind band, as an ensemble performance. Your teacher, and the Edexcel moderator, must be able to hear your own individual contribution.

Most people find that it is best to form an ensemble from members of their GCSE group, as this makes it much easier to arrange rehearsals. However, the ensemble could include other students, teachers or family members – it could even be a group that you belong to outside your school or college. But remember that your teacher has to be present when the piece is performed and recorded.

Ensemble improvisation

This is similar to the improvisation option for solo performing, except that you would be improvising as part of a group, such as a small jazz band or rock group.

Multi-track recording

This is another option for those keen on music technology. You will be expected to direct a complete recording session of a piece containing at least three independent parts, from setting up the microphones and other equipment to producing a final stereo mix. You can perform some or all of the parts yourself, or you can record other people. You can include sequenced tracks, providing you have produced them yourself, but at least one of the tracks must be recorded live, using a microphone.

Rehearsing and directing

For this option you are expected to rehearse and direct a group of three or more musicians. You are not allowed to be one of the performers – you are expected to take the role of a coach or, if the group is quite large, a conductor. If you choose this option, the performance and part of a rehearsal will be video recorded for the assessment.

PREPARING FOR PERFORMANCE

Much of the following information applies mainly to those who play an instrument or sing for Unit 1. If you are taking one or both of the music technology options, turn to page 16.

It is likely that you will spend the first part of the course improving your general performing skills, before deciding on the pieces you will present for Unit 1 and then working on those in detail.

You probably already enjoy playing or singing music, but have you ever given a performance? Just learning to get the notes right is only the first step towards performing. You then need to bring the notes to life, and convince your listeners of your own passion for the piece you are presenting.

Many students enjoy performing, but some find that it makes them very nervous. This is often because the piece is really too difficult. If you are constantly worrying about getting the notes right, the listeners will sense your anxiety and will feel uncomfortable. It would be much better to choose something easier, which allows you to concentrate on communicating the music to others.

A few nerves are natural for all performers, but if you get very worried try to find opportunities to perform to others whenever you can – to your relatives at home, or to other members of your GCSE group. Start with simple pieces that you know well. As your confidence increases you will become more relaxed and your playing or singing will improve as a result.

CHOOSING THE MUSIC

Finding the right pieces to present for Unit 1 will help you get the best possible mark. A piece that you really enjoy playing can be a good choice, but there are several other important considerations.

How long should it be?

Each performance should last no more than five minutes. There is no minimum length, but the piece should be long enough for you to show a range of musical skills. That means that it should contain some variety, rather than consisting of the same basic patterns all the way through. For example, music that contains contrasts between loud and soft sections, or between smooth melodies and passages of nimble fingerwork, could work well as a showcase for your talents. If it is difficult to find a single piece with enough variety, you could perform two contrasting pieces providing the total time does not exceed five minutes (this option could be particularly useful for singers).

© educationphotos.co.uk

How difficult should it be?

The most important thing about Unit 1 is how musically you can perform, not how difficult the music is. The Edexcel specification gives indications of three difficulty levels for singers and for various instruments (Easier, Standard and More Difficult). Your teacher will use this guidance to work out the level of the music you choose.

Performing a piece at the More Difficult level can add up to four extra marks (from a total of 30) to the mark you get for each performance. However, if you choose a piece which is really too hard for you, all your attention will be spent on getting the notes right rather than on communicating the spirit of the music – and you risk a low mark if the performance hesitates or breaks down under the stress of formal assessment.

A piece at the Easier level will get a lower mark than a Standard level piece, but again the difference is not large (except at the top end of the mark range, where the maximum possible will be 23 out of 30). Here, too, it is worth remembering that a fluent and musical performance at the Easier level is likely to get a better mark than an attempt at a Standard level piece that is spoiled by hesitations.

Top Tips

You are more likely to get a high mark for a musical performance of a simple piece, than a bad performance of a more difficult piece.

PRACTISING FOR SOLO PERFORMING

The term **dynamics** refers to the varying levels of loudness or softness in the music.

Start by finding out how your chosen music should be performed – the speed, the **dynamics**, the expression and the style. For example, your listeners would not expect to hear a classical song performed like folk music, any more than they would want to hear a heavy rock number played like a piece for classical guitar. Look for clues in the title and the performing directions. If the piece is a gavotte (an 18th-century dance), you will need to make your performance dance. If it has a title such as *Five Finger Blues* it will need to sound like a blues, not like a piece by Bach.

Practise … and practise … and practise. There is no short cut to hard work, but you can make the job easier in several ways:

■ Concentrate on the more difficult sections. It is very tempting to practise the bits you already know, because they give instant satisfaction. But you need to bring the more tricky passages up to the same standard, so work on those instead. Aim to feel totally in control of the music, from beginning to end.
■ Be self-critical. Never practise mechanically – listen carefully to the sound you are making, and think about how it could be improved. Record yourself

and then listen carefully to the results – compare them with a professional recording of the piece if you can.

■ Concentrate on the images you want to convey in your performing, such as rhythmic energy, a dreamy atmosphere, elegant phrasing, dramatic contrasts or subtle blends. Focus on such detail throughout the music. Rather than thinking of a passage as merely 'happy', decide if you mean boisterous, contented, cheeky or just cheerful. If it is 'sad', do you mean tragic, doom-laden, nostalgic, angry or solemn? Don't be content with merely getting the notes right – always think about what the notes are saying.

Sit quietly, without your instrument (or without singing) and imagine yourself giving a perfect performance of the piece. Can you remember it all, rather like remembering a familiar route to school? If not, the parts that are hazy are the parts to work on when practising. How did the perfect performance differ from your own? Again, the answer will direct you to the passages that need more work.

© educationphotos.co.uk

Once you are fully in control of the technical demands of the music, concentrate on effective contrasts between loud and soft, between smooth and detached notes, or whatever other contrasts the piece demands. You will almost certainly have to exaggerate these in performance much more than you might expect if they are to make an impact on your listeners. Look for every opportunity to introduce contrasting areas of light and shade in the work to make your performance as interesting as possible, not only between sections but even between individual notes wherever appropriate.

Remember that your teacher cannot practise for you, but he or she will be able to give you good advice about the style and effectiveness of your performance, as well as on more technical matters such as fingering.

Unless you play a fixed-pitch instrument, such as the piano or electric keyboard, work hard on intonation (the precise pitch of each individual note), as this will be an important factor in securing a good mark.

Practise performing the entire piece to your friends and family. If you become flustered and have to stop and start again, it will not matter for now but you will at least know the places that need extra practice. Regular performance opportunities in class will give you valuable experience in coping with the stresses and strains of the final assessment, when the time comes.

One of the most important aspects of a performance is continuity – in other words, you need to keep going! This can be a real difficulty for less experienced musicians. The natural reaction after making a mistake is to stop and try the notes again – some people even find that they can't continue and have to go back to the start and have another run at the passage concerned (which then often goes wrong again, because anxiety starts to mount).

Hesitations and breakdowns can have a very bad effect on marks, so it's important to work on keeping going despite slips. When practising, try starting the piece from various different places rather than always from the beginning. Eventually you will find that your fluency improves. Remember …

Top Tips
You can get full marks even if you make a few tiny slips, providing they are well hidden. If making a slip causes you to hesitate, or to stop and start again, you are likely to lose marks.

REHEARSING FOR ENSEMBLE PERFORMING

Most of the previous section also applies to preparing an ensemble performance, but you may already have spotted that we used the word 'rehearsing' in the title for this section, not 'practising'. There is an important difference. Practising is what each member of an ensemble needs to do first, in order to learn their own part. Rehearsing is what happens when the group meets to put together their individual parts.

Rehearsals will be very frustrating if some members of the ensemble have not yet learned their parts – the others may well regard it as a boring waste of time if they have to wait while one person struggles through the notes.

Rehearsals therefore need much more organisation than individual practice sessions. If the group is using sheet music, parts need to be made available to learn well before the first rehearsal, and the members need to be aware of their responsibility to each other, by remembering to bring their music and instruments to the correct place at the right time.

In addition to all of the points about solo performing, intonation is especially important in instrumental ensemble playing. In the early stages it is well worth spending a *lot* of time tuning up accurately – check the pitch of several different notes, across the ranges of the instruments concerned.

You will also need to reach an agreement on how the music is to be shaped, concentrating particularly on getting a good balance between the instruments and/or voices concerned.

It is almost inevitable that some planned rehearsals will prove impossible because key players are absent, or have forgotten their instrument, or because a room is not available, or there is a fire drill or school trip. It is well worth planning at least twice the number of rehearsals you think you need in order to overcome such problems.

Top Tips
Ensemble performing is a co-operative venture that needs a lot of commitment from everyone involved. Be prepared for it to take much more time to prepare than solo performing.

THE PERFORMANCE

Your teacher is required to supervise your preparation for Unit 1 regularly, but the amount of time you spend on practising and rehearsing is largely up to you – the more you do, the better your mark is likely to be.

However, the recording of your performances has to be done under controlled conditions. You have up to 10 hours, supervised by your teacher, in which to complete each recording. This should be ample, although getting the ensemble together at the right time may take longer than you expect.

Try to arrive fully prepared for the performance – discovering at the last minute that you have a broken string or reed, or that you have forgotten your music or some piece of essential equipment, can be an unsettling experience that may make you nervous at the very time when you need to be as calm as possible.

Just as an athlete needs to warm up to give their best, so does a musician. Spend a few minutes playing something familiar before your turn to perform, so that you don't have to start up from cold.

If you need to tune to the piano, or to other members of an ensemble, take as much time as you need – don't rush the process. Remember the advice on the previous pages about vivid contrasts, and aim for a real sense of style and mood in your performing. Also be aware of the following important points:

- You can only receive marks for how you perform on the day
- A good posture helps singers and all instrumentalists to perform at their best
- Even, relaxed breathing helps to calm nerves and also helps to secure a good performance
- Contrasts in the music need to be made really clear
- Expect to be a little nervous and remember that mistakes will probably occur – it's not the mistake that matters so much as how you react to it. Don't stop or hesitate – forget about it and concentrate on what happens next.

Everything comes down to preparation. If you are well prepared, the experience will be fun (or at least painless!) – if you skimped on the practice, the performance will be a worry, and the anxiety will almost certainly lead to an escalating number of mistakes.

Expect to be a little nervous but remember that the more experience you can get of performing to others during the course, the more natural and enjoyable it will become. Blind panic will only normally set in if the music is under-rehearsed or too difficult and this, as we have explained, can be avoided by selecting suitable music and preparing it thoroughly.

HOW IS PERFORMING MARKED?

Each performance is marked out of 30, divided into two categories:

12 marks for accuracy

This includes accuracy of intonation and the fluency of your performance, as well as correct notes. A few tiny slips may not affect the mark providing they are hardly noticeable. If you make a number of mistakes or hesitations, it will be difficult to obtain half of the 12 available marks, even if you manage easier passages well.

In the case of improvisation, marks in this category are awarded for how well you use the stimulus, as well as for fluency and intonation.

18 marks for interpretation

These marks are awarded for the sense of style and conviction in your performance, including effective contrasts and phrasing. A really convincing performance that makes the listener want to hear more should gain full marks. Providing there is *some* shaping of the piece and awareness of style, you are likely to receive half of the available marks, but if there is little beyond the basic notes in much of the performance, you are likely to receive less than seven of the 18 available marks.

In the case of ensemble performance, marks in this category also include your skill in ensemble playing. An ability to react to the other musicians in the group, and to adjust your own performance accordingly, helps to achieve a maximum mark. If you show little awareness of the sounds around you, a low mark must be expected.

The full mark scheme, including specific detail for each option, is printed in the Edexcel specification. We will look at how the music technology options are marked at the end of this chapter.

The specification can be downloaded from the Edexcel website: www.edexcel.com.

AFTER THE RECORDING

For each performance, your teacher will need one of the following items to send to the Edexcel moderator, along with your recording:

- For traditional performances and sequences: a score of the piece that you performed or, if there is no score, a professional recording of the work
- For improvisations: a copy of the stimulus used

■ For realisations: your own detailed written commentary, showing what you intended to achieve and how you went about creating the work, and listing any source material (such as sound samples or tracks by other people) that you have included.

Scores need to contain detailed pitch and rhythm information. Guitar tab is acceptable, providing it includes rhythm information, but lyric sheets or vague descriptions are not allowed. If you submit a description, it has to contain enough detail for the accuracy of the performance to be assessed.

If your performance deliberately differs from the score or recording, you or your teacher needs to add a note to explain how and why.

Top Tips

This requirement is very important. The Edexcel specification makes it clear that performances which 'are not accompanied by acceptable scores or recordings will not be assessed'.

You will also have to sign an authentication statement to confirm that the performances are your own work.

THE MUSIC TECHNOLOGY OPTIONS

If you choose sequencing for solo performance and/or multi-track recording for ensemble performance, you are likely to spend the first part of the course becoming familiar with the equipment you will use, and working short exercises.

SEQUENCED PERFORMANCE

Choosing the right piece for your exam submission is just as important for this option as for any other. Music for sequencing must contain at least three independent, simultaneous parts. Music with clear rhythmic patterns, especially moderately fast dance music, often sequences well. If you choose contemporary dance, make sure the piece is not too repetitive, otherwise it will be difficult to show a range of sequencing skills. Older dance music, including 18th-century dances and ballet music, can often be a good choice. Slow, expressive pieces, and music intended for voices, are best avoided as they can often be difficult to sequence convincingly. As in traditional performing, look for music that contains some clear contrasts in dynamics and **articulation**.

Your sequence will be marked along similar lines to other performances, so your task is not only to input the notes correctly, but also to shape them musically by taking great care over the dynamics and articulation. If you are a skilled keyboard player, you may be able to do much of this shaping as you input the notes in real time. However, if you need to input the music at a slow pace, or to use step-time input (such as playing

Articulation refers to the precise way in which notes are performed. A passage articulated smoothly, with no gaps between the notes, will sound different to the same music played in a detached way, with tiny gaps between each note.

the notes in individually or selecting them with a mouse), you will need to spend much time editing the results so they sound musical and not mechanical.

Remember that you will need to assign appropriate voices and to **pan** them in the stereo sound field (left, right and centre being the obvious choice if there are three parts in your music). For many types of music, especially fast-moving pieces, sounds that speak promptly (such as oboe or pick bass) tend to produce better results than sustained, atmospheric sounds with names such as 'angels' or 'windbells'. Unless the style of the music suggests that panning should change during the course of the piece (as in some modern dance music), the panning should be set at the start of the piece and then not changed – otherwise it will sound as if your synthesised musicians are wandering around as they play!

Sequences are assessed in a similar way to other performances, with a mark out of 12 for accuracy and a mark out of 18 for interpretation. The latter includes appropriate articulation and well-shaped phrasing, dynamics, **timbre** (the sounds you select) and an effective use of panning.

Take particular care over the stereo recording of your final sequence. Mains hum or distortion can easily spoil an otherwise good piece of work, so use your ears critically when checking the results, and re-make the recording if you are not satisfied.

MULTI-TRACK RECORDING

For this option, you can either act purely as the engineer, recording a performance by a group of your friends, or you can also perform one or more of the tracks yourself. Remember that you can include sequenced tracks, providing that you have input the sequence yourself and that at least one of the other tracks is performed live and recorded using a microphone.

If you are recording other people, the choice of music will depend on what they can reasonably manage. It is important not to be over-ambitious – even with the best will in the world, your friends may not have a lot of time to help with your own coursework, especially as group performances usually need a number of rehearsals. If much of the recording time has to be spent getting the notes right, you may have little opportunity to concentrate on producing a good recording. However, whatever music is chosen, it is again important to find something that has plenty of variety, particularly contrasts in dynamics for this option.

Learning techniques of recording is like learning to play an instrument. Practice is vital in order to become familiar with the equipment and to understand its potential. When it comes to the actual recording session, remember that you will need to be there before the performers, to ensure that everything is set up for them, with microphones in the correct positions, and with seats, music stands and good lighting for the musicians. You may need to study special techniques for microphone placement when recording singers and instruments such as drum kits and pianos. For some types of music, microphones need to be placed very close to the instruments concerned, but not in a position where they could be knocked by the performers.

The acoustics of the room in which you record are also important. Some classrooms are so reverberant that echoes obscure the clarity of the sound – you may need to discuss with your teacher whether curtains plus a carpet on the floor might be possible to reduce problems of this sort. Even more difficult in schools are unwanted sounds from adjacent rooms, from outside or even from bells or radiators in the room itself. Again, discuss with your teacher how these can be minimised.

Depending on the type of music you may need to use various electronic effects. You will almost certainly need to add **reverberation**, as most recording is best done in a very 'dry' (echo-free) acoustic, with reverberation added after the basic tracks have been checked for accuracy.

As the recording engineer, you will be responsible for ensuring the unity and balance of the ensemble. If players get out of time or make mistakes, it is your job to politely point out the errors, get the musicians to rehearse the passage until you are happy, and then re-record.

Multi-track recording is marked in a similar way to the other options. There are 12 marks for accuracy – this will be your own best track if you yourself have performed in the recording, or the accuracy of any sequences if you have included sequenced material, or the success with which you have directed the other musicians towards an accurate performance. The other 18 marks, to make the total of 30, are awarded for recording skills. To get a good mark here, you must aim for:

- A strong, noise-free signal, without distortion
- Use of the full frequency range, without being over-bright in the high range or boomy in the bass
- Good balance between the musicians, with effective placing of the various parts within the stereo field
- Appropriate and well-controlled use of effects such as reverb.

Remember that you will have to submit a score, professional recording or detailed commentary of the music used for sequencing and multi-track recording, just as has to be done for the other performing options.

For this unit you have to create and submit either:

▪ Two compositions
▪ Or two arrangements
▪ Or one composition and one arrangement.

Whichever combination you choose, the two items *together* should total between two and four minutes playing time.

For each item you have to submit:

▪ Either a notated score (handwritten or printed) or a written commentary detailed enough for others to perform your work
▪ Plus a recording of the piece (on CD, MiniDisc or MP3).

The time-scale is similar to that for performing. You will probably spend some time at the beginning of the course improving your composing skills by working on exercises and short pieces. After that you will need to start preparing the two submissions for this unit. They need to be virtually complete by about halfway through the year in which your teacher will submit them for assessment in order to allow time for final polishing and recording. Your teacher will need to send work to the Edexcel moderator by the start of May in your exam year, so there will be very little time in the final summer term if you haven't completed everything before Easter.

As with performing, the secret of success is advance planning. Work out a timetable with your teacher that gives you several spare weeks to repeat work if anything should go wrong, such as your work being lost, deleted or stolen, or people needed for the recording being absent. Then be sure to stick to that timetable.

FIRST DECISIONS

RELATING YOUR WORK TO UNIT 3

The works you submit must be related to the music you study in Unit 3. As we shall see, these pieces are divided into four areas of study, and each item you produce for Unit 2 must relate to a *different* area of study. There are several different ways to make this link:

You could write something in the style of one of the set works that you enjoy. This can work well in the case of music written in the last 60 years or so. For example, if you enjoy Bernstein's 'Something's Coming' (from *West Side Story*) you might feel inspired to write your own song for a show. This is not a good idea in the case of older music, because it can be very difficult to write convincingly in the style of long-dead composers such as Handel or Mozart. Just imagine being asked to write a poem in the style of Shakespeare or to paint in the style of Michelangelo!

You could choose to make use of some of the ideas or techniques that you have studied in a set work, without trying to copy the style. For example, the musical depiction of raindrops in Chopin's Prelude No. 15 might inspire you to write a totally different type of piece that refers to some aspect of nature, such as a sunrise or a storm. Or Handel's various ways of writing for accompanied choir in *Messiah* might suggest ways to use similar techniques, but in a very different style in your own piece for accompanied voices.

Instead of relating your submission to an individual set work, you can relate it to some aspect of the entire area of study. This gives you enormous scope because the areas are very broad: Western Classical Music 1600–1899, Music in the 20th Century, Popular Music in Context, and World Music. This means that you are free to draw on any aspect of music in the period concerned. You could make use of a structure, such as variations, that was common throughout the period 1600–1899, or a style such as the waltz that was popular in the 19th century, or a 20th-century technique such as Minimalism, or a style of 20th-century pop music that you enjoy such as reggae.

Remember, your two submissions for this unit must be related to music from *different* areas of study.

Various composing ideas are included in the sections on set works later in this guide, which can be used as exercises or as a basis for developing into compositions. These are only suggestions and in general it is better for you to make your own links with the areas of study, as you can then use the techniques, forms or styles that interest you most.

WHO DO I WRITE FOR?

You are free to use whatever resources you wish. It is often best to write something for yourself to perform, as you will know the capabilities of your instrument or voice. However, unless your instrument is one that can play chords (such as the piano or guitar), writing for between two and four people will give you much more flexibility. There's nothing other than time to stop you composing for a large ensemble – even a choir or orchestra – but that can be a seriously big challenge and won't necessarily get you any more marks. Another possibility is to write a piece for electronic sounds that you can generate with the help of a computer.

Composing music for yourself plus some other members of your GCSE group is fun: it will allow you to try out ideas in class and will simplify the task of recording the piece. Note that items submitted for this unit must be written entirely by you alone – group compositions are not allowed for GCSE.

COMPOSITION OR ARRANGEMENT?

At first glance, writing an arrangement of some existing piece seems much easier than writing a composition. After all, instead of beginning from scratch you can start from music that someone else has already created!

Unfortunately – and perhaps as you guessed – life is not that simple! Simply taking a piece and giving its parts to different instruments will get few marks.

If you choose to make an arrangement, you will need to be very creative in order to get a good mark. First, you need to find a piece that has the potential to work well in a very different context. Something quite simple, such as an unaccompanied folk tune, can often lead to a more interesting arrangement than a fully worked-out composition. This will give you plenty of potential to develop your own variations and harmonies, and to arrange it for the instrument(s) of your choice.

If you do decide to start with an existing composition, you will need to consider carefully how you can successfully re-compose the music in a totally different way. For example, you might take a short dance by Handel (one of the composers of the set works, so making the essential link with an area of study), and give it a jazz arrangement (thus also perhaps making an additional link with the jazz set work by Miles Davis).

How? Could the melody be adapted for a jazz singer or an instrument such as the saxophone? How will it sound jazz-like? Could some jazzy rhythms be included? Perhaps the bass line would work well on bass guitar or plucked double bass? How would you make the harmony sound like jazz rather than like Handel? The chords will surely need to be changed – perhaps reduced in number but some are likely to need extra notes to get the right sound. Could you add jazz-like melodic features to the existing tune? What about adding a part for a jazz drummer?

As you can see, choosing an arrangement instead of a composition is not an easy option if you hope for a good mark. Edexcel has allowed arrangements as an alternative to compositions in GCSE for some years, but it's worth reading what the examiners have said about this choice …

'Arrangements … were very rare this year and tended to be either very good or quite poor … the best candidates created new pieces from their original source material. The music was often rescored for new instrumentation with different harmonies and often included some original melodic parts, countermelodies etc. The weak candidates simply transcribed the original for another group of instruments preserving the melody, rhythm and harmony parts from the original version. These were only awarded low marks.'

COMPOSING YOUR PIECE

Some composers begin by planning the overall structure of their piece, some start with a chord pattern, some prefer to begin with an idea for a melody or rhythm, and yet others start by thinking about how to make best use of the resources (instruments and/or voices) available. Most would agree that getting started is one of the hardest parts of composing!

You are eventually going to have to think about *all* of these elements as the work proceeds – real multi-tasking! – but one good way to get started is simply to doodle musical ideas on your instrument or with your voice. You don't need fully-formed melodies – aim for a few notes that have a distinctive shape and rhythm, and that have the potential to be worked into something longer.

Once you have a few notes, what do you do with them? This is where listening to other music becomes really important. It could be music that you play or enjoy hearing in your leisure time, although the set works for Unit 3 are perhaps the best place to start. Whatever you choose, you need to listen with full concentration for how the composer:

- Begins the piece
- Establishes musical ideas and varies them
- Creates specific moods
- Introduces contrasts
- Paces the music to include areas of tension and relaxation, and points of climax
- Unifies the work, so that it sounds like a satisfying whole rather than a succession of unrelated ideas
- Ends the piece.

Getting the right balance of ideas is one of the most important tasks for a composer. Too much exact repetition and the piece will sound boring. Too many new ideas and it will not gel. Careful listening will show you how composers throughout the ages have evolved various techniques to get the balance right. Learn from them – you are not expected to re-invent the wheel!

Seven tips for better marks

1. Have a clear vision of what you piece is intended to do for the listener. Is it to thrill them? To relax them? To frighten them? To inspire them? To impress them? To paint a picture in sound for them? A well-chosen title (such as *Midnight Rave* or *Sun and Surf*) will make your intentions much clearer than a vague heading like *Composition 1*, and will also help to keep your own eye on the ball.

2. A short piece rarely needs more than two or three different ideas. It is much better to make full use of a small amount of material than to keep introducing new ideas. Explore ways to vary, extend and *occasionally* repeat your opening idea, so that it really sticks in the mind of the listener, before introducing them to anything new.

3. You are likely to need a contrast once the opening material has had a good airing. But make sure that anything new fits logically with the music that has gone before – it shouldn't sound as if a different piece has suddenly burst its way in. You might, for instance, be able to re-use the opening few notes, but continue in a different way. You could use another part of the instrument's range or a different instrument. A change of dynamic and articulation would provide contrast, as would a shift to another (but related) key. Changing both the time and the speed, on the other hand, might prove too disruptive for a contrasting section in a short piece.

4. Many short pieces end by referring back to their opening material. This can be effective, but it is where 'cut and paste' can really limit your marks. If you repeat the opening section, try to do something new and imaginative with it – add extra parts, vary the patterns and change some of the chords. Perhaps you could shorten the repeat, or alternatively you could lengthen it in order to reach a big climax and an extended ending.

5. Aim to write in an **idiomatic** way. For example, the highest notes of the flute are good for loud, brilliant music while the lowest are better for quiet, smooth melodies. Research what is most idiomatic for the instrument you play, and for any others that you include in your composition. If you are writing for a group of friends, get them to demonstrate what they find easiest and most effective (and what they find most difficult), and keep notes of what you learn for your future reference.

> This means that you should write in a style that is characteristic of (and feels natural for) the instruments and/or voices concerned.

6. Rests are as important as notes. They can add contrast and lightness to your music, and are essential to give wind players or singers somewhere to take a breath. Even if you are writing for just a keyboard, one hand can sometimes rest while the other plays alone. If you are writing a solo with accompaniment, let the accompanist take the spotlight for a few bars while the soloist has a rest. If you are writing for a small group, break your melody into fragments and divide them between the players – they shouldn't all be playing continuously.

7. Try out your ideas frequently as your piece progresses – and get your friends to try them out, if they are also involved in the piece. Be prepared to make many changes along the way – composing is not something that most people can do quickly, and many pieces need to go through a lot of re-drafts and improvements before they reach their final form. (The composer Brahms once said that it took him 21 years to complete his first symphony – but you'll be in trouble if your GCSE compositions take that long!)

SUBMISSIONS AND MARKING

SCORE OR COMMENTARY?

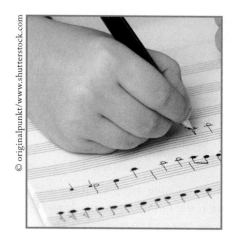

If possible, write your music in the format normally used for the type of music concerned. In many cases, a score in stave notation gives the most detail as it shows exactly what is to be sung or played. It can be hand-written or prepared with notation software on a computer and then printed out (for more on computer-printed scores, see opposite). If your piece is for more than one performer, the parts should be written or printed above one another to make a complete score – this is much easier to read than submitting each individual part on a separate piece of paper.

If you are not very experienced in using stave notation, writing a score will mean quite a lot of work to get to grips with the basics in the early stages, but it is definitely worthwhile as the ability to read and write stave notation is an important skill for many musicians.

Jazz and rock music are often written as a lead sheet. This consists of a melody line in stave notation (with the words if it is a song), plus chord symbols precisely positioned above the music to show the harmonies required. If you write a lead sheet, try to add as much detail as possible, including the speed and a few words to describe the accompaniment style (such as 'heavy rock' or 'country-style finger picking'). If you are a guitarist, you can add guitar grids (showing the fingering of the chords), but remember to include the chord names (such as F or G^7) above the grids.

Guitar tab, which shows the notes as finger positions, can be used for guitar parts if you are familiar with this type of notation, but include the rhythms (as headless notes) above the tab.

Some types of music don't suit traditional stave notation, including experimental pieces, those that contain random elements and those composed for non-western instruments. These are best written up as a commentary, perhaps supplemented with diagrams or track lists. Really precise detail is essential. Edexcel's *Teacher's Guide* for GCSE Music indicates that a written commentary 'must contain sufficient performance directions to allow for a realisation of the piece'. In other words, it must be so detailed that other musicians could perform the piece from your description. Don't spend time saying how you wrote it or who influenced it.

Describe the notes to be played, how they are to be played (including matters such as speed, dynamics and articulation), the way in which the piece is to be assembled by the performers, and what the end result should sound like.

Be aware that a score or a written commentary is an essential requirement, not an option – if you don't submit one, your work will not be moderated.

WHAT TO INCLUDE IN THE SCORE

The following are essential in almost all types of music – use this as a checklist when completing your scores:

- ☑ The title and your name at the head of the first page (you will probably also have to add your centre number and candidate number before submitting the work)
- ☑ The precise names of the instruments (or types of voice) required before the start of the first set of staves
- ☑ The speed at the start, and at any place where it changes
- ☑ The opening dynamic, and all later changes in the dynamics
- ☑ An indication of the style or mood at the start
- ☑ A **clef** and (if required) **key signature** at the start of every stave
- ☑ A **time signature** before the first note of the piece, and any place where the time signature changes
- ☑ Phrasing and marks of articulation (such as **staccato** dots and accents) as needed
- ☑ A clear layout with gaps between each line of music (or a blank stave if you are writing the score by hand), but not so widely spaced that page turns are needed every few seconds
- ☑ Page numbers on each sheet (bar numbers are also useful when rehearsing the piece prior to recording).

If you wish, you can use common Italian terms (such as 'Allegro' for fast or 'legato' for smoothly), but English is just as good. It is much more important that all your performing directions make musical sense and are not just sprinkled around randomly. For instance, a contrasting section might be marked with softer dynamics, a climax might be emphasised by **crescendo** marks and well-placed accent signs, and the ending might need to be marked 'slowing down' (or 'ritardando' if you're keen on Italian) with a pause sign on the last note.

COMPUTER-PRINTED SCORES

Computer-printed scores *can* look very neat, but you need to understand the software, otherwise the results may be disappointing. There are two main types of program, each with a different purpose:

- ■ Sequencing software (such as Cubase) is designed for recording, producing and mixing sounds, although most such programs also have limited facilities to notate the results as a score

■ Notation software (such as Sibelius) is designed for creating and printing-out scores, although most such programs also have limited facilities to work as a **sequencer.**

At the time of writing, no program does both jobs equally well – and if one ever appears, it will undoubtedly be very complicated. The main disadvantage of using a sequencer to notate music is that the program records note lengths very precisely, just as they are played. The result may look something like the upper stave shown left, whereas the performer needs to see something instantly recognisable (smooth quavers and separated crotchets), as shown on the lower stave.

It is not that the software is wrong, but that it's attempting to display note lengths in too much detail for a performer to interpret. Most sequencer software has facilities such as 'score quantization' to help achieve more acceptable results, but you will still need to check the results carefully for eccentric note lengths, overlapping notes, unnecessary rests and unwanted ties.

Software designed for notation is more likely to get note-lengths correct, but may have only limited facilities to make the subtle variations to note lengths needed to achieve musical results when the sequence is played.

Here are some more points to remember when using software to produce a score:

☑ Use a small stave size so that you can get a reasonable number of bars on each page. This saves paper and avoids the inconvenience of having to turn the page every few bars
☑ Use repeat signs instead of printing out repeated sections in full – again this could save paper and unnecessary page turns

- ☑ Experiment to see whether your piece looks better in portrait (upright) or landscape (oblong) format
- ☑ Check that you have used the correct clefs to minimise the number of notes that have to be written above or below the staves. Remember that very low instruments (such as the bass guitar and double bass) are written an **octave** higher than they sound, and that music for the ordinary guitar is written an octave higher than it sounds in the treble clef
- ☑ Adjust the space between the lines of music so there are small gaps for clarity, taking special care that information on one stave doesn't overlap with anything on the staves above or below
- ☑ Make sure that you've made the best choice of key signature(s) in order to minimise the number of **accidentals** needed in the score
- ☑ Label the staves at the start with the instruments, voices or synthesiser sounds required
- ☑ Be sure to add all necessary performing directions, including the speed, dynamics and articulation (phrase marks, staccato dots, accents and so forth).

If your composition or arrangement is intended for live performers, rather than for electronic resources, check that the parts are within the range of the instruments or voices concerned, and that you haven't written anything impossible such as two notes at the same time for a single wind player. Some notation software can be set to warn you of anything that is likely to be impossible.

CONTROLLED CONDITIONS

You have to produce the final recording and score (or commentary) of your work under controlled conditions – in other words, under supervision at your school or college. You will have 10 hours to complete each of the two items required for this unit. Your teacher will decide how and when these hours are allocated.

Although 10 hours sounds like a lot of time, you will need to have become reasonably efficient at writing up your music by this stage of the course. And if the recording involves a number of other people, remember that it may take much longer than you expect. If you don't have the necessary live performers to record your piece, it is acceptable to produce a synthesised 'mock up' using a sequencer, but make it clear in the score or commentary that the work is intended for live performance and is not supposed to be a piece of electronic music.

You are expected to have done most of the work before the controlled conditions start – tasks such as research (listening to relevant music), devising suitable ideas, producing rough drafts, trying out the music in performance, and so on. It is only the final stage of turning your plans into final written form and recording the music that has to be done under controlled conditions.

You will have to sign an authentication statement to confirm that the work is your own. This is very important as you cannot be awarded a mark without it. You must also submit a copy of the source you used for any arrangements.

HOW IS COMPOSING MARKED?

It is well worth understanding how marks are awarded, because this could influence some of the decisions you make about the work you create. Although you have a very wide choice in what to write, it is important to remember that you are composing for an exam. As well as the requirement that each item you submit must be related to a *different* area of study, the mark scheme expects certain features to be present in your work in order to get a good mark.

Each piece is marked out of 30, and half of these marks are always awarded for the following three elements:

A. Use and development of ideas (5 marks)

You could get all five available marks if you have shown imagination in developing the main musical ideas in your work. You are likely to get very few marks if your ideas are not developed, either because they are continually repeated without variation or because the piece constantly shifts through a succession of unrelated ideas.

Precisely what is expected will depend on the type of music you have chosen from the area of study. For example, in Minimalist music there *seems* to be a great deal of repetition, but there is normally a process of small but continual change (as we shall see when we study Reich's *Electric Counterpoint*). Examiners will therefore be looking for that process of gradual transformation if you write in a Minimalist style.

B. Exploitation of the medium (5 marks)

This is about how well you have used your chosen resources. Idiomatic writing is one of the important considerations here. If you have designed your music to suit the character and range of the voices and/or instruments concerned, you should do well. If the music is poorly suited to the resources, it will be difficult to get marks for this element.

C. Structure and form (5 marks)

Marks in this category are awarded for the overall structure of your piece. An imaginative musical design, with good balance between repetition and contrast, should do well. If the piece is meandering and lacking in shape, it will be difficult to pick up marks in this area.

In the case of an arrangement, marks in this category are awarded for an appropriate choice of piece to arrange and for how well the music works in its new version. If the original has simply been transferred to different instruments with hardly any other changes, very few marks will be available in this area.

The other 15 marks are awarded for whichever three of the following categories you and your teacher think best fit the type of music you have written (5 marks per category). For instance, if you have composed a piece for unaccompanied flute, you might choose melody, rhythm and dynamic contrasts – you probably wouldn't choose harmony (as there is no accompaniment), nor texture (as there is only a single melodic line) nor use of technology.

D. Melody (5 marks)

Melodies that have shape and real character will get good marks for this element. In the case of arrangements, this category is used for new melodic parts that you've added to the original piece – if you've not added any, no marks can be awarded in this section.

E. Harmony/accompaniment (5 marks)

Simple, basic harmonies that work well will get around half marks, but for all five marks you need a good range of chords and some effective patterns in your accompaniment if you choose to be marked in this category.

F. Texture (5 marks)

Texture is explained in more detail near the start of the next chapter, but essentially it refers to the way that the various simultaneous lines in a piece relate to one another. Showing awareness of how texture can be used to provide contrast and contribute to the structure of the music should attract a good mark.

G. Tempo/rhythm (5 marks)

A good choice of tempo (speed) and some exciting, inventive rhythms will score well in this category. This could include successfully using an unusual time signature, or combining rhythms in unexpected ways, or simply exercising careful control of rhythm to mark out the different areas of a composition. If you write entirely in crotchets, forget about rests or use rhythm in a random way, you will get few marks in this category.

H. Dynamic contrasts (5 marks)

If you use dynamics sensitively to underpin the contrasts and structure of your music, you will get a good mark. Forgetting about dynamics or sprinkling them around randomly will get few, if any, marks.

I. Use of technology (5 marks)

The marks in this category are only for use of technology in the creation of the music – in other words, for electronic music. There are no marks for using technology to produce the score, commentary or recording.

J. Technical problems (5 marks) – this category is only available for arrangements

The marks here are awarded for how well you have overcome the various technical problems that arise when arranging music for a different medium. If you've shown awareness of the need to adapt the original to suit the new resources, perhaps by moving sections into a more effective octave or by changing accompaniment patterns to suit the types of instrument you have used, you should get a good mark.

INTRODUCTION TO UNIT 3

Unit 3 is based on the study of 12 short and highly contrasting set works. At the end of your course there will be a 1½ hour written paper in two sections. In Section A you have to provide short answers to questions on extracts from eight of the set works, played to you several times each on CD. These questions account for 68 of the total 80 marks available, and you will have to answer questions on all eight extracts.

Section B is worth 12 marks and will require a longer answer about at least one work (which won't be on the CD). Here you will be able to choose one of two different sets of questions.

This means that almost all of the set works will appear somewhere on the paper – you won't know which, though, so it is essential to get to know all 12 really well, especially as you will not have scores to refer to in the exam.

As you read about each set work you will find 'test yourself' questions which you can use to check that you have understood the text. At the end of each section are some sample questions to give you practice in answering exam-style questions. If you have difficulty with any of these, you will find the right answers by carefully re-reading the preceding pages. There is a separate section (starting on page 167) that explains how to tackle the extended answer needed in Section B of the paper.

All 12 set works are available in a single book (with CD) called the *Edexcel GCSE Anthology of Music*, published by Heinemann (Score ISBN: 978-1-846904-05-9, CD ISBN: 978-1-846904-06-6). If you need to obtain your own copy, make sure you get the edition first published in 2009 with the ISBN numbers given above, as previous editions do not contain set works for the current exam.

The abbreviation GAM in this book refers to the *GCSE Anthology of Music*, and references to track numbers relate to the two CDs that accompany the anthology.

WHAT WE WILL STUDY

In the exam, the questions will focus on the music you have studied. Although we need to explore the context and style of each set work, and that will sometimes mean looking at related pieces, you are not expected to memorise chunks of general music history, biographies of composers or lists of singers' albums.

You will, though, need to know the set works very thoroughly – how the music is constructed and how it makes its effect. Some of this information can be put to good use in your composing and, as you get to know more about the inner workings of music, it will all help to improve your performing skills and increase your understanding when you are listening to music. All of what you learn will be extremely useful if you intend to study the subject beyond GCSE, as it will help you focus on what is important in many different types of music.

You will need to recognise (and use) the correct technical terms to describe in detail what you hear. There will also be some questions on the music notation used in the set works, including a few where you may have to complete some missing notes on a stave or identify a few of the chords you hear. You don't need to rely on memory to answer such questions, as the music will be played on CD during the exam.

BEFORE WE START

When you see a reference such as bar 3^2 in this book, it is short for bar 3 beat 2 in the score. A reference such as 2:15 means the music that you hear when your CD counter shows 2 minutes, 15 seconds.

When referring to dates, you need to remember that '18th century' means a year whose four digits begin 17.. , while '19th century' means a year whose four digits begin 18.. . It will help if you remember that we live in the 21st century, but its years begin with 20 (such as 2011), not with 21. Make a special note of this point, because it is easy to get wrong in the heat of the moment when answering a question about when a set work was written.

One of the most frequently misspelled words in English is 'rhythm' – for a musician to get such an important word wrong is hugely embarrassing! If you find it difficult …

Top Tips

To spell rhythm correctly, memorise the phrase:

Rhythm Helps Your Two Hands Move.

The term 'classical music' has two different meanings. For most people, it is the type of music found under the heading 'classical' in listings magazines and on CD racks – works that have become part of the cultural history of western civilisation, because successive generations have found them to be of long-lasting interest and value.

It is important to realise that classical music is not the pop music of the past – it was always something different. At its best, it is music that the composer knew would be listened to with concentrated attention. As a result, classical music often seems to want to be explored – not just heard – even if these days it does sometimes just drift past us over the sound system in a shopping mall or restaurant.

Musicians more often use the term 'classical' to mean one of several major styles within this tradition. Area of Study 1 includes works from the Baroque, Classical and Romantic periods:

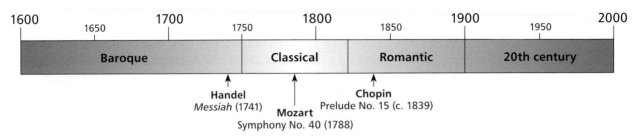

Don't take the dates of the periods too literally. People didn't burn their harpsichords, throw away their Baroque music and dash out to buy the latest Classical piece in January 1750. Change happened slowly. Some composers preferred to remain faithful to the familiar traditions of the past, while others were keen to explore the latest trends, so in reality each style blends into the next over quite a number of years.

Style

Style is surprisingly difficult to define. If you've ever said something like 'she's got style', have you thought about exactly what you mean? It is rarely one single thing, such as a haircut, a way of speaking, or a piece of clothing. It's a combination of factors, which you know when you see it.

Style in music is similar. We will see that certain features of the set works are typical of the style of their time, but there is no neat formula to tell us what to expect in, say, all Romantic pieces – music is simply too diverse for that. For example, our first set work is from a large-scale Baroque work for voices and orchestra. But some Baroque music is very short, and written for just one or two performers. The more music you listen to and find out about, the easier it becomes to recognise style – you know it when you hear it!

SET WORK 1: 'AND THE GLORY OF THE LORD' FROM *MESSIAH* BY HANDEL

Our first set work was written towards the end of the Baroque period, an era that saw the development of the earliest orchestras in the modern sense as well as the first large-scale musical works for the stage, known as operas. Some of the best-known Baroque composers today are Bach, Handel, Purcell and Vivaldi.

Typical features of the late-Baroque style include:

- **Movements** that maintain the same basic mood throughout
- Short melodic ideas that are spun out to form long and highly decorated melodies
- Orchestras based largely on the string family, with only limited use of wind
- The use of instruments such as the harpsichord, organ and lute to fill out the music with chords
- Simple, mainly **diatonic** harmonies in major or minor keys
- Clear contrasts between loud and soft (known as **terraced dynamics**), rather than gradual changes of dynamic.

The Baroque style was not limited to music. Its highly decorated nature, in which almost no surface is left bare, can be seen in this picture of the private chapel of the Prince-Bishop of Würzburg in Germany, completed a year after the first performance of Handel's *Messiah*:

> A **movement** is an independent section within a longer piece of music. The chorus we are studying is the fourth movement in *Messiah*.
>
> **Diatonic** means notes belonging to the current key, as opposed to chromatic notes, which are outside the key.

© German Places

Wurzburg chapel

GEORGE FRIDERIC HANDEL (1685–1759)

© Harriet Power

In 1723 Handel rented this newly-built house in Brook Street, just behind London's famous Oxford Street. It remained Handel's base for the rest of his life. Although the ground floor is now a shop, the rest of the building is a museum about Handel that is open to the public: see www.handelhouse.org.

Handel was born in Germany, where he learnt to play the violin, harpsichord and organ. In his early 20s he spent several years in Italy, which had been the powerhouse behind Baroque music for more than a century. On his return to Germany he secured a post as court conductor for the Prince-Elector of Hanover. Handel was always ambitious, and he was twice allowed leave to visit London, where he saw there were great opportunities to introduce the English to the latest Italian musical styles that he had mastered. Handel was so taken with London that he didn't return to his job in Hanover after his second visit.

By an odd twist of fate, the Prince-Elector of Hanover became King George I of Great Britain in 1714. There seems to have been no ill-will over Handel's neglect of his conducting duties in Germany, as the composer was soon engaged to provide music for royal occasions, including the *Water Music* (written for the King's parties on the River Thames) and four anthems for the coronation of his son, King George II, in 1727.

Occasional works of this sort did not provide a regular income, and for many years Handel made his living largely from writing and staging operas in Italian for the wealthy audiences of London theatres. He was a good businessman and, despite sometimes losing a lot of money, he died leaving a sum equivalent to several million pounds today. England much loved its adopted composer, and over 3000 people attended his funeral in Westminster Abbey, where his memorial can still be seen.

ORATORIO

An **oratorio** is a large-scale composition for solo voices, choir and orchestra, usually on a Biblical subject, but intended for concert performance. Handel wrote more than 20 oratorios, of which *Messiah* (1741) is the most famous.

At first Handel wrote oratorios to perform during the religious season of Lent, when theatres were not allowed to present staged works on certain days. Concert performances were allowed, and oratorios enabled Handel to keep the singers and orchestra of his Italian opera company employed on these days. There were no costumes, scenery or acting in an oratorio, but musically these works were similar in style to his operas and, at around three hours in length, they provided a full evening of entertainment, just as opera did.

There are, though, two important differences. In Handel's oratorios the words are in English rather than Italian, and, unlike most of his operas, there are a number of movements for chorus, whose frequently dramatic music went some way to compensate for the lack of acting. By the late 1730s, the novelty of Italian opera had worn thin in London, and so Handel concentrated mainly on writing and presenting oratorios during the later part of his life.

MESSIAH

Most of Handel's oratorios are based on poetic versions of dramatic stories from the Old Testament of the Bible. *Messiah* was rather different. For Christians, its title refers to Jesus and from the outset there was concern about making the central figure of Christianity the subject of a work to be performed in theatres and concert halls. In fact there was little to worry about. The words were selected by Charles Jennens (who had supplied Handel with texts for other oratorios), and most of them come from prophecies of the Messiah in the Old Testament, with few taken from the narrative accounts in the New Testament. The result is a work that is far more reflective (and less theatrical) than Handel's other oratorios – and it is a work that today is as likely to be heard in a church as a concert hall.

© Nicholas Bunning

A harpsichord is a keyboard instrument on which strings are plucked when keys are pressed

Handel completed *Messiah* in just over three weeks during the late summer of 1741. Although a few movements were adapted from earlier works, and he was well used to working at breakneck speed, this was an extraordinary achievement for a work lasting over two hours. The first performance was given in Dublin, where Handel gave a series of concerts at a newly opened concert hall, on 13 April 1742. It received an enthusiastic welcome, unlike the first London performance at the Covent Garden Theatre in London the following year, where there were still doubts about the suitability of presenting such a subject in a theatre. It was not until Handel started giving annual performances of the work in the chapel of the Foundling Hospital (a London orphanage that he generously supported) from 1750 onwards that *Messiah* started to take its place as the most famous of all major choral works.

Handel had very limited resources available in Dublin for the first performance of *Messiah*. There were no more than 16 singers in all, including the soloists (who sang with the choir in the choruses). The orchestra consisted of probably less than ten string players, supported by organ and **harpsichord**. There were also two trumpets and timpani, but these play in only a very few movements.

Pitch refers to the highness or lowness of a note or piece of music.

Can you sing falsetto? It's a technique used by many pop singers for high notes, but it takes a lot of practice to do well. Start by singing out 'coo–ee' as high and gently as you can.

The recording by the Scholars Baroque Ensemble on CD 1 Track 1 tries to get as close as possible to the sound that would have been produced by this relatively small group. As well as using instruments and playing techniques modelled on those of the day, the performance is a **semitone** lower than the score. This is because scholars have determined that **pitch** in the 18th century was a little lower than it is today. In addition, the **alto** part is performed by men (known as male altos or countertenors), as it was in the first performance. They use a vocal technique known as **falsetto** to get the high notes and pure tone needed.

Handel made many changes to *Messiah* for later performances, adding oboes and bassoons to the orchestra, replacing and cutting some movements, and changing others to suit different singers. After his death, there was a tendency to perform the work on a large scale, often with hundreds of performers and adapted for a much bigger orchestra. The work became (and remains) very popular with amateur choirs because of its large number of choral movements. In the last 30 years, professional performances informed by historical research (such as the one on CD 1 Track 1) have become popular because of the way in which they reveal the clarity of Handel's original ideas.

Test yourself

1. In which country was Handel born?
2. Which country did Handel visit to learn about the latest musical fashions of his day?
3. Name two types of music for which Handel is famous.
4. In which century was *Messiah* written?
5. Which of the following best describes the style of *Messiah*?
   Romantic   Classical   20th-century   Baroque
6. In what sort of building was *Messiah* first performed **(a)** in Dublin and **(b)** in London?
7. Where else might you hear it performed now?
8. What type of instrument is a harpsichord?
9. What is the name of the singing technique used by male altos?

'AND THE GLORY OF THE LORD'

The first part of *Messiah* forms a musical journey from darkness to light, illustrating words which are about the promise that Christ will come to save the world. The oratorio begins with an overture (an orchestral introduction) in the sombre key of E minor. This is followed by two movements in the much warmer key of E major, in which a **tenor** soloist calls on the world to prepare for the arrival of a saviour.

'And the Glory of the Lord' comes next, so it is the fourth movement of the work, and the first in which the choir sings. It forms a joyful response to the prophecy of good news, with dancing triple-time rhythms in the bright key of A major.

Following the score

> A **system** is a group of staves that are played simultaneously.

The score in GAM is laid out in **systems** of eight staves. The top pair are for violins, divided into two groups (first violins and second violins). Below them comes the stave for violas (large violins). Because these are mid-range instruments they use the alto C clef (𝄡), in which the middle line of the stave represents middle C. Next come the four choir parts in descending order of pitch (soprano, alto, tenor and bass, abbreviated to SATB).

Top Tips

Memorise the order of the voice parts in an SATB choir. Examiners often ask questions such as 'Which voice part is lower than soprano but higher than tenor?'

Notice that the tenor part has a small 8 at the bottom of its clef. This indicates that, although the notes are in the treble clef, they sound an octave lower than they are written.

The lowest stave, marked 'Continuo bass', is played by the cellos and also usually by double basses (sounding an octave lower than the cellos). This stave is also used by keyboard players (harpsichord and/or organ) as the basis from which to improvise accompanying harmonies. The word **continuo** refers to the combination of chordal and bass instruments that play this part, as well as to the part itself, and is something found only in Baroque music. There are sometimes figures and other symbols below the continuo part to indicate the chords required, in which case the part is known as a figured bass.

Like most Baroque composers, Handel included very few performing directions in his scores. Here the **tempo** is Allegro (fast) and doesn't change until the last four bars, which are marked Adagio (slow). On CD 1 Track 1 the Allegro is fast enough to give the impression of 'one in a bar' (one dotted minim beat per bar, rather than three crotchets), and the Adagio is only a little slower than the rest of the movement.

Top Tips

When asked to comment on tempo in an exam, students often lose marks by writing about dynamics or other features. Make a point of remembering that tempo refers to *speed*.

The dynamic markings in GAM have been added by a modern editor to reflect the typical **terraced dynamics** found in much Baroque music.

LISTENING GUIDE

A **motif** is a short, distinctive melody or rhythm that is used in various ways to form a much longer passage of music.

The entire chorus is based on four **motifs**, one for each phrase of the text, that are repeated, varied and combined in many different ways. Listen to the recording, without following the score, and make sure that you can recognise the distinctive shape of each one:

Motif A starts with leaps that outline the key chord of A major (A, C♯ and E), and ends by moving stepwise up the last three notes of an A-major scale. These pitches clearly define the key of the music, and the ascent from low A to high A creates a mood of great confidence. The word-setting is **syllabic** (one note per syllable), with the rather unusual feature of two syllables run together in the middle of the third bar.

shall   be   re - veal - - ed,

Motif B, in contrast, has a smooth, descending outline and the setting of the word 'revealed' is **melismatic** (several notes per syllable). The **dotted rhythm** in the first complete bar is repeated a step lower in the next bar, forming a **sequence**.

> A melodic sequence is a motif that is immediately repeated in the same part, but at a higher or lower pitch.

and   all   flesh___   shall   see__   it   to - ge - ther,

Motif C consists of a repeated figure, spanning the interval between the **dominant** (E) and the **tonic** (A) above.

for   the   mouth   of   the   Lord   hath   spo - ken   it.

Motif D consists of much longer notes, most of which are on the same pitch, like a solemn chant to reflect the importance of the words.

Top Tips

In the descriptions above, notice how to write about melody and rhythm. Instead of describing every note (which would take ages and be very boring!), try to identify the main features. For example, state if there is an overall direction to the melody (up or down), whether it moves by **step** or **leap** (or stays mainly on the same note), whether it supports the meaning of the words (if there are any), and if there are characteristic features in the rhythm, such as long notes or dotted patterns. We will learn more on writing about music in the section that starts on page 167.

Handel builds the whole movement from these four motifs, often pairing A with B and C with D. Before we look at how he does this, we need to learn about a term that students often get wrong in exams. **Texture** refers to how the different simultaneous layers in music are combined. In a **homophonic** texture there is a tune and an accompaniment. In a **contrapuntal** texture, two or more melodies are heard at the same time. As we shall see, much of this chorus is based on the contrast between these two textures. Let's have a look in detail at the opening sections.

Bars 1–11 (0:00 to 0:12)

This orchestral introduction starts with A followed by B, and is extended to end in a **perfect cadence** in the tonic key of A major. The approach to the cadence (bars 9–10) features a type of **syncopation** known as a **hemiola**, in which two bars of ³/₄ time are played as if they were three bars of ²/₄ time. This lively rhythmic device is typical of many Baroque triple-time movements. See how many more you can spot in this chorus.

Sounds like:

Bars 11–17 (0:12 to 0:19)

Motif A is sung by the altos alone, and the whole choir responds by repeating it in a homophonic texture. Can you spot which voice sings the tune (that is, motif A) in bars 14–17?

Bars 17–38 (0:19 to 0:41)

Imitation occurs when a melody in one part is copied a few notes later in a different part (and often at a different pitch), while the melody in the first part continues.

Motif B is sung by the tenors alone but, before they have finished, the basses enter with the same motif at a lower pitch – a technique known as **imitation**. The sopranos also enter in imitation and then Handel pulls a clever trick – in bar 22 the tenors enter with motif A while the other parts continue with entries of motif B. This overlapping and combination of melodies forms a contrapuntal texture to contrast with the opening homophonic entry of the choir.

Modulation is the process of changing key.

Handel has a second way of introducing contrast in this section. From bar 21 onwards D♯ appears in almost every bar. This is a sign that the music is modulating to a key with four sharps (three in the key signature plus D♯). That key is E major, the dominant, and this **modulation** is confirmed by a perfect cadence in E major in bars 37–38.

Bars 38–43 (0:41 to 0:46)

This short orchestral interlude, based on motif B, is the second half of the introduction moved into the dominant key.

Bars 43–57 (0:46 to 1:02)

Motif C is announced by the altos, and then by the tenors. They don't overlap, so this is not imitation. Motif D follows immediately, made all the more solemn because the tenors double the basses for the first seven notes. Handel again combines two motifs in counterpoint when the upper voices enter with motif C (bar 53) before the lower voices have finished motif D.

By now, you have probably spotted that the movement is based on the contrast between alternating homophonic and contrapuntal textures. The latter often includes imitation and the combination of two different motifs. Here are some more points to explore about the movement:

■ When the choir are singing, the orchestra mainly doubles their parts, although it also supplies the bass in bars where the basses are not singing. Sometimes the doubling is in a different octave – for example, in bars 35–38 the first violins sound higher than the sopranos because they double the alto part at the octave above.

- The orchestral introduction can be described as a *ritornello* (Italian for 'little return'), because little bits of it return later, between the choral sections. Can you find where this happens?
- In the choir's homophonic passages, the tune is often in the bass (for instance, in bars 76–79, motif A is in the bass).
- Further variety of texture is created through different combinations of voice parts – as well as using all four parts together, Handel sometimes uses just one voice part, or various combinations of two parts (TB, SA, AT and so on), or (in bars 116–119) just the three lower parts without sopranos.
- Further variety of key occurs in bars 65–102, where Handel passes through the dominant (E major) on the way to a long section in B major (the dominant of the dominant key). He comes back the way he went, returning to E major in bar 93. After the perfect cadence in E in bars 101–102 the music is in the tonic key of A major until the end.
- The entry of motif A at bar 107^3 (1:56) is remarkable because Handel uses a **monophonic** texture (a melody on its own) in which the sopranos are taken to their highest note in the chorus – a real test of the brave!
- Handel achieves a great sense of energy by making the last chord of each section serve as the first chord of the next section so that there are no gaps (look, for instance, at bar 38).
- Phrases of the text are repeated a number of times, helping to make the words clear to listeners even in contrapuntal passages.
- The final bars contain one of Handel's most characteristic endings – a total silence (sometimes known as a **general pause**) breaks the flow and is followed by a slow, sustained cadence. Here the cadence is **plagal** (a chord of D followed by a chord of A, forming the progression IV–I in A major), sounding like a grand 'Amen'.

Top Tips

Examiners often ask about important cadences. The final cadence in this work is important because it is so typical of Handel and because plagal cadences are not very common in music. Be prepared!

Test yourself

1. Name three instruments that might play from a continuo part.
2. How many different motifs are there in this chorus?
3. Look at the alto part in bars 29–32. What term describes the type of word setting in these bars?
4. What is the meaning of the small 8 printed below the treble clef in the tenor part?
5. Which one of the following statements is true?
   (a) The tenor melody in bars 47–50 is exactly the same as the alto melody in the previous four bars.
   (b) The tenor melody in bars 47–50 is a 4th higher than the alto melody in the previous four bars.
   (c) The tenor melody in bars 47–50 is a 5th lower than the alto melody in the previous four bars.
6. In which bars does Handel use a monophonic texture?
7. What musical term describes the texture in the last four bars of the movement?

Further listening

To broaden your knowledge of Handel's music, here are some more works that you might enjoy:

- Other choruses from *Messiah*, particularly the **'Hallelujah'** chorus that ends the second part of the oratorio. It is one of the most famous pieces of choral music ever written, and it contains many of the features we have studied, including contrapuntal and homophonic textures, imitation, the combination of different motifs and another example of Handel's favourite ending for fast choral movements.
- *Zadok the Priest* is one of the four anthems that Handel wrote for the coronation of George II – it has been sung at every British coronation since. You may recognise its famous opening, designed to create an overwhelming feeling of expectation for the entry of the choir.
- **The Hornpipe in D major** from Handel's *Water Music* – no voices in this famous movement, but a good example of the composer's ability to write a memorable tune with some very catchy rhythms.
- *Dixit Dominus* is one of Handel's earliest works, written when he was in Italy. It has a Latin text because it was written as sacred music for the Roman Catholic Church, but it contains some of Handel's most dramatic and colourful writing.

Composing ideas

While studying 'And the Glory of the Lord' we have come across a number of techniques that could be used in your own compositions. These could be effective in most styles of music – you are not required to write in the style of Handel. You might try:

- A piece for choir in which you use contrasting textures – all four parts together, each part alone, different pairs of parts (such as SA, AT and TB), and three of the four available parts (such as ATB or SAT). If you include an accompaniment, remember that it can be used to give the singers a breather between sections, perhaps basing these passages on the choir's music, as Handel does.
- A piece for whatever resources you wish that has a great sense of forward movement because each new section starts on the last note of the previous one, like the overlapping sections in Handel's chorus.
- A piece for keyboard, or for two or more performers, which contrasts homophonic and contrapuntal textures. If you fancy including imitation, remember that it doesn't have to last for more than a few notes to make its point.

Sample questions for Section A

Listen to the first 41 seconds of CD 1 Track 1 four times, with short pauses between each playing, as you answer the following questions. Don't consult the score or any other information before writing your answers.

1. The tempo of this music is marked 'Allegro'. What does Allegro mean?

.... (1)

Questions that ask you to name a 'device' expect you to give a technical term such as sequence or pedal. Here you should name the rhythmic device used.

2. Name the rhythmic device heard at the end of the orchestral introduction.

.... (1)

3. Here is the first sung phrase. Complete the four missing notes (the rhythm is shown above the stave). (4)

And the glo - ry the glor - ry of the Lord,

4. What type of voice sings this first phrase? .... (1)

5. When you first hear the words 'shall be revealed', the tune is copied by other voices so that it overlaps with itself. What musical term describes this technique?

.... (1)

6. This extract begins in A major. In what key does it end?

.... (1)

7. Name a keyboard instrument that plays in this extract.

.... (1)

(Total 10 marks)

Top Tips

Some questions (like number 3 above) may ask you to complete a few missing notes or chords in a passage. Although there won't be many such questions, they often carry more marks than single-word answers, so it is well worth getting as much practice as you can on this type of question. Make sure that you write notes on staves clearly, either in a space or on a line. If the examiner can't be sure what you've written, you won't get a mark.

Another type of question that is likely to carry four marks is one that asks you to name four important features of Baroque music. What answer would you give? In this type of question, the features you list don't have to come from the set work.

Sample questions for Section B

Before tackling this section read the information on writing extended answers, on page 167. Then complete your answers without consulting any notes or the score, and without listening to the recording.

The following questions are about 'And the Glory of the Lord' from *Messiah* by Handel.

(a) In which century was this music composed? .... (1)

(b) From what type of longer piece is this chorus taken? .... (1)

(c) Comment on how Handel uses the following musical elements in this chorus:

> Remember, tonality is about the keys used, not about tone colours, and texture is about the way that the various simultaneous lines in a piece relate to each other.

→ Tonality and harmony
→ Texture
    Melody
    Rhythm and tempo
    Word setting (10)

Use correct musical vocabulary where appropriate and remember that the quality of your writing, including spelling, punctuation and grammar, will be taken into account in this question. Write your answer on a separate sheet of paper.

(Total 12 marks)

SET WORK 2: SYMPHONY NO. 40 IN G MINOR, K. 550 (FIRST MOVEMENT) BY MOZART

> K. 550 is the number of this work in the catalogue of Mozart's compositions that was compiled by the Austrian scholar Ludwig Köchel.

Our second set work dates from the middle of the Classical period. Although it was composed less than 50 years after *Messiah*, much had changed in the world of music during that time. Orchestras had grown larger, particularly with the regular use of woodwind and brass as well as strings. The wide range of tone colours this provided made orchestral music much more popular in the Classical period. New instruments, such as the clarinet, horn and piano were now sufficiently reliable for regular use – in fact, the harpsichord quickly disappeared once composers had discovered the very expressive capabilities of the piano. The style of composition also changed, with more emphasis on simplicity and clarity, but also an interest in creating dramatic contrasts rather than relying on a single mood throughout a movement.

The four best-known Classical composers are Haydn, Mozart, Beethoven and Schubert. They all lived and worked in and around Vienna in Austria for parts of their lives, so the music of this period is sometimes described as 'Viennese Classical'.

Typical features of the Viennese Classical style include:

- A preference for homophonic textures (melody and accompaniment)
- Pairs of balanced phrases that can sound like questions and answers
- Increasing use of wind instruments in orchestras
- The use of the piano as the preferred keyboard instrument

- Mainly simple harmonies, but a tendency to modulate more widely than most Baroque music
- Expression markings in scores, including features such as accents and crescendo signs
- The use of contrasting moods within longer movements.

The Classical style was not limited to music. The visual arts of the period drew their inspiration from ancient Greece and Rome (the original meaning of 'Classical'). Nobody knows what music sounded like 2000 years ago, so this was not possible for composers, but their music reflects the elegant proportions and balance of the age.

Compare the following picture of a German Classical palace in Berlin, completed just two years before Mozart wrote this symphony, with the picture of the German Baroque chapel on page 33:

There is far less surface decoration, and much more concentration on a perfectly balanced form – even nature has been brought under control, as you can see from the carefully clipped conical hedges!

The preference of the period for elegant form can be seen in this piece of tableware, made just after Mozart wrote his fortieth symphony. Decoration is muted in colour and consists mainly of bands of clearly balanced patterns. The focus of the design is on the graceful shape of the object, just as it often is in the music of the Classical period.

WOLFGANG AMADEUS MOZART (1756–1791)

Mozart was born in the city of Salzburg in Austria. His father was a professional musician and gifted teacher, but even he was surprised at his son's early and rapid progress in music. By the age of four the young Mozart was playing easy keyboard pieces, and he soon began to compose and to start learning the violin.

By the time Mozart was six, his father was taking the boy (and his talented elder sister) to nearby cities to perform for royalty and other important people. It was clear that the young Mozart was a child prodigy – a young person of exceptional talent – and the next year the family set out on a European tour that was to last over three years, including more than a year spent in London. Everywhere they went, the public were astonished at the talents of the boy wonder, and further long tours followed.

Mozart's childhood home in Salzburg is now one of several museums devoted to the life and work of the composer

In 1773 Mozart secured a post as a court musician to the Archbishop of Salzburg. This provided a modest income, but he found the opportunities in the small city very limiting, and was soon on the road again, this time looking for a new job. He had no success, but in 1781 Mozart resigned from his Salzburg post to try his fortunes as a freelance musician in the much larger city of Vienna.

At first Mozart had much success as a performer in Vienna, but he found it difficult to get enough composing commissions to make an adequate living. By 1788, when he wrote his fortieth symphony, he was in debt and writing letters to his friends to beg for loans.

Despite the difficulties, Mozart composed some of his finest music in these last years and his financial situation slowly began to improve. But he died in 1791 at the age of only 35, probably from rheumatic fever, a disease of the immune system from which he had suffered several times since childhood. He left over 600 compositions of almost every type then known, from solo piano pieces to large-scale operas.

THE SYMPHONY

A **symphony** is a type of large-scale orchestral work that first became popular in the Classical period (the movement we are to study comes from a symphony that lasts about 25 minutes in total). Haydn was the first major composer to explore the potential of the symphony, writing over 100 such works between 1759 and 1795. By the end of this period, the typical symphony had four movements, in the order:

- Fast (often quite serious, but not solemn)
- Slow
- Minuet (a triple-time dance-like movement)
- Fast (often lighter in style than the first movement).

All four of the Classical composers we've mentioned (Haydn, Mozart, Beethoven and Schubert) wrote symphonies – the nine by Beethoven are particularly fine examples. During the Romantic period, symphonies tended to become longer and more elaborate, but they continued to be one of the main types of orchestral music for many composers well into the 20th century – an indication that the basic design was flexible enough to survive many changes in musical style.

The symphony became so important that many orchestras have used the description 'symphony orchestra' in their title, even though they play many other types of music. The most likely place to hear a symphony today is in a concert hall – a typical orchestral concert will often include at least one symphony.

SYMPHONY NO. 40 IN G MINOR

By the late 18th century, almost every public concert in Vienna began with a symphony, and wealthy aristocrats would often commission composers to write symphonies for their own private orchestras to play. Mozart wrote his three last symphonies in a little over six weeks, during the summer of 1788. They were not commissioned, and it seems likely that he wrote them for a series of three concerts he was planning to revive his failing fortunes, perhaps followed by publications of the three works as a set.

There is little evidence that these concerts ever took place, but the fact that Mozart later went to the trouble of rescoring this symphony to include clarinets suggests that he had at least one specific performance in mind. The recording on CD 1 Track 2 (by the Capella Istropolitana from Bratislava, near Vienna) is of this later version.

Although we know nothing of the first performance, we do know that the symphony was first published in 1794, soon after Mozart's death. Performances followed and it quickly became well known, and by 1804 a leading music magazine was hailing the work as a masterpiece. Mozart remained a respected figure during the 19th century, although his music was not as widely performed as it is today. However, during the 20th century this symphony became a standard concert work, frequently played by orchestras around the world, and it remains well known to many members of the public today.

Following the score

The full list of instruments is printed at the start of the score. The woodwind come first, in order from high to low (reading down the page): one flute, plus two each of oboes, clarinets and bassoons. Next come the brass: two horns, which have a separate stave for each player. Finally come the strings, again from high to low. The string parts are laid out in a similar way to those in *Messiah* – remember that the violas use the alto C clef, and that the double basses play the same notes as the cellos, but sound an octave lower.

There is no continuo part – the larger number of wind instruments in Classical music means that there was rarely still a need for a keyboard instrument to fill out the harmonies. Many symphonies of this period also included parts for trumpets and timpani, but Mozart clearly decided that their additional power was not needed in this intense, passionate work.

As the number of wind instruments increased, orchestras tended to need more string players to balance them out. Although this symphony doesn't need the huge orchestra that we shall see is required for set work 4, Mozart would probably have wanted about 25 instruments in total, 16 of which would have been strings. Today, we call a group of this size a **chamber orchestra** – an ensemble suited to a large room ('chamber') or small concert hall.

© Vienna Mozart Orchestra

The Vienna Mozart Orchestra – a modern chamber orchestra

The clarinet was invented around 1730 and had become a standard instrument in many orchestras by the end of the 18th century. Woodwind instruments at this time had far fewer keys than their modern equivalents. In the case of the clarinet, which has a wide range, this meant that it was not easy to play some notes. To get round this problem, players had instruments of slightly different sizes to suit the key of the music.

A 'clarinet in C' works like most instruments – if a C is played, the note C sounds, and the same applies to all of its other notes. If the key of the music required a 'clarinet in B♭', the composer would write the music a tone higher, so that when C is played, B♭ sounds. All other notes similarly sound a tone lower than written. Clarinettists thus didn't have to learn new fingerings for the B♭ clarinet, but composers did have to learn how to **transpose** – that is, to write music at a consistently different pitch.

Look now at bars 133–138 in GAM 2. The clarinets are playing exactly the same notes as the oboes, but their stave looks different because parts for clarinets in B♭ have to be written a tone higher than they sound.

Top Tips

When an instrument is described as being 'in x', x is the note that sounds when C is played. From this, we can work out how it transposes. So, a 'clarinet in B♭' sounds B♭ when C is played: B♭ is a tone below C, so we now know that the music for a clarinet in B♭ will sound a tone lower than written.

The horn was another new arrival in the Classical orchestra, and proved ideal for sustaining the harmonies that keyboard instruments had provided in the Baroque period. The type of horn used in the 18th century is called a **natural horn** – it didn't have the finger-operated valves of modern horns to help produce different pitches, and so players had to rely mainly on using their lips. This meant that only a small selection of pitches was available. The only ones that appear in the horn parts of the set work are those on the top stave below.

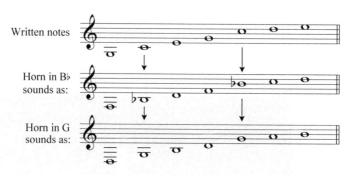

However, horn players could insert an extra piece of tubing (called a crook) to change the pitch of the entire instrument. If a B♭ crook is used, the notes on the top stave sound as shown on the middle stave. If a G crook is used, they sound as shown on the lowest stave.

To maximise the number of pitches that can be used in the horn parts, Mozart pulls a clever trick – he asks one player to crook in B♭ and the other player to crook in G. Even so, we can see that most of the available notes are too widely spaced to allow either horn to play a melody, which is why the instrument is used mainly for sustaining harmonies and for adding weight in the louder sections of the movement.

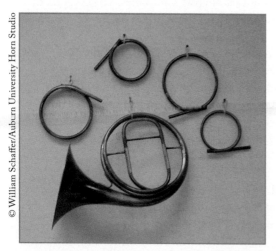

A natural horn with different sizes of crook

Because the crook did the job of transposing notes to the required key, horn parts were always written in C major, without a key signature. This means that the natural horn is a transposing instrument, and it follows the rule in the tip above. When the instrument is 'in B♭', the note B♭ (a tone below C) sounds when C is played – and all other notes sound a tone below their written pitch, like the clarinet in B♭. When the instrument is 'in G', the note G (a 4th below C) sounds when C is played – and all other notes sound a 4th below their written pitch.

Let's see how this works in practice. Take a look at bars 153–160 in GAM. The first horn plays E in every one of these bars. Because it is crooked in B♭, the notes will sound a tone lower than written – in other words, they will all sound as D. Now look at the second horn part. It plays G in every one of these bars. Because it is crooked in G, the notes will sound a 4th lower than written – in other words, they will also all sound as D, but an octave below the first horn.

The score is more difficult to follow than the one for the first set work because, after the first system, staves are omitted for instruments that are not playing to save space. This means that the number of staves in a system frequently varies. You may find it easiest to follow the first violin part, letting your eye take in other staves when something interesting happens in a different part.

The score shows how composers were starting to add a lot more performing directions. As well as detailed dynamics, there are curved slurs over notes to be played **legato** (smoothly), dots or wedges over notes to be played **staccato** (detached) and **accents** (the sign *sf* in bars 34–37) on notes to be played forcefully. The **crescendo** marking in bar 63 means gradually get louder, and is a reminder that dynamics were not limited to the simple contrasts between loud and soft that were common in Baroque music. The tempo direction (Molto Allegro) means very fast.

Other signs and abbreviations in the score include:

- ■ 'div.' in bar 1 of the viola part, which indicates that the players are to divide into two groups, one playing the upper notes and the other playing the lower notes
- ■ 'a 2' (for example, in bar 28 of the bassoon part), which indicates that both players are to play the same notes
- ■ '1' (for example, in bar 45 of the clarinet part), indicating that only one player is required – in other words, a solo
- ■ The symbol *tr* (for example, in bar 65 of the first violin part), which stands for a **trill** – a type of ornament in which the printed pitch is rapidly and repeatedly alternated with the note one step above
- ■ The double bar line (with pairs of dots) at the end of bar 100, which indicates that the first 100 bars are to be repeated.

Test yourself

1. Why is the city of Vienna important in the history of Classical music?
2. Mozart is sometimes described as a child prodigy. What does prodigy mean?
3. What is a symphony and in what sort of venue would you expect to hear one played?
4. How does a natural horn differ from the type of horn used today?
5. What does the term 'crescendo' mean?

Consult the score in GAM to answer the following questions:

6. What two notes are played by the violas on the first beat of bar 1?
7. Which of the following best describes the solo played by clarinet and bassoon in bars 45–46?
   (a) They play in unison
   (b) Apart from the fourth note, they play the same tune
   (c) They play in octaves.
8. What does 'a 2' mean in bar 91 of the clarinet part?

Listen to the first part of the recording up to 1:52, without following the score, and see if you can identify the following four features:

A	0:00	A quiet tune in a minor key that begins with repeated falling semitones
B	0:32	A loud major-key motif that starts with rising leaps (ending with a total silence at 0:48)
C	0:49	A quiet tune with falling phrases in a major key, shared between violins and woodwind, leading to a big build up that suddenly ends with a quiet descending scale
D	1:21	A return of the falling semitones from the opening melody, ending with a series of cadences

Sonata form was used for the first movement of sonatas, symphonies and many other types of instrumental music from the Classical period onwards. Composers sometimes also used it for other movements (three of the four movements in this symphony are in sonata form) and for single-movement works such as overtures.

What you have heard is the opening section of a movement in **sonata form** – the most important large musical structure in the Classical period and for many years beyond. This section is known as the **exposition** because it presents (or 'exposes') the main ideas of the whole movement.

The two main melodies in sonata form are known as 'subjects'. The **first subject** is the tune in G minor that you heard at the start (**A**), and the **second subject** is the tune in B♭ major (the relative major) that you heard at **C**. The journey between the two is known as the **transition** and, as noted in **B** above, it contains a short but distinctive motif of its own. The exposition comes to an end with a **closing section** in the key of the second subject and is, in this work, based on a motif from the first subject.

Here is the exposition in graphic form. The main keys are represented by blue for G minor and green for B♭ major:

Bar number	1	**A**	28	**B**	44	**C**	72	**D**
Exposition	First subject		Transition		Second subject		Closing section	
Track timing	0:00			0:32	0:49		1:21	

Now listen to the complete movement. The whole of the exposition is repeated, which takes us to 3:44 on the CD. Try to spot the following features in the rest of the movement:

E	3:45	Chords lead to a series of new versions of the first subject that sound increasingly weird as the key shifts rapidly and unpredictably. Agitated quavers accompany the loud version of the first subject, after which it fragments until only repetitions of its first three notes remain.
F	4:55	The music from the exposition is heard again, in the same order as before, but with several changes. In particular, the transition is much longer and the second subject is now in a *minor* key.

Section **E** is known as the **development**, and is the part of sonata form in which the composer transforms material from the exposition using a variety of different keys.

Section **F** is known as the **recapitulation** – a word we often shorten to 'recap.' but that should always be spelled out in full for music exams. In it, the music from the exposition is repeated, but changed so that most of it stays centered on the tonic key throughout.

Sonata form is really about **tonality** – the use of keys – to structure music. The exposition starts in the tonic (here, G minor) but soon moves to a related key (B♭ major, the relative major). The development creates instability by passing rapidly through a range of keys, although it ends by preparing for the return of the tonic. The recapitulation restores order by staying focused on the tonic key. We can see this in the following diagram, in which the turmoil of keys in the development is indicated by the colour red:

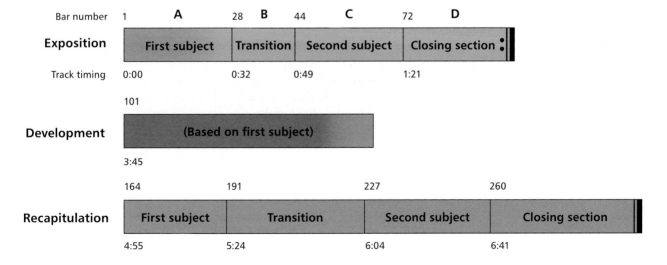

Now that we have established the main signposts in the movement, we'll look in detail at each of its sections.

Exposition

First subject

Mozart starts with a quiet accompaniment pattern, played on divided violas, above which the first subject begins on the last beat of the first bar, creating an **anacrusis** – the technical term for a weak-beat opening. There are three statements of the important falling semitone motif, the last followed by an upward leap and a short rest. Mozart then balances these eight beats with a downward descent to the same rhythm:

Already we can see the Classical preference for balance at work (remember the building pictured on page 44). This becomes even clearer when Mozart repeats the opening four-bar melody a step lower in sequence (bars 5^4–9^3):

> A **pedal** is a sustained or repeated note, often in the bass, heard against changing harmonies.

- The first four-bar phrase (bars 1^4–5^3) is underpinned by a **pedal** on the tonic (G), and has an inconclusive ending that makes it sound like a question
- The second four-bar phrase (bars 5^4–9^3) ends with a perfect cadence that makes it sound like an answer.

This is the balanced, question-and-answer phrasing that is typical of the Classical style.

Mozart extends his first subject with a continuous eight-bar phrase (to balance the first eight bars), which ends with the entry of the entire orchestra for the chords in bars 16–20. Woodwind lean up to the dominant chord of D (notice the *rising* semitone in the flute), while strings hammer out the rhythm of the opening motif on D, forming a dominant pedal.

This heralds a repeat of the opening of the first subject, which starts over the top of the bassoons' link in bar 20, forming a seamless overlap. But there's an important change – F♯ no longer appears, and warm **seventh chords** start to usher in the relative major key of B♭. Using another overlap to avoid any gaps that would interrupt the flow, Mozart makes the last chord of the perfect cadence in bars 27–28 also serve as the first chord of the …

Transition

The transition in sonata form is also known as the 'bridge passage' because it bridges the gap between first and second subjects. Although short, it has its own distinctive theme (which will become important later):

Unlike the drooping semitones of the first and second subjects, it is loud and confident, consisting of rising leaps between notes of chords. It starts on a strong beat, rather than with an anacrusis, and it is accompanied by amusing burbling quavers on bassoons and lower strings. This is a good place to point out that, while much of the movement seems emotionally highly charged, part of Mozart's skill lies in his ability to change mood in an instant.

The transition ends with rising scales (bars 34–37) over that persistent semitone (C–D♭ in the bass), followed by chords over a dominant pedal in B♭ (bars 38–42). Both the scales and the chords suggest B♭ *minor*, but a general pause (bar 43) clears the air, ready for the …

Second subject

The second subject begins in bar 44 with another pair of balanced phrases, the first ending in an imperfect cadence and the second in a perfect cadence. Both phrases start with a **chromatic** descent (introducing those falling semitones again), but the cadences make the key of B♭ *major* crystal clear.

Top Tips

The use of balanced phrases is described as **periodic phrasing**. If you need to explain this important feature of the Classical style, the second subject makes a good example, because the imperfect cadence at the end of the first phrase helps to make it sound like a question, while the perfect cadence at the end of the second phrase creates the feeling that an answer has been given.

Notice the scoring of the second subject. Like the first subject, it is played in octaves, but here the first phrase is shared between strings and woodwind. It starts on violins but the clarinet and bassoon take over the third note, and then hand the phrase back to the violins in bar 46.

Another similarity with the first subject is the use of mainly descending phrases, but the rhythm is totally different. There is no anacrusis, the insistent quaver–quaver–crotchet pattern has gone, and the tune is accompanied by simple chords rather than throbbing quavers. The melody moves mainly by step and has a more relaxed, lyrical character.

Mozart uses a standard chord pattern known as the **circle of 5ths** in part of the second phrase – each new chord is a 5th below the previous one (G is a 5th below D, C is a 5th below G, and so on):

Circle of 5ths

A short link played by clarinet and bassoon (bar 51) leads to a repeat of the second subject, in which roles are reversed – the first phrase is now mainly in the woodwind, with violins chipping in for the six notes originally played by clarinet and bassoon.

> A **syncopated** rhythm is one in which the main notes fall on weak beats (look at the flute and bassoon parts in bars 58–61 and the second violins in bars 64–65).

In bar 58 the second phrase is interrupted by falling semitones pitted against **syncopated** rising semitones on the flute. Continuous quavers return in the accompaniment and a big build-up begins in which the harmony, having been stuck on the same pair of chords for five bars, bursts free to rise through a dramatic chromatic chord (the **diminished 7th** in bar 63) to reach a powerful perfect cadence in B♭ major during bars 64–66.

It seems like another build-up is to follow as strings climb chromatically in octaves in bars 66^2–68^1, but it is not to be – the second subject ends in a delicate descending scale of B♭ major in bars 70–72^1.

Closing section

Mozart starts with a major-key version of his opening three-note motif, played on clarinet and echoed an octave lower by bassoon. This type of interchange is often described as a **dialogue**:

Notice that the original falling semitone in this motif is now a falling *tone*, creating a much gentler effect in the key of B♭ major. At the end of bar 76, first violins reintroduce the original minor-key version of the motif, but it is quickly overtaken by a cadence in B♭ major (bars 79–80).

> A **coda** (Italian for 'tail') is a rounding-off section at the end of a movement. A **codetta** ('little tail') is a similar passage at the end of a main section.

In bars 80^4–84^3 Mozart repeats the dialogue – but can you see how it is different? This is again followed by a brief appearance of the minor-key version of the motif, and this time the B♭-major cadence (bars 87–88) leads to a passage of descending scales and repeated perfect cadences. This final section (bars 88–99) is called a **codetta**, and its purpose is to reinforce the new key centre of the piece, B♭ major.

In bar 100, the solitary loud chord is the **dominant 7th** of G minor, preparing for the return of the home key when the exposition is repeated.

Development

Mozart uses a short link to move from G minor at the start of bar 101 to the remote key of F♯ minor in bar 105. Before the link has finished, the first subject returns, but it is already starting to mutate. We hear only its first four bars, the last two notes of which are altered, and these four bars appear three times in all, in descending sequence. Below the sequence, the bass moves down in steps (F♯, E♯, E♮, D♯) and there are no clear cadences to clarify the key.

At the end of bar 114, Mozart introduces a **contrapuntal** texture in which the first subject is played by low strings and bassoons, above which the violins have a staccato **countermelody**. Roles reverse at the end of bar 118 – the first subject moves to the violins and the countermelody to the bass. Mozart continues this alternation (with upper woodwind supplying supporting harmonies) through a succession of rapidly changing keys.

At bar 138 the dynamic drops to **_p_** and Mozart presents the opening of the first subject in **imitation** between first violins and upper woodwind. Notice how he lightens the texture by avoiding low instruments in this passage. The first subject fragments still further, until only three notes are left (which sometimes rise rather than fall, as in the woodwind parts of bar 148).

At bar 153 Mozart begins a long pedal on D, the dominant of the home key of G minor, started by the horns and taken over by the bassoons. This is known as **dominant preparation**, and is a signal used by most composers of the period that the recapitulation is getting near. Above the pedal, fragments of the first subject descend chromatically but, before they or the dominant pedal have finished, the first subject sneaks back in (bar 164[4]). The recapitulation has begun.

Recapitulation

The start of the recapitulation sees the return of the tonic key (G minor) as well as the reappearance of the complete first subject. This final section in sonata form follows the order of the exposition, but there have to be some changes because the movement would sound unfinished if it ended in the relative major key like the exposition. In particular, the second subject and closing section have to be rewritten to stay in the tonic.

In fact, Mozart starts making small changes (such as the new bassoon part in bars 168–172) almost immediately. That one is probably to add variety, but the changes to both the melody and the harmony from bar 185 onward are part of the composer's advance preparation for re-locating the second subject to the tonic key.

Mozart generally prefers to hold his listeners' attention by varying material rather than repeating it exactly, and this is particularly clear in the transition (starting in bar 191). It begins in a similar way to its first appearance in bar 28, except that it is a 5th lower, in E♭ major. However, we've not heard its distinctive melody since the exposition, and so Mozart seizes the opportunity to develop the section into more than twice its original length. This enlarged transition includes:

■ Presenting the melody in the bass against a counterpoint of quavers in the violins (starting in bar 198)

■ Detaching four of the melody's notes to use in close imitation over a circle-of-5ths harmony (Fm, B♭, E♭, A♭, Dm, G and Cm in bars 203–209), while the second violins continue the quaver counterpoint:

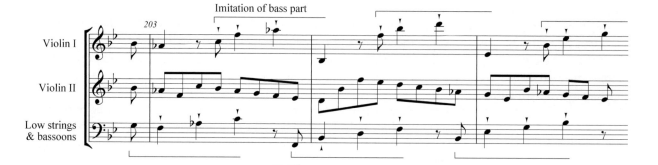

■ Shifting the whole of the original transition to the home key of G minor in preparation for the entry of the second subject in this key (bars 211–226).

The second subject returns in bars 227–259. The first part is similar to the exposition, although the change from B♭ major to G minor makes a big difference to the character of the music. However, at the point where Mozart originally introduced a 'dramatic chromatic chord' (bar 63) to break free from the repetitions of the previous bars, he now goes much further. Bar 246 corresponds with bar 63 (the diminished 7th chord), but Mozart then adds five extra bars over a chromatically rising bass (with further diminished 7th chords in bars 247, 249 and 251) to winch-up the tension before the perfect cadence in G minor in bars 252–254[1]).

The first 21 bars of the closing section (starting in bar 260) are taken from the similar passage in the exposition, transposed down to G minor. At bar 281 Mozart introduces a short, highly dramatic outburst. Above and below a tonic pedal in the second horn (also played in syncopated rhythm by the violas), woodwind ascend with a syncopated chromatic scale, which is also picked out in dotted rhythm by the other strings.

The discordant clashes between pedal and rising chromatic notes end as quickly as they began, but Mozart has still not finished with development, even this late in the movement. The first subject is given a new ending (second violins, bars 285[4]–288) which is imitated by first violins, violas and (opening notes only) woodwind. Finally, a brief coda (bars 293–299) brings the movement to a close with repeated perfect cadences in the key of G minor.

Test yourself

1. The phrases of the first subject begin with an anacrusis. What does this term mean?
2. What name can be given to the total silence in bar 43?
3. In sonata form, what name is given to the section between the exposition and the recapitulation?
4. What two things return at the *start* of the recapitulation in sonata form?
5. What type of ornament is played by the first violins in each of bars 247 to 250?
6. What is the main difference between the second subject in the exposition and the second subject in the recapitulation?
7. This movement contains several chromatic passages. What does chromatic mean?
8. Mozart often creates new tone colours by doubling a melody in a different octave. For example, the clarinet phrase in bars 14–16[1] is doubled an octave higher by the flute and an octave lower by the bassoon. Explain how the following passages are doubled:
    (a) Strings in bars 44–45
    (b) Woodwind in bar 51
    (c) Woodwind in bars 70–72[1].

Further listening

To broaden your knowledge of Mozart's music and of the Classical symphony, here are some more works that you might enjoy:

- **The other movements of this symphony.** The second movement (in E♭ major) is slow and lyrical, and is another sonata-form structure (without a transition between first and second subjects). The third movement is a stormy minuet in G minor – totally different from the normally elegant style associated with this dance. It is included in the original (2002) edition of GAM. The last movement (still in G minor) is very fast, and is again in sonata form.
- **Mozart's Symphony No. 41** in C major, K. 551 (nicknamed the 'Jupiter'), finished less than three weeks after the G minor symphony. The grand, celebratory style of its first movement could hardly be more different from our set work, despite the fact that it, too, is in sonata form.
- **Haydn's Symphony No. 104** in D major (nicknamed the 'London'). Composed in 1795, seven years after Mozart's G minor symphony, and first performed in London. The first movement includes two features found in some sonata-form movements, although not in our set work: it starts with a slow introduction before the exposition, and the second subject is simply the first subject in the dominant key (a reminder that contrast of keys was at least as important as contrast of tunes in the early history of sonata form).
- **Beethoven's Symphony No. 5** in C minor, first performed in 1808, is perhaps even better known than Mozart's Symphony No. 40. The first movement is in sonata form and makes intensive use of its famous four-note opening motif.
- **Schubert's Symphony in C major**, D. 944 (nicknamed the 'Great' C-major) was completed in 1826 and shows some of the influences of the Romantic style that was then starting to develop, including larger orchestras, longer movements and more emphasis on melody. Both the first movement and the (very exciting) last movement are in sonata form.

Composing ideas

While studying the first movement of Mozart's Symphony No. 40 we have come across a number of techniques that could be used in your own compositions. These could be effective in most styles of music – you are not required to write in the style of Mozart. You might like to try composing:

- A piece that uses different keys to define its various sections. This wouldn't necessarily have to be sonata form. You could, for instance, write a piece in ternary form (ABA) in which the A sections are in the main key, while the middle B section passes through a variety of different keys, perhaps ending with a passage of 'dominant preparation' in readiness for the return of the A section.
- A piece based on just one or two motifs that are developed with some of the techniques used by Mozart, such as varied repetition, sequence, fragmenting a motif and using it in imitation.
- A song that includes a section with chords based on the circle of 5ths (but note that this progression is rather over-used in some types of pop music, so just one such passage in the song would probably be enough!).
- A piece in which melodies are shared between instruments (like the start of Mozart's second subject) rather than being played continuously on the same instrument.

Sample questions for Section A

Listen to the section of CD 1 Track 2 from 0:49 to 1:14 four times, with short pauses between each playing, as you answer the following questions. Don't consult the score or any other information before writing your answers.

1. Here are the first eight bars of the melody. Add the rhythm (only) of the tune in bar 2. (2)

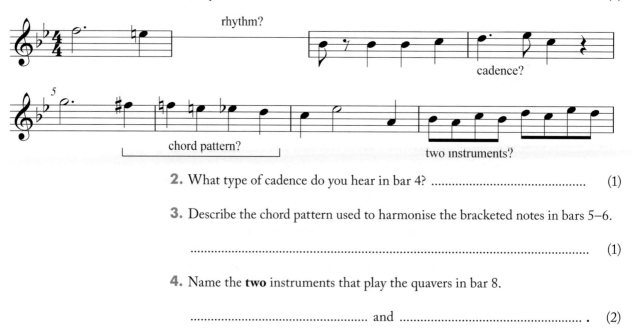

2. What type of cadence do you hear in bar 4? .... (1)

3. Describe the chord pattern used to harmonise the bracketed notes in bars 5–6.

.... (1)

4. Name the **two** instruments that play the quavers in bar 8.

.... and .... (2)

5. After bar 8, the first six bars above are repeated. State **two** ways in which these bars differ when repeated.

(a) ....

(b) .... (2)

6. What rhythmic device do you hear in the bars immediately after this repeat?

.... (1)

7. Underline the term below that best describes the texture of this extract.

contrapuntal   homophonic   imitative   monophonic   (1)

(Total 10 marks)

Top Tips

If you are asked to state from which part of the movement this extract comes, remember that the second subject is major in the exposition and minor in the recapitulation.

Don't forget that you could be asked to name some of the main features of the Classical style. Could you name four?

Sample questions for Section B

Before tackling this section read the information on writing extended answers, on page 167. Then complete your answers without consulting any notes or the score, and without listening to the recording.

The following questions are about Symphony No. 40 (first movement) by Mozart.

(a) In which century was this music composed? .... (1)

(b) What style is this piece of music written in? .... (1)

(c) Comment on how Mozart uses the following musical elements in this movement:

> Don't forget to mention balanced phrases and chromatic writing. →

> Include the various types of woodwind doubling, the role of the horns and the different string textures Mozart uses. →

Structure and tonality
Melody
Texture
Dynamics
Use of instruments   (10)

Use correct musical vocabulary where appropriate and remember that the quality of your writing, including spelling, punctuation and grammar, will be taken into account in this question. Write your answer on a separate sheet of paper.

(Total 12 marks)

SET WORK 3: PRELUDE NO. 15 IN D♭ MAJOR, OP. 28 BY CHOPIN

Op. is an abbreviation of *opus* (Latin for 'work'). This piece is from a set of preludes that Chopin labelled as his 28th work.

Our third set work dates from early in the Romantic period. This doesn't mean that the music of the age was all about love (although some was) – but it was a time when many composers explored the power of music to affect the emotions.

Some Romantic composers used music to paint pictures in sound (orchestral pieces known as tone poems), often depicting vivid scenes from nature. Some wrote pieces of extreme difficulty to impress their fans with technical skill. A growing awareness that Italy and Germany were not the only countries capable of producing great music led to musicians from other parts of Europe becoming widely known as composers. Many of them included elements from their own national traditions in their music. Chopin, for example, was born in Poland and wrote a number of works based on traditional Polish dance styles such as the mazurka and polonaise.

The Romantic period was also one of extremes, with music ranging from long works for huge numbers of performers to short piano pieces and songs suitable for the growing market of music-making in the home. The industrial revolution brought modest prosperity and increased leisure time to a new middle class, who became major consumers of music, replacing the aristocrats who had employed composers in earlier centuries. Industrial processes also helped to make printed music cheaper, allowing many composers to work as freelance musicians, earning a living from the publication and performance of their works.

Well-known composers of the early Romantic period include Schumann, Mendelssohn, Chopin and Berlioz. Later generations include Wagner, Verdi, Liszt, Brahms, Grieg, Tchaikovsky and Dvořák.

Typical features of the Romantic style include:

- Large orchestras (often including a full range of woodwind, brass, percussion, harp and strings)
- Increasing technical difficulty in some types of music
- An emphasis on melody, supported by more complex chords and more daring modulations than in earlier periods
- A tendency to use descriptive titles to suggest a mood or an idea behind the music
- An ability to evoke a wide range of human emotions, from horror, fear, grief or unfulfilled love to triumph over despair and overwhelming joy
- Works that explore pure fantasy, such as music about trolls, witches, fairies, medieval knights or mythical heroes, and pieces that suggest vivid natural images, such as a moonlit night or a fearsome storm at sea
- Less formal structures than earlier periods and greater freedom of expression
- A wide dynamic range, from the almost inaudible to the overpoweringly forceful.

Neuschwanstein castle in Bavaria, Germany

As with the other styles we've looked at, we can use the visual arts to get a clearer picture of Romanticism. The photo above looks at first sight like a remarkably well-preserved medieval castle. It is nothing of the kind. It's a purely Romantic fantasy, built for King Ludwig II of Bavaria in the late 19th century. The spectacular hilltop setting reflects the age's love of the grandeur of nature, while its towers almost seem made for imprisoning Rapunzel, the subject of one of the famous fairy tales collected by the brothers Grimm that became so popular during the Romantic period.

The drama of nature was also a common theme in Romantic paintings. Unlike the formal head-and-shoulders portraits of the 18th century, the solitary figure in this landscape by Caspar David Friedrich has his back to the viewer, so we are forced to use our own imagination in deciding whether he is master of this wild scene, overawed by it, or simply terrified of it.

We mentioned earlier that Romantic music is a style of extremes, and that small-scale music for domestic consumption (such as our set work) existed alongside works of heroic proportions. The new middle class market is perfectly reflected in the German style known as *Biedermeier*. The interior scene pictured on the next page reflects the type of house in which cultured amateurs might perform songs by Schumann and piano pieces by Chopin, for their own pleasure or for the entertainment of their family and friends.

'Wanderer Above the Sea of Fog'

This is no aristocratic palace – the rooms are not large, the furniture is simple and functional, and the walls are hung with framed prints rather than original paintings. But on the other hand, fitted carpets, elegant draperies and echoes of the classical style around the door and on the ceiling reflect the comfortable life style of the type of family that would become an important market for the smaller-scale compositions of the Romantic period.

FRÉDÉRIC CHOPIN (1810–1849)

Chopin was born in a small Polish village in 1810, but while he was still a baby his family moved to the city of Warsaw. There, Chopin showed early talent as a pianist and by the age of eight he was performing at society gatherings and had had his first two compositions published.

The only known photograph of Chopin, taken shortly before his death in 1849 and so dating from the very earliest years of photography

Although his early years sound like those of Mozart, they were actually far more ordinary. Instead of concert tours around Europe, Chopin went to school in Warsaw, and generally he much preferred playing to small groups of appreciative people rather than giving public concerts.

Chopin left Poland when he was 20 and eventually settled in Paris where he felt very much at home (his father was French and Chopin himself, like many cultured Poles, spoke fluent French). Although he continued to avoid public concerts as much as possible, he performed to private gatherings in the salons of Paris, where his playing was famed for its beauty of tone and singing quality of its melodies, and he was soon making a good living from the high fees he was able to command as a piano teacher. At the same time, publication of his compositions (most of which are for solo piano, and all of which include the piano) started to attract international attention.

In 1838 Chopin began a long and difficult affair with a female French novelist, six years his senior, who wrote under the pen name of George Sand. The pair of them spent the winter on the Mediterranean island of Majorca, where Chopin completed the set of preludes from which our set work is taken. However, by then the first signs of the disease from which he would eventually die had appeared. Chopin was eventually able to return to work, but his health continued to be a matter of concern and his relationship with Sand (which had become the subject of much public gossip) gradually deteriorated. He died in Paris at the age of 39 from tuberculosis, the biggest killer of the age, for which there was no cure before the discovery of antibiotics a century later. By the time of his death, Chopin's reputation as one of the greatest composers of piano music was secure. His works continued to grow in popularity through the 19th century and are now played by many pianists around the world.

THE PIANO

Unlike a harpsichord, the dynamics of individual notes on the piano can be varied across a wide range, resulting in the very first pianos being described as keyboards with *piano e forte* ('soft and loud'). This eventually led to the new type of instrument being called the pianoforte, which we now shorten to piano.

The piano was invented in the early 18th century, but it was not until the Classical period that the mechanism became reliable enough for it to replace the harpsichord, which it then did surprisingly quickly. The pianos of Mozart's day had a smaller range of notes than modern instruments, and a softer, clearer tone. However, the invention of the iron frame in the 19th century allowed strings of much greater tension to be used. This gave a fuller tone and greater sustaining power, and enabled the range of the piano to be extended to more than seven octaves.

Various other developments in the first part of the 19th century included improvements to the mechanism to allow notes to be repeated very rapidly – something that was exploited in a lot of the more technically demanding piano music of the period, although not in our set work.

There are three strings per note on a piano, reducing to two for the lower notes and just one for each of the very lowest notes. When a key is pressed, a hammer strikes the strings to produce the required note. Releasing the key allows a felt-covered damper to fall back on the strings to stop them vibrating.

Pianos have at least two pedals, operated by the performer's feet. The right-hand one is known as the sustaining pedal (although often incorrectly described as the loud pedal). When pressed, all of the dampers are raised from the strings, allowing notes to ring on after their keys have been released. The left pedal is known as the soft pedal and, on a good piano, it moves the hammers slightly sideways so that only one string per note is struck, producing a softer, muted tone.

© Sefik Yüksel

Pianist İdil Biret standing next to Chopin's last piano, in the Chopin Museum in Poland

Chopin's Op. 28 consists of 24 preludes, one in each of the 12 major and 12 minor keys. They are arranged so that those in major keys form a **circle of 5ths**, each of which is followed by one in its relative-minor key, thus: C major, A minor, G major, E minor, D major, B minor and so on.

Other composers had written sets of preludes in every key – those by Bach, in particular, were studied by Chopin. However, the term prelude suggests an introduction to something else, and each of Bach's preludes is followed by a type of contrapuntal movement called a fugue. Chopin's preludes, in contrast, are short, self-contained movements (No. 15 is the longest), each with a different character. Although all 24 are sometimes performed as a complete set, Chopin played only individual preludes (or a small group of them) in his own concerts.

The preludes were first published in 1839, and Chopin dedicated the work to Camille Pleyel, a fellow pianist and owner of the company that made Chopin's favourite type of piano. They vary in difficulty, and some are as likely to be played by amateur pianists at home as by professionals in the concert hall. The performance on CD 1 Track 3 is by the Turkish pianist İdil Biret, who has recorded all of Chopin's piano music.

You may see this prelude described as 'programme music' – that is, a piece which tells a story or suggests an image. However, there is not the slightest evidence that Chopin intended it to suggest raindrops, and it is clear from his letters that he strongly objected to programmatic titles being added to his music.

Unlike many of his contemporaries, Chopin was not keen on giving descriptive titles to his music. The nickname 'Raindrop' arose from a story told by George Sand that slowly dripping water on the roof of the building where they stayed in Majorca caused the sickly Chopin to imagine, as he composed, that he had drowned in a lake and heavy drops of icy water were falling on his dead body. She, of course, had the imagination of a Romantic novelist, while he thought the whole idea was stuff and nonsense. Nevertheless, the nickname became associated with the persistent repeated quavers that dominate this piece (even though we don't know for sure which particular composition Sand was referring to!)

Following the score

A quick comparison with the scores of the first two set works shows that Romantic composers continued the practice of adding ever more detailed performing directions to their music.

The long curved lines are phrase marks, indicating passages that should sound as a continuous **legato** statement. The direction 'Ped.' below the bass stave shows where to press the sustaining pedal, while the star-shaped sign shows where to release it in order to stop different chords from blurring into each other.

As well as the abbreviation 'cresc.' Chopin uses 'dim.' (short for **diminuendo**, meaning gradually get quieter). He also uses signs that musicians nickname 'hairpins' to indicate similar dynamic changes: if the lines open out (as seen between the staves in bars 2–3) there should be a small crescendo, while if they close up (as in bars 3–4) there should be a small diminuendo.

The word at the start (sostenuto) is Italian for 'sustained'. It's not really a tempo direction, but it does suggest a fairly relaxed pace. The time signature **C** means the same as $\frac{4}{4}$ time – four crotchet beats in a bar.

The left hand in bar 28 is marked *sotto voce* (Italian for 'under the voice' and implying the musical equivalent of a whisper) – some pianists choose to use the soft pedal at this point, to get the right sort of hushed tone. Three more Italian words appear in the final bars. In bar 79, *smorzando* means 'dying away'. Two bars later, the direction *slentando* means becoming broader (which here might mean both slower and louder). In bar 88, ritenuto means immediately slower.

The small numbers on many notes are suggestions for fingering which have been added by an editor rather than the composer. The vertical bracket in bar 9 instructs the pianist to use the right hand to play the top note in the chord on the bass stave, because it involves too wide a stretch for the left hand alone.

There are several unusual rhythmic features. The group of seven notes with the figure 7 above in bars 4 and 23 is called a **septuplet**: in each case, all seven notes have to be fitted into a single beat. A similar rhythmic effect occurs in bar 79, where ten notes have to be fitted into the last beat of the bar. The notes in small type in bars 11 and 15 are called **grace notes**, and the time they take is deducted from the previous note in each case.

In bar 42, the unusual symbol ✗ is called a double sharp – a note that is two semitones higher than the natural note. Here, F✗ is the same note as G natural.

The term cantabile (Italian for 'singable') is often used to describe the song-like nature of Chopin's expressive melodies.

One important feature of Romantic piano music that is not notated in the score is called **rubato** – an Italian word meaning 'robbed'. It refers to creating an expressive rhythm by making some notes fractionally longer than notated, at the expense of others that are made fractionally shorter. Chopin explained that rubato should only be used in the 'singing hand' (the hand playing the tune), adding that the accompanying hand should always keep strict time. However, many pianists today ignore this advice – listen to İdil Biret's performance of the septuplets in bars 4 and 23, for example.

Listen to the recording on CD 1 Track 3, without following the score, and see if you can identify the following three main sections in the piece:

A	0:00	A section in a major key with a long, elegant melody, heard several times
B	1:38	A contrasting section in a minor key with a rather plodding melody mainly in the bass, and containing several loud climaxes
A	4:33	A shortened version of the opening section

Because the sections flow into each other, and are not self-contained like those in most ternary-form pieces, and because the final A section is very short, you may see the structure described as rounded binary form: two main sections, the second of which is rounded off by a reference to the opening material.

This is known as **ternary form** – a sort of musical sandwich, in which the two outer sections surround a different filling in the middle. We could describe it as ABA[1] (where A[1] means that the second A section is not identical to the first one). It is a structure that was popular for short piano pieces in the Romantic period.

Two other features that you may have spotted while listening to the prelude are:

- A repeated note (mainly on the same pitch) that acts as a **pedal** throughout most of the piece and that perhaps suggests raindrops
- A **coda** which starts at 4:58 (where the pedal briefly stops), that brings the prelude to a close with some drawn-out perfect cadences.

There is no counterpoint in the piece – the texture is **homophonic**, with a short **monophonic** passage in bars 82–83. The song-like melody in the outer sections is supported by **broken chords** in the left hand, while in the middle section the melody is rather more plain, and mostly in the left hand.

A **broken chord** is a chord in which some or all of the notes are sounded separately rather than together.

Section A

Chopin gives the opening four-bar melody an elegant shape by starting with a descent through the key chord, followed by a stepwise ascent that ends by falling back to the tonic:

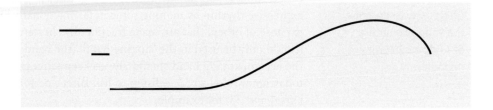

The distinctive rhythm at the start of this melody (see left) consists of a dotted pattern followed by a gently syncopated minim. The same rhythm is used to different pitches in bar 3, helping to unify the melody.

These opening four bars are then repeated almost exactly, with the septuplet in bar 4 providing a link between the two phrases. The harmonies are entirely based on the tonic and dominant chords of D♭ major, with a dominant pedal running throughout, and perfect cadences in bars 4 and 8.

The new phrase that starts on the last beat of bar 8 also features a syncopated minim (bar 9). Again, the phrase is repeated although its second appearance starts differently (on the second beat of bar 12). A third version follows, with rather more changes. These phrases are harmonically more varied than the first eight bars, and they visit two related keys. This means that the A♭ pedal cannot always be used, although its persistent 'raindrop' rhythm does continue.

In bars 20–27 the opening phrase returns and is heard twice, with an important change in bars 26–27, where the cadence is imperfect, not perfect, in order to lead into the middle section of the prelude.

We can thus see that not only is the whole piece ternary in form, but also that its first section uses a small-scale ternary structure.

Section B

The minor key with the same tonic note as a major key is known as the tonic minor or parallel minor key. For example, C minor is the tonic minor of C major. In the set work, D♭ minor has been written enharmonically as C♯ minor to reduce the number of accidentals needed.

The repeated A♭s in bar 27 become repeated G♯s from bar 28 onwards. A♭ and G♯ sound the same and are therefore known as **enharmonic equivalents**. The key signature also changes at this point, but the effect is not as startling as it might look. Chopin has simply moved from D♭ major to C♯ minor – the same tonic note, now written enharmonically as C♯, but the key is now minor and is known as the **tonic minor** of D♭ major.

Top Tips

Make sure you are really clear about the meaning of enharmonic and the tonic minor key – ask your teacher for help if you're puzzled – as these are the sort of features that you could be asked about in the exam.

The dominant pedal continues, now written as G♯, but the minor key darkens the mood. The absence of a 3rd in some chords (such as the bare 5th heard throughout bar 31) gives the music a stark character, especially when combined with a lack of perfect cadences in the new key, and the ominous crotchet tread of a bass melody that has no clearly memorable shape.

Bar 36 sees a repeat of the first four bars of section B with the pedal now doubled in octaves, extra notes to thicken the texture and an enormous crescendo. The next four bars (bars 40–43, starting at 2:16) are new – a noisy outburst on a chord of E major, in which thunderous raindrops move up to the note B, and that ends with a perfect cadence in the dominant key (G♯ minor).

The whole of the first 16 bars of section B are then repeated in bars 44–59, after which Chopin introduces a new phrase of narrow range in bars 60–67. The varied repeat of these eight bars (bars 68–75) includes more dissonance and a final climax

(f in bar 70), before dying away to end on the dominant chord of C# minor (a
G#m chord). This chord is the enharmonic equivalent of the dominant of D♭
major, providing a smooth link to the …

Final section

The opening of the prelude (in D♭ major) is repeated but, after a more decorative
link in bar 79, its second phrase is cut short to make way for a short **coda**. Like
many of Chopin's codas, this maintains the listener's interest until the very end
of the piece by giving a tantalising hint of something new – the unaccompanied
melody starting at the end of bar 81 on the highest note of the piece. But the
vision vaporises as quickly as it arrived, and the melody sinks to the middle of the
texture to disappear amid the two perfect cadences that end the prelude.

If we use lower-case letters to represent the different parts of the main sections
that we have identified, we can finish by taking an overview of the entire structure
of the prelude in the following diagram:

Bar number	1	9	20	28	44	60	76	82
	a	b	a	c	c	d	a	coda
Track timing	0:00	0:29	1:09	1:38	2:30	3:26	4:33	4:58

A	B	A
D♭ major	C# minor	D♭ major

Test yourself

1. Chopin was born in Poland, but in which city did he eventually settle?
2. How did the pianos of the 19th century differ from those of Mozart's time?
3. What is the meaning of the word 'sostenuto' in bar 1 of the score?
4. The pianist is instructed to use the right-hand pedal in this piece. What is the correct name for that pedal and what effect does it have on the performance?
5. What other meaning of the term pedal is important in this piece?
6. What word best describes the texture of most of this prelude?
7. Which note is the enharmonic equivalent of **(a)** G# and **(b)** F𝄪?
8. What is meant by rubato?
9. What term best describes the form of this prelude? (There are two possible answers.)
10. What is unusual about the coda?

Further listening

To broaden your knowledge of Chopin's music and of Romantic piano music in general, here are some more works that you might enjoy:

- The other preludes in **Chopin's Op. 28: No. 7** (in A major) and **No. 20** (in C minor) are short and fairly easy, so you might be able to manage a performance if you (or someone in your class) can play the piano. The ferociously exciting **No. 24** (in D minor) on the other hand, is enough to strike fear in the hearts of even professional pianists.
- Two famous piano pieces by Chopin (both with nicknames that he would have disapproved of) are the **'Revolutionary' Étude**, Op. 10 No. 12 (a stormy work that elevates the humble pianist's study to a concert piece) and the **'Minute' Waltz** – a jolly dance that some pianists attempt to play in 60 seconds.
- Although Chopin disliked descriptive titles, many of his contemporaries wrote short piano works known as 'character pieces' because they aim to depict the mood or image suggested by their title. Look out for Schumann's collection called *Scenes from Childhood* (containing pieces with descriptive titles such as 'Dreaming', 'Frightening' and 'At the Fireside') and Mendelssohn's 'Spring Song' from his *Songs Without Words*. Three of the Schumann pieces are in Edexcel's *A-level Anthology of Music* and many pianists who study for grade exams are likely to have learned at least one 19th-century character piece. Two of Schumann's piano pieces from his *Album for the Young* are in the previous (2006) edtion of GAM.

Composing ideas

While studying this prelude we have come across a number of techniques that could be used in your own compositions. These could be effective in most styles of music – you are not required to write in the style of Chopin, nor does your own work have to be for piano.

The type of structure used in this prelude is sometimes described as 'nested' ternary form, because a miniature ternary form is nested within the first section of its overall ternary form. At its most extreme, you could write a piece with sections in the order ABA – CDC – ABA. However, exact repeats of long sections can be boring, and it is worth remembering that Chopin makes only a brief reference to A in his short final section. Another way to avoid the obvious is to vary material when it returns, rather than copying it out exactly.

How about writing a character piece for your instrument? You might, unlike Chopin, decide to make your intentions clear with a descriptive title – *Sweet Revenge, Night on the Town, A New Puppy* – use your imagination, and think carefully about how you could introduce contrasting sections without spoiling the overall mood of the piece.

Chopin uses a homophonic texture throughout almost all of the prelude, but it varies considerably, from long melodies with broken-chord accompaniment to gruff motifs in the bass beneath a repeating pedal note. Could you create something similar? Perhaps you might be inspired by Chopin's unusual coda, in which the music of the final section is interrupted to give a hint of something new at the very point where the listener thinks that the piece is about to end.

Remember that although your compositions must be related to the areas of study, you don't have to base them on ideas from the set works. In the case of this area of study, it is enough for your work to be related to any typical aspect(s) of western classical music in the period 1600–1899.

Sample questions for Section A

Listen to the section of CD 1 Track 3 from 4:58 to the end four times, with short pauses between each playing, as you answer the following questions. Don't consult the score or any other information before writing your answers.

Here is an outline of the right-hand part at the start of this extract.

1. Complete the melody in bar 2 (the rhythm to use is shown above the stave). (4)

2. Underline the term below that best describes the texture of the passage marked with a bracket.

   contrapuntal   homophonic   imitative   monophonic   (1)

3. Name the cadence heard in bars 3–4. .... (1)

4. Describe what happens to the tempo in the last two bars of the extract.

   .... (1)

5. This extract is from the end of the prelude. What is the correct technical term for this section?

   .... (1)

6. This prelude was composed in the Romantic period of western classical music. State **two** features of Romantic music.

   (a) ....

   (b) .... (2)

(Total 10 marks)

Top Tips

In questions such as number 6, be sure to give features that are important in the named style. You won't get marks for features that are common in many styles, such as cadences or sequences.

Sample questions for Section B

Before tackling this section read the information on writing extended answers, on page 167. Then try to complete your own answers without consulting any notes or the score, and without listening to the recording.

The following questions are about Prelude No. 15 in D♭ major, Op. 28 by Chopin.

(a) In which century was this music composed? .... (1)

(b) Where might you hear this type of music performed?

.... (1)

(c) Comment on how Chopin uses the following musical elements in this movement:

> Don't forget to include the role of the repeating pedal note.

Melody and rhythm
Tonality and harmony
Texture
Dynamics
Structure (10)

Use correct musical vocabulary where appropriate and remember that the quality of your writing, including spelling, punctuation and grammar, will be taken into account in this question. Write your answer on a separate sheet of paper.

(Total 12 marks)

The key feature of 20th-century music is its diversity. The invention of recording and radio, the ease of international travel, and the commercialisation of popular music meant that composers and audiences encountered a much wider range of music than ever before. As a result, many different styles developed, enabling listeners to choose from a much greater variety of new music.

In the early decades of the century, composers such as Elgar and Rachmaninov continued to write in a Romantic style. Others, such as Schoenberg (composer of our next set work) and Stravinsky looked for new ways to express themselves through music. Some composers, such as Bernstein (composer of the second set work in this section) were influenced by jazz and others by folk music from around the world. From about 1950, pre-recorded and electronic sounds started to play a role in some of the new music of the time.

After about 1960 there was a reaction against the dissonance and concentration on technique found in some of the music of earlier decades. A number of composers started to write works that had a wider appeal because they used simple material in new ways. We shall meet an example by Reich in the third of our set works.

We therefore cannot speak of a 20th-century style, although for much of the century composers used dissonance more freely than before, and often explored unusual rhythms and tone colours.

Here are the dates of the three set works in this area of study – the shaded grey areas represent the two World Wars that had such a devastating effect in the first half of the century:

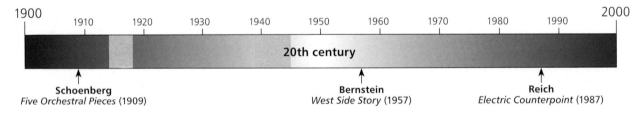

SET WORK 4: 'PERIPETIE' FROM *FIVE ORCHESTRAL PIECES*, OP. 16 BY SCHOENBERG

The word school in this context means a group of people whose ideas and work have much in common – it doesn't mean that they all went to the same school.

When studying the Classical style, we noted that the music of that period is sometimes described as 'Viennese Classical' because so many of its composers lived in or near Vienna. The Austrian city continued to be famous for its music during the Romantic period and then, in the first half of the 20th century, three of its composers became known as pioneers of a totally new style. These were Schoenberg and his pupils Berg and Webern. Together they are known as the Second Viennese School – the first being the Viennese composers of the Classical period.

ARNOLD SCHOENBERG (1874–1951)

Schoenberg learnt the violin as a child, and taught himself the cello, but his involvement in music was as an enthusiastic amateur until the age of 24, when his first substantial work received a private performance. He had almost no formal training in composition, but the experience encouraged him to leave his job as a bank clerk in order to concentrate on music.

Schoenberg's grave in Vienna reflects the modernism of his music

Almost from the beginning, Schoenberg's highly original approach to composing attracted controversy. Performance opportunities were rare, and at first he earned a living from orchestrating popular operas – another skill that he taught himself, largely by careful observation, aided by a keenly analytical ear. Later he established a reputation as a gifted teacher of composition, working on his own music in the summer holidays. In 1925 he accepted a teaching post in Berlin, but was forced out in 1933 because of his Jewish background. Realising that there was no future for him in Nazi Germany, Schoenberg and his family moved to America. Although he found it difficult to settle there at first, he was able to resume his life of teaching and composing. After some years of ill health, he died in Los Angeles at the age of 76.

In Schoenberg's early years, the dominant figure in Viennese music was Gustav Mahler, whose symphonies and songs are typical of the late-Romantic style in their chromatic writing and expressive melodic lines, as in this short fragment from Mahler's fifth symphony, completed in 1902:

Schoenberg detested the term atonal, because 'lack of key' sounds so negative. He preferred to describe his work as 'pantonal' – music that brings together all keys. However, it's not a term that ever really caught on.

Schoenberg's first works were in a similar style, but he came to the conclusion that the expressive power of this type of writing comes from its dissonances, which occur on almost every beat in the example above. Anchoring the music to a key, as Mahler does, meant that tensions were periodically resolved by cadences which for Schoenberg interrupted and diluted the emotional impact of the music.

From about 1908, Schoenberg started writing music that is **atonal** – without key. Our set work is an early example of this.

Atonality introduced a number of problems, the least of which (for Schoenberg) was public acceptance of its unfamiliar sound world. The most pressing need was how to structure a long movement without sections in different keys – remember that all three of the set works we have studied so far use related keys to give variety and shape to the music. Because there was no call for lengthy sections to establish keys, ideas could be introduced and developed very rapidly and so composers of the Second Viennese School often found it difficult to write pieces of any great length.

A second problem was how to make the music sound truly atonal – because, however hard one tries, certain notes can easily sound more prominent than others and so have a 'gravitational' pull that makes them sound like a modern version of a key note. Schoenberg eventually solved this problem by developing a technique known as serialism, in which every one of the 12 notes in an octave is given equal status. It proved influential for decades, and was adopted by many composers for at least some of their works.

However, this was some years away when Schoenberg wrote his *Five Orchestral Pieces*. Our movement is structured around a kaleidoscope of linked motifs that constantly re-appear in different guises – it is atonal, but it is not serial.

EXPRESSIONISM

An Expressionist self-portrait by Egon Schiele (1912)

Schoenberg was an amateur painter who, at the time he wrote *Five Orchestral Pieces*, was well aware of the latest artistic trends in Vienna. The period leading up to the First World War was dominated by **Expressionism** which, in painting, meant using distortion, bold brushwork and non-naturalistic colour to express the artist's state of mind, rather than aiming for photographic reality. In Vienna, the Expressionists were influenced by the work on psychology pioneered by Sigmund Freud, and their paintings often explore the darker side of the human subconscious.

Expressionism also had an impact on the drama of the period. Kokoschka's play *Murderer, The Hope of Women* was first produced in Vienna in 1909, and caused as much controversy as Schoenberg's *Five Orchestral Pieces*, completed in the same year. The deeply disturbing drama revolves around a power struggle between man and woman that encompasses torture, imprisonment, a stabbing and ritual slaughter. There was virtually no script – much of the horrific drama was conveyed through movement, improvisation, hissing and screaming, supported by costumes and scenery painted in vivid red and black.

It is important to remember that Expressionism is not entirely about dark and gloomy subjects. It is a style in which inner feelings are outwardly expressed as intensely as possible. Sometimes these could be feelings of fantasy and joy, as in the Expressionist architecture of this German astronomical observatory, started in 1919.

The Einstein Tower, Potsdam, Germany

Its rounded, organic shape playfully reflects the purpose of the building (exploration) by using a very modern architectural language – perhaps it could be a submarine, perhaps even a futuristic space ship that could be imagined visiting the universe that the tower is built to observe. At the same time, the colour and positioning of the building within its shady woodland background is designed to maximise the typically Expressionist element of dramatic contrast between dark and light.

The observatory has little in common with the architectural language of earlier buildings we have looked at, just as Schoenberg's totally chromatic musical language in the set work bears little resemblance to the tonal styles of the previous set works we have studied.

FIVE ORCHESTRAL PIECES

Schoenberg wrote his *Five Orchestral Pieces* in the summer of 1909, at the suggestion of the German composer Richard Strauss, who then declined to conduct them as they were too daringly experimental for the audiences of the day. There seemed little prospect of any performance, given the enormous orchestra required, but in 1912 three of the five pieces were presented in an arrangement for four pianists at two pianos, although this could hardly have conveyed the vivid colours that the composer had in mind.

The full score was published in 1912, and Schoenberg lost no time in sending copies to conductors who he hoped might perform the work. There were no positive replies but then he discovered that the British conductor Sir Henry Wood had obtained the music and planned to give the first full performance of the work during his famous summer festival of promenade concerts (the Proms) in London. It took place on 3 September 1912: many of the audience were baffled, others hostile, and some of the newspaper reviews were scathing. However, there was enough interest in the work to warrant a second London performance in 1914, which Schoenberg himself conducted.

A few further performances followed, and Schoenberg made some changes for a new edition of the work in 1922 (this is the version in GAM). One of these was adding a title for each movement at the request of his publisher, who felt that pieces without titles were difficult to market. Like Chopin, Schoenberg much preferred his music to speak for itself, and he made the point that the titles don't reflect any meaning in the music. Here are translations of the five deliberately obscure titles that Schoenberg chose, along with a brief note about each piece:

1. 'Premonitions': A fast and furious explosion of musical ideas.

2. 'The Past': A more relaxed piece with vague hints of more traditional musical techniques.

3. 'Colours', to which Schoenberg later added the sub-title 'Summer Morning by a Lake': A slow movement based on altering the tone colour of sustained notes through subtly changing instrumentation.

4. 'A Sudden Reversal': 'Peripetie' is the German equivalent of *peripeteia* – a Greek word referring to a sudden change of fortune for a character in a drama. Another fast movement, full of driving energy and startling contrasts.

5. 'The Obligatory Recitative': Schoenberg's meaning is particularly obscure, but it could be loosely paraphrased as 'the unending story'. Fragmentary melodies pass from one instrument to another, like shadowy figures in an atonal waltz. After a final, strident climax the piece dies away in a very quiet ending.

One of the obstacles to performance was always the large orchestra needed for such a short work: the entire recording from which CD 1 Track 4 is taken (played by the London Symphony Orchestra) takes less than 17 minutes but requires at least 90 players. Schoenberg later produced a slightly-scaled down version, as well as an arrangement of four of the movements for a small chamber orchestra. However, it is widely agreed that the 1922 revision shows the work in its best light, offering a full range of orchestral colour. *Five Orchestral Pieces* has been recorded many times, but it still doesn't appear in concert programmes as frequently as might be expected for one of the great orchestral masterpieces of the early 20th century.

Test yourself

1. What is the name of the European city in which Schoenberg was born and first worked?
2. Complete the following sentence:
   Schoenberg and his pupils are often described as the
   .... school of composers.
3. Where did Schoenberg work in the last part of his life?
4. The *Five Orchestral Pieces* are atonal. What does atonal mean?
5. In which decade of the 20th century was this work written?
6. What does 'Op. 16' mean?
7. In which famous festival of music (still going) was this work first performed?
8. Suggest two reasons why Schoenberg found it difficult to get his *Five Orchestral Pieces* performed.
9. Schoenberg later gave the set work the title 'Peripetie'. What does this word mean?
10. The style of the set work is Expressionist. What does this term mean?

Following the score

This is the most complex of any of the scores in GAM and is not easy to follow. Schoenberg gives us a helping hand by bracketing the main melodic ideas, with the sign ⌐ ⌐, which stands for *Hauptstimme*, German for 'principal part'. The symbol ⌐ ⌐ (trumpet in bars 28–31 and woodwind in bar 29) stands for *Nebenstimme* – a part of secondary importance.

The instruments are named in full at the start. Surprisingly, this is not the complete orchestra – several instruments required in other parts of Op. 16 are silent in this movement. Thankfully, parts for transposing instruments are printed at **sounding pitch** in this score (with a few exceptions listed below) despite being labelled 'in B♭', 'in F' and so on.

The score is laid out in the usual way, with woodwind at the top, followed by horns, then the rest of the brass, percussion and strings. Within each family, the instruments are ordered from high to low.

Piccolo and 3 flutes	The piccolo is a small flute that sounds an octave higher than shown in the score
3 oboes and cor anglais	The cor anglais is related to the oboe but has a lower range
5 clarinets	There are three (standard) clarinets in B♭. The clarinet in D is smaller and higher, while the bass clarinet has a range an octave lower than the standard instrument
3 bassoons and contrabassoon	The contrabassoon (or double bassoon) is a very large instrument that sounds an octave lower than printed
6 horns	
3 trumpets	
4 trombones	
Tuba	
Xylophone	A tuned percussion instrument with wooden bars
Cymbals	A cymbal is played with a cello bow (bars 63–64) and then struck with a mallet (bar 65)
Tam-tam	A large gong
Bass drum	
First violins	
Second violins	
Violas	As usual, most of the viola part is printed in the alto C clef
Cellos	Note that much of the cello part is very high and written in the treble clef
Double basses	The double basses sound an octave lower than printed

A quick glance through the score will show that there are more performing directions than ever in music of this period. Schoenberg was meticulous in his use of dynamics to get precisely the balance he required. There are also a number of directions in German, which are translated for you in the score.

There are several other points to note:

- Directions such as 'a 3' (bassoons, bar 1) mean that all three bassoons play the same notes.
- *Divisi* at the start of the string parts means that the players in each string section divide into groups, each of which plays a different note of the chords.
- In bar 3 of the violin and viola parts, 'pizz' is short for pizzicato and means pluck the strings. Two bars later, the Italian word arco ('bow') is a direction to return to bowing the strings.
- The bracketed '6' in the woodwind parts of bar 3 is a sextuplet – six semi-quavers, rather than the normal four, have to fit in the first beat of this bar.
- 'Bell up' in bar 34 of the trumpet part is an instruction for the players to point their instruments upwards in order to produce a loud, brassy sound.
- '1 solo' in the cello and bass parts of bars 44–45 means that each part is to be played by a single musician – the others join in at the word tutti ('all') in bars 53 and 55.
- In bars 62–63 the three note beams under the semibreves in the cymbal part indicate a tremolo – which in this case means that the cello bow should be rapidly stroked across the edge of a cymbal. The tremolo on the very high double-bass chords in the final bars also indicates rapid bow strokes, which Schoenberg here specifies should be played on (or rather very close to) the bridge, which produces a very thin and icy shimmering sound.
- The + signs on the horn notes in bar 65 tell the players to insert their hands further than normal into the bell of the instrument to produce a thin, nasal sound.
- In addition, you will see that the strings and brass have to play with mutes in a number of passages.

LISTENING GUIDE

Listen to CD 1 Track 4 without following the score and then debate the following questions with the other member of your GCSE group.

- Does 'Peripetie' sound as though it was written some 100 years ago? If not, why not?
- What were your reactions to the piece? If you thought it was unpleasant, explain why you think that music should always be pleasant. Can't music sometimes be scary or even horrifying?
- Are there aspects of the piece that remind you of more familiar types of music, such as contrasting sections and recognisable ideas that return in different ways?

When answering the third question, you probably spotted the contrasts but may well not have noticed how closely all of the main ideas are related. In fact, few of us can do so on a single hearing. An important part of Expressionism is its intensity, in which ideas come so thick and fast that they can only really be absorbed by the subconscious.

One of the unifying elements in 'Peripetie' is a **hexachord** – a set of six pitches that can be used as a chord or a melody. We first hear them in the opening woodwind fanfare, where the sixth note is the G♯ at the bottom of the woodwind chord in bar 2 (the first five notes, incidentally, are based on the chord at the end of the previous piece in Op. 16).

If we write the notes of this hexachord in scale order, we can see the intervals between each of its notes (½ = semitone, 1 = tone, 1½ = one and a half tones):

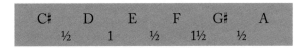

Now look at the sustained horn chord in bars 8–13. If we write the notes of this six-note chord in scale order, we have a hexachord in which the intervals between the notes are exactly the same as in the hexachord at the start of the piece:

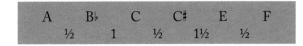

Schoenberg has moved the notes of the first hexachord to a new pitch level, and distributed them differently, but it is essentially the same type of **dissonant** chord.

Next look at the chord for six horns in bars 37³–39¹. Again, we'll list its notes in scale order: A, B♭, C, D♭, E, F. This is the same hexachord as the previous one (D♭ is the enharmonic equivalent of C♯).

Finally, look at the chord in the last two bars of the piece, scored for the extraordinary combination of very high double basses and very low horns. Here are its pitches written in scale order:

You've guessed! It's that hexachord again, on yet another pitch level. There are many other examples of hexachords in the piece, some of which use different sets of six pitches.

Now we need to look at some of the other material that Schoenberg uses in this short piece. 'Peripetie' consists of five sections, which are shown below with an indication of their content and dynamic outline:

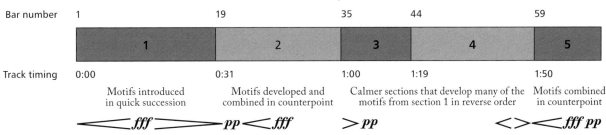

Schoenberg presents his main ideas in the first section. These return in reverse order (and with some other changes) in the middle section. In sections 2 and 4, new ideas are combined with some of those already heard. In the last section Schoenberg works a number of these earlier motifs into a loud climax.

The overall structure could be described as **rondo** – a sort of double sandwich with the structure ABACA. However, the lack of tonality and the changes of rhythm when an idea returns means that the piece is nothing like the well-contrasted rondos written in the Classical period.

Top Tips

If you are asked to describe the structure, use the expression 'free rondo form' to show that you realise it is not a traditional type of rondo.

It would take a long time to show how all of the motifs in the piece are related, and you won't be expected to go into that sort of detail, so we'll just look at some specific examples of the ways in which material from the opening section is used later in the piece.

In the first 18 bars, Schoenberg introduces a number of short motifs in quick succession, which we'll identify with letters:

Motifs (a) and (b)

The hexatonic opening fanfare (a) lands on a different hexachord (b) in bar 2 (the note G♯ is common to both). This entire idea is repeated at a higher pitch level in bar 3, with the notes of the fanfare now in **diminution** (i.e. half their previous lengths).

The two fanfares are separated by **contrary motion** chromatic scales from the brass in bar 2. The speed is so fast that this sounds like a smear of colour – indeed, Schoenberg marks the trombone parts 'gliss.' (short for **glissando**) to exaggerate the effect.

Both of these ideas return later. For example, versions of motif (a) are used in **imitation** during bars 19–21 (look for the triplet brackets), followed by the normal and diminished versions together in **counterpoint** in bar 22 (look for the ⊓ ⊐ signs). Hexachord (b) follows immediately on the first beat of bar 23.

The most spectacular reappearances of (a) occur twice in the low brass parts of bars 32–35 and once more in bars 63–64[1]. In each case, the original motif is turned upside down (a process known as melodic **inversion**), so that instead of rising, the fanfare plunges into the depths – on the final occasion ending with a terminal thump from the percussion department.

A **contrary motion** scale is one in which the rising and falling versions of the scale are played at the same time.

A **glissando** is a continuous glide in pitch between notes, here produced by the trombone's slide.

Motif (c)

Returning to the opening, at the end of bar 3 all six horns announce a very angular idea in triplets that we'll call motif (c).

Schoenberg adapts this idea so freely that some of its later appearances are far from obvious: one very loud version from the horns starts on the last beat of bar 27, while a very quiet version forms the bassoon solo in bars 44–45. This is also the motif with which the piece ends, forming the quiet clarinet gurgle in bars 64–65.

Motif (d)

Motif (d) is formed from the rapidly repeated hexachords in bars 5–6. The distinctive rhythm of this motif is easy to spot by looking at the score or by listening: see how many examples you can find.

In the trumpet parts of bars 61–63, Schoenberg lops away half of the hexachord, leaving just three pitches that form an **augmented chord**. As the music gets louder, these repeated chords climb part of a **whole-tone scale** that ends in bar 63 with a similar chromatic smear to the one heard in bar 2.

A normal chord of F major consists of the notes F, A and C. An **augmented chord** of F major consists of F, A and C♯, as seen in the trumpet parts during the first half of bar 62.

In a **whole-tone scale** the interval between every note is a tone: D♭, E♭, F, G, A, etc.

Motif (e)

Motif (e) is the quiet, rhythmically simple idea started by the horns in bar 6 that ends on the sustained hexachord mentioned earlier (again, look for the ⌐ ¬ mark).

Sometimes this returns in a greatly hyped-up version (the horns' semiquaver triplets in bars 32–33), but elsewhere Schoenberg extends the original, placid version of the motif (bars 37–44, again in the horns).

Motif (f)

Motif (f) is the twisting chromatic figure introduced by low woodwind in bar 8 against the horns' hexachord.

Again, Schoenberg sometimes energises this motif with a much faster rhythm, as in the low woodwind parts of bars 32–33. Later, it is transformed into the quiet little melody for muted trumpets in bars 45–47.

Motif (g)

Finally a much longer melody (g), consisting mainly of wide leaps, is announced by a solo clarinet in bars 10–18.

Schoenberg's sketches for 'Peripetie' suggest that this may have been the composer's first main idea for the piece, from which much of the other material was derived. Again, it appears later in very different guises. In bars 32–34 we hear only its first two notes, played six times in succession by first violins and cellos in unison. This

© Florence Homolka

Arnold Schoenberg

leads straight into a version of the first half of (g), played in unison by all the strings (except double basses), in which a prominent change is made to its climactic sixth note.

We have only touched on a few of the dozens of connections between motifs that shoot past in the two minutes or so that this piece lasts. However, if you have followed at least some of the description above, you will have a good idea of the sheer intensity of Schoenberg's Expressionist style, which is as much for the subconscious as for the ear to absorb.

Before we leave 'Peripetie', there are some final points to note:

Schoenberg was later fascinated by the idea of constantly changing the tone colour of a melody by assigning individual notes to different instruments – a technique known as *Klangfarbenmelodie* (tone-colour melody). Its origins lay in the third of his *Five Orchestral Pieces*, 'Farben' (Colours) although there is little use of this technique in 'Peripetie'.

■ Many of Schoenberg's melodic lines sound very angular because of his use of **octave displacement**, in which one or more notes are shifted into an unexpected octave. Clear examples occur in the clarinet melody (g) that begins in bar 10. Try playing it with the second note (A♭) and the eighth note (D♭) an octave lower than Schoenberg wrote them.

■ The constantly changing instrumentation is one of the highlights of the piece. Notice how Schoenberg often uses instruments in extreme parts of their range (very high or very low) to get the colours he wants. He often uses blocks of similar tone (the six horns, the five clarinets, and so on) and, while parts are often doubled in unison, there is relatively little of the octave doubling that we saw in the set work by Mozart.

In a **canon**, the same melody appears in two or more different parts, each slightly out of step with each other, as happens when you sing a round.

■ The contrasts in dynamics (summarised in the diagram on page 79) are supported by the instrumentation, which is quite sparse in the calmer mood of sections 3 and 4. These sections include many of the ideas from section 1 in reverse order (is this the 'sudden reversal' of the work's title?): motif (g) comes first (bar 35, strings), then the hexatonic chord from bar 8, followed by motif (e) in the horns, references to (f) and (c) in the quiet melodies of bars 44–47, and finally motif (a) returns in the clarinet and bassoon parts of bar 48.

■ Counterpoint plays an important part throughout, but especially in sections 2 and 5. In fact, in section 2 Schoenberg develops six of his main ideas virtually simultaneously. Section 5 is perhaps even more impressive. The enormous build up is formed from three simultaneous **canons** that begin in bar 59:
  ▪ Third clarinet and second violins play the opening of motif (f) in repeating canon
  ▪ The horns play motif (e) in canon
  ▪ First violins and violas (both divided) play a canonic version of the motif first heard in bar 24.

The effect of a cello bow being drawn across a cymbal, as marked in bars 62–63, can produce an eerie penetrating whistle. However, as in many performances, this cannot easily be heard against the full orchestra on CD 1 Track 4 – perhaps it is one of the rare cases where Schoenberg miscalculated his orchestral balance.

■ Distorted memories of other things we've heard before swirl around these canons: rising versions of motif (d) in the trumpets, merging into a repeat of that chromatic smear, repetitions of motif (a) in the other woodwind parts and then, as the visions reach their climax in bar 63, the doom-laden inversion of (a) descending into the depths of the heavy brass as the horns shriek out the opening of motif (f) in triplets.

■ And then it stops. The quick reminder of motif (c) from low clarinets in the final bars, set against the icy hexachord, seems almost like blinking your eyes as dawn breaks. Have we awoken from a nightmare? The only certainty is that we have experienced a fine example of Expressionist music.

Test yourself

1. Which instrument normally uses the alto C clef?
2. What is the lowest instrument of the brass family?
3. What is unusual about the cymbal part in this piece?
4. In the score, what does the sign H ⌐⌐ mean?
5. What do you think Schoenberg meant when he used the dynamic marking *fff*?
6. Name the main way in which the second section of 'Peripetie' differs from the first section.
7. What is meant by octave displacement?
8. What musical term best describes the tonality of 'Peripetie'?
9. What musical term describes the texture in the last section of this piece?
10. What does melodic inversion mean? Where do you hear melodic inversion in 'Peripetie'?

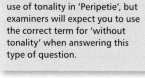

Strictly speaking, there is no use of tonality in 'Peripetie', but examiners will expect you to use the correct term for 'without tonality' when answering this type of question.

Further listening

To broaden your knowledge of Schoenberg's style, and of other music written in the early decades of the 20th century, here are some more works that you might enjoy:

- One of Schoenberg's most famous Expressionist works is **Pierrot Lunaire**, composed in 1912. It consists of 21 poems about a clown who is obsessed with the moon and driven to madness. The poems are set for a narrator (who declaims the words in a style between speech and singing) and five instrumentalists. No. 5, 'Valse de Chopin' (Waltz of Chopin) is in the previous (2006) edition of GAM. No. 7, 'Der Kranke Mond' (The Sick Moon) is included in the Edexcel *A-level Anthology of Music*.
- An extract from the Expressionist opera **Wozzeck** (written by Schoenberg's pupil, Berg, between 1914 and 1922) is included in the 2006 edition of GAM.
- Less than nine months after the first performance of *Five Orchestral Pieces*, audiences in Paris were shocked by **The Rite of Spring** (1913), the latest ballet score by the Russian composer Igor Stravinsky. Although it is very dissonant, the musical language is likely to seem more familiar than that of 'Peripetie', and rhythmically it is extremely exciting, especially in its final 'Sacrificial Dance'.
- In 1914, the English composer Gustav Holst heard Schoenberg conduct *Five Orchestral Pieces* in London and set to work on his famous orchestral suite **The Planets**. He was influenced by both Schoenberg and Stravinsky but, while Holst's style was modern, it was far less extreme than that of either continental composer. As a result, the work quickly became popular with a wide public – the first movement ('Mars') is particularly well known.

Composing ideas

While studying 'Peripetie' we have come across a number of techniques that could be used in your own compositions. You could try writing in an atonal Expressionist style, but our study of the set work should indicate that it is not just a question of writing as many discords as you can! The style needs fast-changing colours, vivid contrasts between areas of high and low tension, and great intensity. Remember that octave displacement frequently features in Schoenberg's melodies, and that motifs are closely related, with each idea quickly morphing into new versions.

Other features of 'Peripetie' that could be used in various different styles of music include:

- The use of rondo form (a structure such as ABACA). Remember that exact repetition of the A section can be boring – while you may not want to make the repetitions of the opening section quite so unobvious as Schoenberg, some variation when it returns is a good thing.
- Combining ideas in counterpoint (perhaps even using imitation and canon) can make a very exciting section for a piece, although it is not easy and needs careful planning. In tonal styles of music, it is often easier to start with a chord pattern, and then write two or three different melodies to fit it before trying to combine them.
- Using an idea in diminution is another good way of creating excitement in a piece. Did you notice that in 'Peripetie' Schoenberg sometimes uses a motif in diminution when it occurs in a high range?

Sample questions for Section A

Listen to the first 27 seconds of CD 1 Track 4 three times, with short pauses between each playing, as you answer the following questions. Then complete your answers without consulting any notes or the score, and without listening to the recording.

1. In what style is this music? .... (1)

2. Name **two** features of the style you have given above.

    (a) ....

    (b) .... (2)

3. Much of this extract is based on hexachords. What is a hexachord?

.... (1)

4. The extract starts with a fast flourish played by the woodwind. What type of scale is played by the brass immediately after this flourish?

.... (1)

5. Which brass instruments play a loud, jagged melody shortly after the opening?

.... (1)

6. Name the instrument that plays the solo at the end of this extract.

.... (1)

7. Write X in the box next to the statement below that best describes this solo:

The melody moves mainly be step ☒
The melody moves mainly by leap ☒ (1)

8. Give **two** *musical* reasons why you like **or** dislike this piece.

(a) ....

....

(b) ....

.... (2)

(Total 10 marks)

Top Tips

Questions such as number 8 need special care. Examiners are not bothered whether you like the music or not – they want to know the musical reasons behind your opinion. You will get no marks for saying that you dislike it because you think it is weird or that you like it because it is exciting. To get marks you need to say *why*. For example, you might say that you dislike this piece because the ideas come and go too quickly for you to recognise them, or that you like it because of its vivid and rapidly changing orchestral colours.

Sample questions for Section B

Before tackling this section read the information on writing extended answers, on page 167. Then complete your answers without consulting any notes or the score, and without listening to the recording.

The following questions are about 'Peripetie' from *Five Orchestral Pieces* by Schoenberg.

(a) In which decade of the 20th century was this music composed? Put a cross in the correct box.

1900s ☒   1910s ☒   1920s ☒
1930s ☒   1940s ☒   (1)

(b) Complete the sentence below by adding one of the following words in the space provided: first   second   third   fourth   fifth

'Peripetie' is the .... piece in Schoenberg's *Five Orchestral Pieces*.

(1)

(c) Comment on how Schoenberg uses the following musical elements in this piece:

Tonality and harmony
Melody
Rhythm
Texture
Timbre

(10)

Timbre (pronounced *tam-bruh)* refers to tone colour. Here you should write about the different colours Schoenberg obtains from the instruments of the orchestra.

Use correct musical vocabulary where appropriate and remember that the quality of your writing, including spelling, punctuation and grammar, will be taken into account in this question. Write your answer on a separate sheet of paper.

(Total 12 marks)

SET WORK 5: 'SOMETHING'S COMING' FROM *WEST SIDE STORY* BY BERNSTEIN

Some modern musicals are just glitzy showcases for the back-catalogues of old pop stars. The type of musical referred to in this section is dramatically very different, and often differs from opera only in that the music is in a more popular style, designed to be sung by actors rather than professional singers.

In the late 19th century, increasing prosperity created a demand for popular entertainment suited to ordinary people. In response, dozens of new theatres opened in cities such as New York and London to provide variety shows that consisted of an assortment of songs, dances, magical illusions and comedy acts.

These often included short sketches, presented in costume and with scenery, which used a simple storyline to link a selection of songs and dances. Such productions developed into 'musical plays' and 'musical comedies', from which the modern musical takes its name.

In the early 20th century, many musicals consisted of a succession of good songs held together by an often implausible plot. However, three works showed that the musical could be a new art form in which music, dance and drama work together to totally engage the audience: *Show Boat* (1927) by Jerome Kern, *Porgy and Bess* (1935) by George Gershwin (a work that the composer described as a 'folk *opera*') and *Oklahoma!* (1943) by Rodgers and Hammerstein.

West Side Story (first staged in 1957) is a direct descendent of these works, taking the musical into a new dimension in which age-old ideas of gang violence, ambition, humour and love are interpreted in terms that seem as modern today, half a century on, as they did in the late 1950s.

LEONARD BERNSTEIN (1918–1990)

Leonard Bernstein in 1945

Bernstein grew up in the U.S.A., where he started learning the piano at the age of ten. He went on to study music at Harvard, one of the famous American universities, and by the age of 25 he was conducting one of the country's most famous orchestras. Bernstein was not only a highly skilled musician but also wide ranging in his musical tastes, enjoying the latest jazz of the day. He established a reputation as a superb pianist, conductor, broadcaster and composer, writing works for the concert hall as well as the theatre.

Bernstein's first musical was *On The Town* , a work with a strong element of dance, that was first staged in 1944 on Broadway (the part of New York where many of the theatres present musicals). It was turned into a film in 1949 and the stage version has been revived many times ever since.

Several other stage works followed, of which *West Side Story* (1957) is undoubtedly the best known. It was made into an award-winning film in 1961, and in the same year Bernstein arranged nine of the numbers from the musical as a very popular orchestral work for performance in the concert hall, under the title *Symphonic Dances from West Side Story*.

Strangely, Bernstein never conducted a recording of his most famous work until 1984, when he embarked on an ambitious project to make a studio recording with famous opera singers rather than the singing actors for whom the work was written. The powerful operatic voices and large orchestra sound totally different from recordings of the stage show. The whole process of rehearsing and recording the work was filmed, allowing us to witness in detail how Bernstein wanted to interpret his music. If possible, try to see the film, which is available on DVD from Deutsche Grammophon (*The Making of West Side Story*) – it will give you many insights into how a great conductor works and the tensions of the recording studio, as well as throwing new light on *West Side Story*. This DVD shows only the recording of the soundtrack. The film version of the entire show (which doesn't include all of the music in the stage version) is also available on DVD from MGM (their special edition, which includes various additional background material, can often be purchased at a bargain price).

You can find out more about Bernstein from the website www. leonardbernstein.com.

WEST SIDE STORY

The idea of a musical based on Shakespeare's play *Romeo and Juliet* was suggested to Bernstein in 1949 by Jerome Robbins, who had arranged the dance sequences for *On The Town*. The setting was changed from renaissance Italy to modern-day New York; Romeo and Juliet, the young lovers who defy a running feud between their families, become Tony and Maria from rival teenage gangs, the Jets and the Sharks; and Shakespeare's famous balcony scene is mirrored by the meeting of Tony and Maria on the fire escape of a bleak New York apartment.

Some early sketches were made in 1949, but it was not until 1956 that Bernstein began work in earnest on the project. The playwright Authur Laurents was engaged to write the script, since the musical is based only on Shakespeare's plot and doesn't use his text. The **lyrics** (words of the songs) were supplied by Stephen Sondheim, who was later to compose his own musicals, including the famous *Sweeney Todd, The Demon Barber of Fleet Street*.

Bernstein himself made an important contribution by insisting that the conflict at the heart of the drama should revolve around racial tensions in New York caused by a large influx of immigrants from Puerto Rico, rather than making the rival gangs Catholic and Jewish, as originally proposed. This may well have been because it gave him an excuse to base many numbers on the exciting Latin-American dance rhythms that he encountered on holidays with his South-American wife, as well as on the Afro-Cuban jazz that he enjoyed. But he was probably also aware that the drama in *Showboat*, *Porgy and Bess*, and *Oklahoma!* had all centred on conflict between different communities. Whatever Bernstein's reasons, the decision to expand Shakespeare's story of family rivalry into the broader field of tensions arising from immigration makes *West Side Story* as relevant in the 21st century as it was in 1957.

The Jets in a production of *West Side Story* by Leighton Park School

Much else about *West Side Story* was revolutionary. Instead of the sweet romanticism of many earlier musicals, it is a story of doomed love. Extended dance sequences convey the drama and, in place of rousing finales, both acts end in murder. The music is highly integrated, using techniques borrowed from opera, such as ideas in the orchestra that foreshadow the drama that will unfold. These give the audience an insight into future events beyond the experience of the characters on stage. The work is held together with motifs and melodies based on a **tritone** – an interval of three whole tones. Its harsh sound has been associated with evil for centuries, and Bernstein weaves it into the fabric of *West Side Story* to act as a unifying device and a musical symbol of the tragic fate that will befall the two teenage lovers at the heart of the story.

The original production was fraught with difficulties. Actors were not used to singing in the very contemporary styles that Bernstein demanded, the extensive dance sequences needed weeks of extra rehearsal, and the financial backers became convinced that nobody would want to see a musical that ends in tragedy and in which the curtain at the end of Act 1 comes down on two dead bodies instead of the usual jolly chorus.

Their fears were largely unfounded. After some trial runs, *West Side Story* opened on Broadway in 1957 and ran for 732 consecutive performances. The London production ran for three years until 1961, when the work was adapted as a film musical. Amateur and professional stage productions have continued ever since.

However, while *West Side Story* seemed to have opened up an entirely new dramatic direction for the musical, it remains unique. Musicals today are more popular than ever, but none match the intensity of this work – and even Bernstein himself was later responsible for one of the greatest flops of all time with his 1976 show, *1600 Pennsylvania Avenue*, which closed after only seven performances.

The plot of *West Side Story* centres on the rivalry between two teenage gangs: the Jets, born in New York, and the Sharks, whose families came from the Caribbean island of Puerto Rico. The tension on the streets is obvious from the moment the curtain rises. The gangs confront each other to menacing music and a fight breaks out. The police arrive and chase the Sharks away, leaving the Jets to plan a final show-down at a dance due to take place that evening.

Tony, who was once the leader of the Jets, has grown tired of this constant violence but is persuaded to go to the dance. 'Something's Coming' is his first song in the show, and in it he expresses his hopes of a better future – something new will happen, maybe tonight … and it does. At the dance that evening, Tony meets Maria, sister of the leader of the rival Sharks gang. It is love at first sight and thus starts a story of betrayal and violence, love against all the odds, and eventually tragedy as Tony is shot and dies in Maria's arms.

Following the score

In a musical, the orchestra (or band) is usually positioned in a sunken area in front of the stage, called the pit, which restricts the number of players that can be used. Nevertheless, *West Side Story* requires a 31-piece band: five woodwind (who have to play a range of instruments), seven brass, five percussion, guitar, piano and 12 string players.

In GAM 'Something's Coming' is printed as a vocal score. This shows the voice part in full, but the band parts are arranged onto two staves, suitable for a pianist to play when accompanying rehearsals. Following a vocal score is relatively simple, but watch out for the repeats:

■ Bar 3 is played five times (to cover movement on stage during the introduction to the song)

To fully understand the drama, and give yourself an evening's brilliant entertainment, try to see a production of West Side Story. There have been many professional productions (a new one opened in New York in 2009, which could transfer to the UK in future years) and the show is regularly presented by amateur and school groups. Alternatively, while nothing matches the thrill of a live performance, try to see the 1961 film version, available on the MGM DVD mentioned earlier.

- Bars 9–30 are sung twice, the second time to different words. On the repeat, bars 26–30 (known as first-time bars and bracketed with a '1') are missed out, so on this second time through the music jumps straight from bar 25 to bar 31 (known as the second-time bar and bracketed with a '2')
- Bars 40–62 are also sung twice, and again the first-time bars (bars 52–62) are omitted for the repeat
- The final bar is repeated as many times as required ('ad lib') to allow the music to fade out beneath the expected applause at the end of the song.

Although many of the notes are carefully marked with staccato dots, accents and slurs, the only unusual Italian terms are *marcato* (meaning 'marked' or 'emphasised') in bar 21, *subito* (meaning 'suddenly') in bar 128 and *sempre* (meaning 'always') in bar 148. Notice the triplet bracket in bar 76 and elsewhere, indicating that three crotchets' worth of notes have to fit into the space normally taken by two crotchets.

The role of Tony is sung by a **tenor** – a high male voice. His music is printed in the treble clef but sounds an octave lower than written. Notice that the word-setting is almost entirely **syllabic**. Do you remember from our study of *Messiah* what this term means?

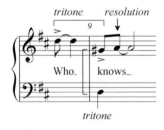

'Something's Coming' was added to *West Side Story* at a very late stage, during rehearsals for the first performance, when it was realised that Tony, the leading male figure in the show, had no song near the start to establish his strongly optimistic character. 'Something's Coming', written in a single day, ideally serves the purpose, but Bernstein was not content to just add a new number without making its *musical* contribution to the drama crystal clear. For that reason, the song not only revolves around the tritone – the symbol of conflict – but it also makes clear that Tony, through his death, will provide the resolution of that conflict. Bernstein does this by resolving the dissonant tritone onto a stable perfect 5th (A above D) as early as Tony's second phrase (see left).

Tony and Maria in Leighton Park School's *West Side Story*

The tritone gnaws away throughout most of 'Something's Coming' and at the very end Bernstein has another trick up his sleeve. To integrate the song into the rest of his drama, Tony's final note is not the tonic (D) but a long-held C♮. Not only is this a note of the blues scale on D, reflecting the jazz-influenced style of *West Side Story*, it is also a pitch (the flat 7th of the major scale) that figures prominently in other songs in the musical. Finishing the vocal part on this unexpected note, with a fade-out ending, gives a deliberate sense of incompletion. For Tony, this is not the end, but the start of something new … something's coming, in fact.

Listen to the performance on CD 1 Track 5, sung by Mark Eldred with the Nashville Symphony Orchestra. Follow the score and identify the three main ideas in the song:

■ **A**: The opening syncopated melody, which starts tentatively but becomes quite snappy at bar 13
■ **B**: A more forceful, punchy idea, first heard at bar 21
■ **C**: A warmer, more legato melody, first heard at bar 73.

Did you also spot that the entire song is based on these three ideas, although they are often not exactly the same when they return? We'll look at the differences later – let's start by looking at each of the three main ideas.

Theme A

The simplest version of theme A is the 12-bar phrase in bars 40–51. It consists of a two-bar motif that starts by resolving the tritone between C in the bass and F♯ in the tune. This motif is heard four times with either a rising or falling ending.

When it occurs for a fifth time (bar 48) the last note is B♭ (the flat 7th of C major), which is sustained to fill the remaining three bars. The main feature of this motif is its syncopated third note, which gives the tune its urgency.

Despite all the F♯s, the music is anchored to the key of C major by the alternating Cs and Gs in the bass. These are heard in all 12 bars, and form a constantly repeating pattern known as a **riff**. Above the riff, the rest of the accompaniment rises and falls between E and G.

Theme B

Theme A is followed immediately by theme B in bars 52–62. Tony excitedly declaims 'Something's coming' to four accented crotchets on the note A. The vocal line then gets very syncopated, but uses only two pitches (F and A). In fact the melody of theme B uses only four different pitches in total, allowing Tony to express his words as clearly as possible. Like theme A, it ends on a long sustained note.

The bass riff moves up to F and C, returning to C and G in the last four bars, but otherwise the accompaniment is similar to theme A. However, notice that while theme A was 24 beats long (12 bars of $\frac{2}{4}$), theme B is 23 beats long (10 bars of $\frac{2}{4}$ and one of $\frac{3}{4}$). So, although the two themes sound balanced, Bernstein actually ups the tension by making theme B slightly shorter.

The Sharks in Leighton Park School's *West Side Story*

Theme C

The legato melody starting on the second beat of bar 73 forms a 32-bar section known as a **bridge** – a contrasting section between the main themes. It contains three similar phrases – the first two are eight bars long and the third is extended to 16 bars by its long final note.

At first this seems very different from themes A and B – the phrases are much longer, higher in range, and more legato. However, notice the similarities. The accompaniment is much the same as before, except that it moves through different chords, and the melody again ends on a long sustained note.

Structure

Once you have these three themes clear in you mind, it will be much easier to follow the overall structure of the song, which is more ingenious than you might have first suspected:

Bars	Theme	Key	Notes
1–20	A1	D major	This first version of A is in ¾ time – the second of each pair of bars in the ²⁄₄ version has been replaced by the third beat of a ¾ bar. The bass riff is still there, but it now consists of falling 4ths. In the accompaniment, the first two notes of A are heard at the start of every bar. The vocal motifs are introduced gradually, with a long note at the end of each, so the song doesn't really seem to get under way until bar 13.
21–30	B1		As the time changes to ²⁄₄, theme B starts in quavers, rather than crotchets as it does later. The time signature reverts to ¾ at bar 27, ready for the repeat.
9–20	A1		Theme A is repeated exactly to different words.
21–31	B1		Theme B is repeated to different words, rising to a high E at the end.
32–51	A2	C major	Bernstein makes a seamless join by starting the accompaniment to the ²⁄₄ version of theme A under the last note of the previous section. From bar 40, A and B are the simple versions that we discussed earlier.
52–62	B2		
32–51	A2		Bars 40–51 are repeated with different words. Note that bars 52–62 are not repeated.
63–72	B3		The same as B2, but a tone higher to prepare for a return to D major.

Bars	Theme	Key	Notes
73–105	C1	D major	This is the bridge, discussed earlier.
106–117	A2	C major	A repeat of bars 40–72, with different words. Theme A starts very quietly, almost whispered, and theme B appears in its third version because the music is again about to return to D major.
118–127	B3		
128–140	C2	D major	The first half only of the bridge, to new words.
141–158	A1		The ³₄ version of A, similar to bars 5–20, using the second-verse words with a few small changes.

Top Tips

It's unlikely that you would need to go into this amount of detail, even in an extended answer. But if you do refer to the three themes, don't describe them as A, B and C without first telling the examiner what you mean by these letters. For instance, you could say that A is the syncopated opening melody, B is the punchy theme sung to 'Something's coming', and C is the legato melody sung to 'Around the corner'.

The table above reveals two important points about this short song:

- It is not atonal like 'Peripetie' – 'Something's Coming' is clearly tonal, despite some pleasant dissonances in the harmony. The song is in D major, with two contrasting sections in C major. These two keys are not closely related, and Bernstein simply slips from one to the other rather than setting up careful modulations of the sort we saw Handel and Mozart use. However, they have huge significance in the context of the musical as a whole, because C is the flattened seventh degree of D major – the interval that, along with the tritone, permeates *West Side Story*.

- There is a lot of repetition of the main ideas (A and B are each heard four times before the bridge appears), but the words are seldom repeated exactly, the alternation of A and B provides variety, and Bernstein uses a range of techniques, from strongly contrasted dynamics to changing the lengths of repeated sections (and even changing the **metre** of A) to avoid too much exact repetition. Notice particularly how he reflects Sondheim's questioning lyrics at the start of the song ('Could be! Who knows?') with well-spaced vocal entries, that are then followed by the rapid-fire excitement of theme B as Tony starts to seize on the potential of a new future.

Metre refers to the number of beats in a bar. This song includes duple metre (the two beats per bar of ²₄ time) and triple metre (the three beats in a bar of ³₄ time).

Did you notice that it is quite difficult to feel the beat at the start of the song? This is because Bernstein suggests Tony's tentative questioning by using a device known as **cross rhythm** – two conflicting rhythms heard at the same time. The syncopated melody sounds more like $\frac{6}{8}$ time, with two main beats per bar, while the bass beneath it has the three beats per bar of $\frac{3}{4}$:

Written:

Sounds like:

Throughout the song, Bernstein's accompaniment acts as a unifying force – from bar 32, where the $\frac{2}{4}$ version of the opening riff starts, the accompaniment patterns are continuous and even keep going during the bridge, just adapted to the different chords required. However, there is a lot of subtlety in the instrumentation. Even though instruments are not marked into the vocal score, see if you can spot the following main points (which only include features that can be heard reasonably clearly on CD 1 Track 5):

- The instruments in the first 15 bars are clarinets (including bass clarinet) and pizzicato strings, supported by a quiet but very busy drum part (played with wire brushes on a snare drum and hi-hat cymbal)
- Muted trumpets enter at the end of bar 17 and continue until bar 28
- From bar 32, the minims in the accompaniment are played by clarinets, with brass added for the louder section beginning in bar 52
- The sustained accompaniment in the bridge is played by high strings, with flutes joining in 'whistling' in bar 82
- In the second bridge, high violins illustrate the words ('The air is humming') – one plays **tremolo** (dividing each note into rapidly repeated pitches), while the other plays sustained **harmonics** (very high, pure notes produced by placing a finger lightly on the string while bowing).

Bernstein uses mainly soft dynamics in the accompaniment, along with techniques such as wire brushes on the drums and mutes for the trumpets, in order not to over-balance the singer. This was particularly important in the 1950s because there were no radio microphones to bolster the voices of the actors who sang in the original show. For the same reason, the texture of the song is entirely homophonic, with no counterpoint to distract from the vocal line.

Test yourself

1. On which play by Shakespeare is *West Side Story* based?
2. On which of Shakespeare's characters is the part of Tony based?
3. The lyrics of the song are by Stephen Sondheim. What is meant by the term lyrics, and for what else did Sondheim later become famous?
4. What musical term describes the texture of this song?
5. The accompaniment at the start features cross rhythm. What does this term mean?
6. Explain how the bridge is both similar to, and yet different from, the other sections.
7. 'Something's Coming' begins and ends in D major. Which other key is used in the song?
8. On what note does Tony finish?
9. How does the music reflect Tony's gradually increasing sense of excitement and expectation?
10. Why did Bernstein have to take special care that the band didn't over-balance the soloist in this song?

Further listening

As well as listening to more of *West Side Story*, look out for the following works by Bernstein and others:

■ Bernstein's first musical, **On The Town** (1944) includes, among a number of wonderful songs, a famous setting of 'New York, New York' and the comic solo 'I Can Cook, Too'.

■ Bernstein's **Prelude, Fugue and Riffs** (1949) is one of his most jazzy and exciting pieces – the riffs are a good deal more complicated than those in 'Something's Coming'. The excellent recording by Simon Rattle is available as an MP3 download from Amazon.

■ Bernstein's **Chichester Psalms** (1965) shows a quite different side of the composer's output. It is a setting of words from the psalms in their original Hebrew, commissioned by Chichester cathedral in West Sussex. Some of it uses ideas that Bernstein originally intended for *West Side Story*, before he decided that the rival gang should be Puerto Rican rather than Jewish.

■ There are countless musicals by other composers that are worth getting to know. Andrew Lloyd Webber's early work **Jesus Christ Superstar** (1970) was as revolutionary in its day as *West Side Story* was 13 years before. Stephen Sondheim went on to write a number of musicals that are dramatically more thoughtful than some of the spectacular 'mega-musicals' of recent years. His **Sweeney Todd, The Demon Barber of Fleet Street** (1979) is as much opera as musical, and has been produced in opera houses as well as theatres around the world.

■ There are songs from the musicals **Oliver!** and **Cabaret** in the original (2002) edition of GAM, and from **Oklahoma!** and **Sweeny Todd** in the 2006 edition.

Composing ideas

While studying 'Something's Coming' we have come across a number of techniques that could be used in your own compositions. A song for a musical could become a really fun project. Don't fall into the trap of spending too much time on the lyrics – it is the music that will get the marks. However, try to imagine a scene in which your song could reflect the mood of the character that sings it. Most musicals include love songs, but why not be more original and try something different – perhaps a comedy number, or a dramatic song to be sung during a raging storm, or maybe even a duet if you feel ambitious?

There is no need to aim for such a complex structure as 'Something's Coming', but there should be some contrast – perhaps different verses, each followed by the same chorus, or maybe a 32-bar song form, which consists of eight-bar sections in the pattern AABA, where B is the bridge. Remember that Bernstein doesn't make his bridge totally different to the rest of the song – the melody is a contrast, but the accompaniment remains very similar in this section.

It's also a good idea to follow Bernstein's example and not have too many exact repeats. When a section returns, think how it could be slightly varied to make it more interesting, perhaps by making the melody rise to a higher note, or maybe by changing the length of a passage when it returns.

You might also think about using some of the techniques that we spotted in 'Something's Coming' – accompaniments based on riffs, melodies that consist of a short motif with different endings, cross rhythms or perhaps the unusual tonal scheme of moving between two keys a step apart.

Sample questions for Section A

Listen to the first 33 seconds of CD 1 Track 5 four times, with short pauses between each playing, as you answer the following questions. Don't consult the score or any other information before writing your answers.

1. Write X in the box that shows the first interval sung by the soloist (to the words 'Could be').

major 3rd	☒	perfect 4th	☒
perfect 5th	☒	octave	☒

(1)

2. The bass part is the same in every bar for more than half of the extract. What is the correct musical term for a pattern that is constantly repeated?

.... (1)

3. What rhythmic device is heard above this repeating bass part?

.... (1)

4. How does the metre change for the section that starts 'It may come cannonballing down through the sky?'

.... (1)

5. Is the word setting in this extract syllabic or melismatic?

.... (1)

6. Name **two** different wind instruments heard in this extract.

.... and .... (2)

7. What type of voice (soprano, alto, tenor or bass) is this song written for?

.... (1)

8. This song comes from a musical. Briefly explain what is meant by a musical.

....

.... (2)

(Total 10 marks)

Top Tips

In the exam, you get time to read through the questions before the extracts are played and to complete your answers after hearing each extract. Use this time to spot and answer questions for which you don't really need to hear the recording, such as 7 and 8 above. This will allow you to concentrate on the other questions while actually listening to the music.

Sample questions for Section B

Before tackling this section read the information on writing extended answers, on page 167. Then complete your answers without consulting any notes or the score, and without listening to the recording.

The following questions are about 'Something's Coming' from *West Side Story* by Bernstein.

(a) In which year was *West Side Story* first staged? Put a cross in the correct box.

1937 ☒   1947 ☒   1957 ☒

1967 ☒   1977 ☒   (1)

(b) In which city was this musical first staged? .... (1)

(c) Comment on how Bernstein uses the following musical elements in this piece:

Metre and rhythm
Melody
Tonality
Texture
Structure   (10)

Use correct musical vocabulary where appropriate and remember that the quality of your writing, including spelling, punctuation and grammar, will be taken into account in this question. Write your answer on a separate sheet of paper.

(Total 12 marks)

SET WORK 6: *ELECTRIC COUNTERPOINT* (THIRD MOVEMENT) BY STEVE REICH

The work of Schoenberg and the other members of the Second Viennese School had an enormous impact on many composers writing for the concert hall until at least the 1960s, particularly because of the way they had shown that music could work without the use of tonality.

However, atonality had only ever appealed to a small number of music lovers and, by the late 1960s, some composers were having doubts about whether such Modernist music was really going to continue to be the path for the future. Little by little, works started to appear in which more familiar elements of music were used, but in new and unexpected ways. This style has become known as **Postmodernism** ('after Modernism').

Modernism: The Royal National Theatre, London

Once again, it can help to understand this new style by looking at similar changes in architecture that were happening around the same time. The building on the previous page is part of the Royal National Theatre in London, designed in 1967. The shapes against the sky are interesting, but the severe lines, stern concrete exterior and well-hidden windows of this rather brutal modernist style don't welcome in the public, which should surely be the main function of a theatre. In fact, it is far from obvious that this construction is actually a theatre at all.

The next picture is a photograph of the National Theatre in Budapest, Hungary, opened in 2002. This Postmodernist building has many traditional features: it is symmetrical, clad in stone, has columns with statues that look like saints on a medieval cathedral, and even has a circle of old-style rounded window arches near the top. But it is not a copy of an earlier style. The roof has gull-like wings, as if it has glided down from the sky, the statues on the columns are not of saints but of the muses (goddesses of comedy, tragedy, history, dance, music and so on), and huge plate-glass windows flood the interior with light. The entire structure is a playful Postmodernist fantasy, intended to attract audiences into the theatre rather than frighten them away with stern modernity.

© Újfalusi Németh Jenő

Postmodernism: The Hungarian National Theatre, Budapest

MINIMALISM

The style most closely associated with Postmodernist music in the last 40 years has become known as **Minimalism**. The term refers to using limited materials in new ways (although some of the techniques derive from non-western traditions, such as African drumming and Indonesian gamelan music).

Some of the typical features of Minimalism used in *Electric Counterpoint* include:

- Diatonic harmony (there are two different keys in *Electric Counterpoint*, but there are no chromatic notes in either key)
- Chords that change very slowly as notes are gradually added and removed
- Little variety in instrumentation (only guitar sounds are used in *Electric Counterpoint*)
- Repeating patterns that gradually vary over time.

You may be tempted to think that Minimalist music consists of little more than hypnotically repeating patterns. However, the last of the points above is crucial – the music is actually in a constant state of change, but its development is organic rather than dramatic. Although Minimalism can seem much more familiar than the atonal styles of the early 20th century, it challenges audiences to think about the nature of music just as much as the music of the Second Viennese School challenged accepted opinions.

Let's conclude this section with a final illustration from the visual arts. The American artist Dan Flavin had worked in a Minimalist style (although he disliked the term) since the 1960s. The photograph below is of part of an art installation that he created shortly before his death in 1996. It uses the simplest of materials (industrial neon tubes) set in a huge darkened hall in which repeating patterns of coloured light reflect off a polished concrete floor – patterns that can and will be disrupted by the viewers of his work. Simple? Yes. Subtle? Well, without light, how would we perceive any kind of visual art? Minimalism challenges its audience as much as Modernism – it just does it in a gentler way.

A Minimalist-influenced installation by the artist Dan Flavin for the Menil Collection, Houston, Texas

STEVE REICH (BORN 1936)

Reich's parents divorced soon after his birth, and he spent much of his childhood travelling between the home of his father (a lawyer) in New York and the home of his mother (who worked in musicals as a singer and songwriter) in California. He learnt the piano when young, and his interest in jazz led to him take up the drums at the age of 14. However, he took a degree in philosophy at university, later going on to study composition at music college.

Steve Reich

Reich's earliest music was in the Modernist style that was still in favour in the early 1960s, but he was always more drawn towards the rhythmic possibilities of music, and he went on to form his own ensemble, based around tuned percussion instruments, to perform his compositions.

In 1970, Reich travelled to Ghana to study African drumming and the following year he completed one of his best known pieces, *Drumming*. The influence of African rhythms permeates the work, as it does in the simpler *Clapping Music* of 1972 and *Music for Pieces of Wood* (1973).

Following studies of Indonesian gamelan music and traditional Hebrew chant, Reich's works became more complex and he later started to incorporate the rhythms and inflections of human speech into his works. *Different Trains* (1988) starts from Reich's own childhood experience of long train rides between the distant homes of his divorced parents, but it moves on to explore the desperate journeys of Jews trying to escape the death camps of Nazi Germany in World War II. To accomplish this aim, the work incorporates poignant phrases from tape-recorded interviews of those who survived the holocaust.

One of Reich's more recent works is *Daniel Variations*, which combines a text from the Book of Daniel in the Bible with the words of Daniel Pearl, an American reporter who was kidnapped and murdered in 2002 by religious fundamentalists in Pakistan. The work received its first performance in 2006 at the Barbican Centre in London.

For more about Steve Reich see his website: www.stevereich.com.

Although it seems surprising now, Reich's early work sometimes attracted as much controversy as Schoenberg's music did earlier in the century. In a 1973 performance of Reich's *Four Organs*, members of the audience in New York's Carnegie Hall repeatedly tried to interrupt the piece with booing and whistling, and one woman reputedly kept banging on the stage, shouting 'Stop, stop, I confess'. Today, so many composers have adopted at least some of the features of Minimalism that it hardly seems out of the ordinary. As well as appearing in concert halls and opera houses, Minimalist music has been used in the soundtracks of films and television programmes, and has influenced many trends in rock and electronic pop music over recent decades.

ELECTRIC COUNTERPOINT (THIRD MOVEMENT)

Electric Counterpoint was commissioned by the Brooklyn Academy of Music in New York for the famous jazz guitarist Pat Metheny, who helped Reich with the guitar writing and who gave the first performance in 1987. Metheny is the guitarist on CD 1 Track 6.

Guitarist Pat Metheny

It is the third in a series of four 'counterpoint' works by Reich, all of which centre on a soloist playing live against a backing, built up in layers, that was recorded earlier. The result is the clever idea of a contrapuntal piece played by a single person on an instrument that would normally play only a single melody line (or, in the case of the guitar, chords). To simplify performance, Reich has made the backing tracks available on tape (now on CD) for those who don't wish to record their own tracks. Alternatively, the work can be performed entirely live by a large ensemble of guitarists.

The work is in three movements (following a conventional fast–slow–fast pattern) and lasts about 15 minutes in total. The first movement is based on a theme derived from African music, and all three movements follow a similar idea of building a complex contrapuntal texture from simple materials.

Like other Minimalist pieces, some of the ideas in *Electric Counterpoint* have influenced pop musicians. In particular, the Orb used an extract from the third movement on their track *Little Fluffy Clouds*, released in 1990 (and re-released several times since).

Following the score

The speed is shown as ♩ = 192. This means 192 crotchets per minute (roughly three a second) – a very fast tempo. The time signature of $\frac{3}{2}$ indicates a triple metre of three minim beats per bar. Reich splits each minim into four quavers, so there are 12 quavers per bar, felt as three groups of four. To make this pattern clear, there are beams over each group of four quavers, even when some of those quavers are rests.

Apart from dynamics (and a pause sign on the last note) there are no other performing directions. We have almost come full circle – like a Baroque composer, Reich lets the performer decide how to interpret the music and so doesn't cover his score with phrase marks, accents, staccato dots, expression markings and so forth.

The only other point to note is that because stave notation for the guitar (and bass guitar) is written an octave higher than it actually sounds, the entire score sounds an octave lower than printed.

Listen to CD 1 Track 6 without following the score and see if you agree with the following points:

0:00	The opening builds up in layers, using notes in the high register of the guitar
0:44	Bass guitars enter, first playing in alternate bars and then continuously
1:06	Guitar chords appear, with falling patterns that later transform into rising patterns
2:18	A sudden change of key
2:33	A return to the original key
2:48	Back once again to the second key
3:02	The two keys start alternating more rapidly
3:33	The bass guitars and chordal parts drop out, leaving only high guitar parts to finish the movement

We could describe this as **ternary form** (ABA), a structure that we've met before. However, unlike Chopin's Prelude No. 15, where the middle section is marked out by a different melody and a contrasting key, the long middle section in *Electric Counterpoint* is distinguished by its different texture (the addition of bass guitars and chords).

We next need to turn to the score in order to understand the detail.

Bars 1–23 (0:00 to 0:43)

The term register is used to describe a particular part of an instrument's range.

We'll start by looking at the four pre-recorded tracks. The movement opens with a one-bar **syncopated** motif played in a high register by guitar 1. This forms an **ostinato** that is heard continuously until the end of bar 73. The motif is **hexatonic** (do you remember what this term means?) – it consists of six of the seven pitches of G major. The missing pitch (C) will not appear in any part until bar 24.

In bar 7, guitar 2 enters on the last note of the same motif (F#). It then continues to play the complete motif as an ostinato until the end of bar 73. Because the beginning of the actual motif starts two quavers later than the motif in guitar 1, the two ostinatos form a **canon**:

Next guitar 3 joins the canon, starting the motif on the fifth quaver of each bar. At first Reich gives it only the last four notes of the motif (the quaver rest and quaver notes in bars 10 and 11), then another four quavers are added in bars 12–14. This process of **note addition** leads to the full motif being heard from the last three quavers of bar 14 onwards.

Finally, guitar 4 enters in bar 16 with the last five notes of the motif, starting its repeats of the full motif from the sixth quaver of that bar. Here are bars 16–17, in which the full four-part canon is now under way, showing how each of the canonic parts plays the same motif (shown with a bracket) but starting in different parts of the bar:

Each bracket above contains the same pitches and note lengths, but each sounds slightly different because the motif starts in a different part of the bar and so the accented notes fall in different positions. This effect is known as **metrical displacement**.

Once you are sure you understand the process of note addition used to build-up the entry of guitar 3, you should be able to see how the live-guitar part works. It too is canonic, starting the complete motif on the third quaver of bar 6. Before this it plays fragments of the motif (four quavers in bars 2 and 3, eight in bar 4, and 10 in bars 5–6). It briefly drops out, and then starts the whole process again in bar 10, this time beginning on the fifth quaver of the bar. This is the quaver on which guitar 4 starts in bar 16, so in bars 16–17 the two parts are in unison: Reich fades out the live-guitar part at this point.

A **resultant melody** is a new melody that emerges when two or more different melodies are played at the same time.

Reich uses a different approach for the live-guitar part from bar 20 onwards. Study the score carefully and see if you can spot how every note of what looks like a new pattern doubles a note in one of the other guitar parts. This is known as a **resultant melody** and has the effect of accenting the doubled notes, giving new life to the ostinato.

In these first 23 bars we have heard some of the most characteristic features of Minimalism:

- ■ The music is entirely diatonic (only six pitches from the key of G major have been used)
- ■ There are no chord progressions – basically, the harmony hasn't changed at all
- ■ There is little variety in instrumentation (only high-register guitar sounds have been used)
- ■ The movement is constructed in layers, starting with a **monophonic** texture that builds up to a four-part canon (decorated by the live guitar)
- ■ Several of these layers feature note addition, in which notes are gradually added until all of the notes of the complete one-bar motif are present
- ■ The layers combine to form elaborate canonic ostinatos
- ■ The music is based on repeating patterns, given variety by metrical displacement, and the different ways in which these patterns build-up and overlap. Otherwise, there is very little rhythmic variety – from bar 7 onwards there is constant quaver movement, with no shorter note-lengths.

There are no cadences or chord progressions to establish a key, but do you agree that the music sounds nothing like the atonality of Schoenberg's 'Peripetie'? This is because the G-major tonality is made clear by the repetition of notes from this key, with no other pitches to confuse matters. There are frequent gentle dissonances, but even these are minimised by Reich's use of a hexatonic scale that omits the note C, thus avoiding the potential semitone clash between C and B.

Bars 24–35 (0:44 to 1:05)

The upper parts continue as before, but the entry of the two bass guitar parts immediately adds depth to the texture. The two bass guitars play the same pitches, but their octave leaps don't coincide, producing an interesting aural effect on the stereo recording where one guitar is panned left and the other right. Their part also has an impact on the harmony, introducing the pitch C for the first time, and outlining a triad of A minor (A, C and E) in a two-bar ostinato below the G major already established by the canonic ostinatos.

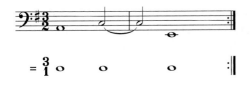

Reich again uses note addition to introduce the bass guitars. Their complete two-bar pattern starts in bar 32, but before this we hear 10 quavers of the pattern in bars 24 and 26, rising to 16 quavers during bars 28–31. When the complete pattern starts in bars 32–33, it adds a new dimension to the rhythm because the pitches change in unexpected parts of the bar (see left), cutting across the prevailing $\frac{3}{2}$ metre.

Bars 36–73 (1:06 to 2:17)

All the previous parts continue and now the final element is added to the texture, this time introduced by the live guitar. It is a pattern of three chords: C, Bm and

Em (the last without a third). Initially, only the first of these appears (bars 36 and 37) but in bars 38–39 we hear the complete two-bar motif for the first time.

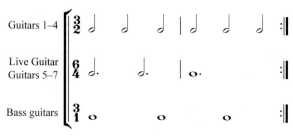

The rhythm of this pattern cuts across the threefold divisions of $\frac{3}{2}$ time just as much as the bass-guitars' pattern did. So, although there is no change in time signature, we now have three conflicting pulses at the same time, producing an effect known as **cross rhythm** (see left).

Guitar 5 doubles the new chordal ostinato in bars 40–41. It then takes over this part, while the live guitar adds to the rhythmic vitality by metrically displacing its first chord to the second crotchet of the bar (bars 42 and 44). By another process of note addition, this builds into a new chordal pattern, first heard complete in bars 50–51. The chords are C, D and Em, and they rise in syncopated rhythm and in **contrary motion** to the falling chords in guitar 5.

Guitar 6 takes over the rising pattern from bar 52 onwards, allowing the live guitar to introduce a final variant of the chord motif. This rises then falls (C, D, Bm) and introduces a new level of metrical displacement because it starts on the third crotchet of the bar. This is taken over by guitar 7 from bar 64. We have now reached the densest texture in the movement, with all ten parts playing:

- ■ A four-part canon in guitars 1–4
- ■ A three-part canonic texture in guitars 5–7 (because the patterns are slightly different, it is not strictly a canon)
- ■ A two-bar ostinato shared by the bass guitars
- ■ A free part for the live guitar which again picks out selected notes from the four-part canon.

Almost immediately, guitars 5–7 fade (bars 68–73) in preparation for the next section.

Bars 74–113 (2:18 to 3:32)

The key signature changes to E♭ major, but there is no modulation – Reich steps directly into this new key. Another important change occurs at bar 82: while guitars 1–4 continue in $\frac{3}{2}$, the other parts move into $\frac{12}{8}$ time. This too has 12 quavers per bar, but they are grouped differently, creating yet more cross rhythms:

Despite these changes, the melodic shapes are similar to those already established, and the rhythms and textures continue as before.

The most important feature of this section is the alternation of key and metre:

- ■ $\frac{3}{2}$ returns to all parts in bar 94
- ■ The key returns to G major in bar 98, but now with $\frac{12}{8}$ rhythms in some parts
- ■ $\frac{3}{2}$ is restored in bar 100, but the key switches to E♭ in bar 102, and so on …

These rhythmic and tonal changes give this section the instability of a development section in sonata form (as we saw in Mozart's symphony), even though the style is totally different.

Bars 114–140 (3:33 to 4:24)

The five lower parts fade out towards the end of the previous section, leaving just the five original parts from bar 114 onwards. However, the alternation of keys continues as does the switch to sections of $\frac{12}{8}$ time in the live-guitar part. In bar 134 all the ostinatos change shape slightly: from here to the end, Reich uses only the five pitches of a **pentatonic scale** (here, G, B, D, E and F♯). Most obvious is the rise in pitch, and the clash between the bright top E and top D that occurs at the start of every bar. Meanwhile, a long crescendo leads to a climactic final chord, in which all five parts simply prolong the seventh quaver of their ostinatos. The only pitches are E and B, so the ending (especially when preceded by purely pentatonic notes) is tonally ambiguous – have we finished in G major or is the piece in a modal version of E minor? Without a cadence or a complete tonic chord, Reich ensures that we are left wondering.

The final chord consists of the outer notes of an Em triad (E and B). However, the key of the work is not E minor, as D♯ is never used. *Electric Counterpoint* is best described as being in the Aeolian mode (A–B–C–D–E–F–G), transposed to start on E, with some sections (those with a key signature of three flats) being in the Aeolian mode on C.

Test yourself

1. In which two decades of the 20th century did Minimalism first start to become popular?
2. What is the importance of Pat Metheny in the creation of *Electric Counterpoint*?
3. What is the form of the third movement of *Electric Counterpoint*?
4. What musical term best describes the texture of most of this movement?
5. State what you understand is meant by **(a)** an ostinato and **(b)** a canon.
6. Briefly explain what is meant by **(a)** note addition, **(b)** metrical displacement and **(c)** resultant melody.
7. Give an example of cross rhythm from the set work.
8. How many notes are there in **(a)** a pentatonic scale and **(b)** a hexatonic scale?
9. Describe the final chord of the piece.
10. What role does music technology play in the performance of this work?

Listening ideas

To broaden your knowledge of Reich's style and of other Minimalist music, here are some more works that you might enjoy:

- Reich composed *New York Counterpoint* (for live and pre-recorded clarinets) in 1985, two years before *Electric Counterpoint*. The second movement is included in the Edexcel *A-level Anthology of Music*.
- Reich's *Clapping Music* (1972) was included in the original (2002) edition of GAM and is well worth performing in your GCSE group. The same book includes one of the earliest well-known Minimalist pieces, *In C* by Terry Riley – Reich discovered that he lived on the same street as Riley, and he took part in the first performance of *In C* in 1964.
- The second (2006) edition of GAM includes part of *Shaker Loops* (this version from 1983) by John Adams, another of the first generation of American Minimalist composers. Also look out for Adams' *Short Ride in a Fast Machine* (1986), which has become one of the most popular of all Minimalist works.
- Lighter types of music have been influenced by Minimalism, including *Still Life at the Penguin Café* by Simon Jeffes, *Principia* and other works by Steve Martland, and *Eliza's Aria* by Elena Kats-Chernin (used in the TV advert 'Lloyds TSB For The Journey': www.lloydstsb.com/forthejourney.asp). Minimalism has also influenced the work of rock artists such as Brian Eno and entire pop-music genres such as trance.

Composing ideas

While studying *Electric Counterpoint* we have come across a number of techniques that could be used in your own compositions. Writing a piece in a Minimalist style makes a good project, but it is essential to remember that simply repeating motifs will not produce interesting work. Reich builds up his movement in layers whose relationship gets ever more complicated through the use of metrically displaced canons, increasing numbers of cross rhythms, changes in texture and changes in chord. It also has a clear shape, with a climax in roughly the third quarter of the piece.

There is one feature of Minimalism that Reich does *not* use in the set work, although it does occur in many other Minimalist pieces. This is known as 'phasing' and involves two similar ostinatos moving in and out of step with each other as they repeat because one is slightly longer than the other. Ask your teacher for help if you want to include this technique in your work.

Other techniques used by Reich, that could be applied to work in other styles, include the use of canon and the idea of writing a piece in which a live performer decorates a group of pre-recorded tracks. The idea of writing a work for a group of similar instruments, such as three clarinets, is another possibility. However, this can be quite restrictive in tone colour unless, like Reich, you can extend the range by adding other instruments from the same family (such as a bass clarinet and/or a high E♭ clarinet).

Remember that although your compositions must be related to the areas of study, you don't *have* to base them on ideas from the set works. In the case of this area of study, it is enough for your work to be related to any typical aspect(s) of Music in the 20th Century.

Sample questions for Section A

Listen to the first 43 seconds of CD 1 Track 6 three times, with short pauses between each playing, as you answer the following questions. Don't consult the score or any other information before writing your answers.

1. Write X in the box that describes the texture at the very beginning of the extract.

homophonic ☒   monophonic ☒   polyphonic ☒   (1)

2. The first bar is repeated throughout the extract. What musical term describes a part that is continually repeated?

....   (1)

3. What musical term describes the relationship between the four parts that accompany the live guitarist?

....   (1)

4. What is the time signature of this music? ....   (1)

5. Write X in the box that best describes this music.

atonal ☒   chromatic ☒   diatonic ☒   (1)

6. In what style is this piece written? ....   (1)

7. List **four** important features of the style you named in question 6.

(a) ....

(b) ....

(c) ....

(d) ....   (4)

(Total 10 marks)

Top Tips

In questions such as number 7, don't make the same point twice – even if you use different words you won't get a mark for just repeating a point.

Sample questions for Section B

Before tackling this section read the information on writing extended answers, on page 167. Then complete your answers without consulting any notes or the score, and without listening to the recording.

The following questions are about *Electric Counterpoint* (third movement) by Reich.

(a) In which decade was *Electric Counterpoint* written? Put a cross in the correct box.

1950s ☒   1960s ☒   1970s ☒   1980s ☒   1990s ☒   (1)

(b) Name the guitarist for whom this work was composed.

....   (1)

(c) Comment on how Reich uses the following musical elements in this piece:

Metre and rhythm
Melody
> Remember to explain how the key (or mode) is ambiguous. → Tonality
Texture
Structure   (10)

Use correct musical vocabulary where appropriate and remember that the quality of your writing, including spelling, punctuation and grammar, will be taken into account in this question. Write your answer on a separate sheet of paper.

(Total 12 marks)

It is important to realise that classical music is not the pop music of the past. Popular music has existed throughout history, but we know relatively little about it before the middle of the 19th century, because songs and dances were learnt by ear and seldom written down. After about 1850 increasing prosperity encouraged the growth of professional entertainment in variety shows and music halls, producing a great demand for new songs. At the same time, the advent of affordable pianos and cheap music printing created a market for printed copies of these songs to perform at home, and so popular music regularly appeared in print for the first time.

Much 19th-century popular music was not greatly different from the waltzes, marches and light classical songs of the period. However, in America the abolition of slavery resulted in excitingly fresh musical ideas coming to public attention as black-American music became more widely known. These included features new to most western ears, such as complex syncopation and blue notes (the flattened third, fifth and seventh of the major scale) that had originally come from Africa several generations earlier via the slave trade.

By the 1890s, ragtime was the rage – a blend of syncopated rhythms ('ragged time') and familiar western harmonies. The mournful style of the blues took longer to catch on – it was rather too closely identified with black music to be commercially successful at first in those racially prejudiced times. However, the invention of the gramophone record led to the rapid spread of all the latest types of popular music in the early 20th century, and an even greater impact resulted from the start of public radio broadcasting in 1920 the first and sound movies by the end of that decade.

By 1920, ragtime was almost forgotten and jazz had become a driving force in much popular music. Unlike ragtime, jazz is not a style of music but a style of performance. In its most common form, jazz consists of mainly improvised variations on a chord pattern and so has proved adaptable to changing tastes for almost a century. In the 1930s, a style of jazz known as swing became one of the most common types of popular music. However, after the Second World War jazz and popular music went their separate ways. Our first set work in this area of study is one of the most famous pieces of jazz from the 1950s. In the same decade, rock and roll had become the latest style in American pop music, soon to be followed by the Beatles and other British rock and pop bands in the 1960s. Ever since, pop music styles have changed rapidly, although the increasing use of music technology and the influence of different types of music from around the world have been two common themes in many new trends. Our other two set works are songs that both date from the 1990s:

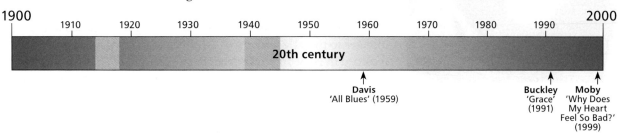

SET WORK 7: 'ALL BLUES' BY MILES DAVIS

MILES DAVIS (1926–1991)

Swing was very popular in the 1930s, but it required big bands in order to be heard in the large dance halls of the day. Improvisation, which is at the heart of all jazz, is not practical for a large group of performers, and by the early 1940s some jazz musicians were developing a new type of jazz called bebop – one of the styles that influenced Bernstein in *West Side Story*. Bebop was played by a small combination of musicians (known in jazz as a 'combo'), allowing much more opportunity for improvisation, and was music for listening to rather than dancing.

Miles Davis grew up in the American Midwest and began learning the trumpet at the age of 13. He made quick progress and was starting to play professionally before he left school. He briefly continued trumpet lessons at the famous Julliard School of Music in New York, but soon gave up his classical studies in order to work professionally with some of the leading jazz musicians of the bebop era.

Bebop was very fast and technically demanding, requiring extended playing at the very top of the trumpet's range. It was not a style that came naturally to Davis, even though he was good at it, and in the late 1940s he gathered together some like-minded musicians to record a series of tracks in a new, more relaxed style that became known as cool jazz.

© Tom Palumbo

Miles Davis in 1955

During the 1950s, Davis produced jazz that was influenced by the blues and by the types of scale known as modes, giving rise to the term **modal jazz** for this period of his work. He continued to be a great innovator throughout his working life, later incorporating electronic instruments into his music and working in new cross-over styles such as jazz-rock fusion (one of the styles in which the guitarist Pat Metheny made his name).

KIND OF BLUE

© CYLU/www.shutterstock.com

An LP record player

Before the introduction of the LP (long-playing) record in 1948, it was not possible to have more than about 3 minutes' worth of continuous music on a gramophone record. The LP allowed more than 20 minutes per side, which was ideal for the relatively long pieces that jazz musicians in the 1950s preferred.

Kind of Blue is an album of five tracks, varying in length from 5½ minutes to the 11½ minutes of 'All Blues', our set work. It was recorded in New York on 2 March and 22 April 1959. **Stereo** sound had only just started to appear on records at this time, so the album was released in both mono and stereo versions.

A sextet is a group of six musicians.

Miles Davis worked with a number of jazz musicians over the years – the sextet employed on this recording includes some of the greatest jazz performers of the age:

- Miles Davis (trumpet)
- Julian 'Cannonball' Adderley (alto saxophone)
- John Coltrane (tenor saxophone)
- Bill Evans (piano)
- Paul Chambers (bass)
- Jimmy Cobb (drums).

In early jazz, the first three of these players would have been known as the frontline and the last three as the rhythm section. Although this distinction was rarely used in modern jazz of the 1950s, it is notable that the three melody instruments each have extended solos in 'All Blues', while the pianist has a shorter solo and the other rhythm instruments don't play individually for any length of time.

© Frank Driggs Collection/Getty Images

Left to right: John Coltrane, Cannonball Adderley, Miles Davis and Bill Evans in the studio, 1959

According to pianist Bill Evans, Davis had planned the tracks only hours before the recording. He gave the members of the sextet brief sketches of the scales and melodic ideas on which to improvise, plus some verbal instructions. Then, with almost no rehearsal, each track was recorded.

Kind of Blue is widely regarded as Davis' finest work. It was influential at the time and was well received, although by 1959 modern jazz was very much a minority interest in the face of the enormous popularity of rock and roll. Appreciation of the album has grown over time, and it is now regarded as the best-selling jazz album of all time – clocking up some five million sales (the majority of which have been since the year 2000).

THE BLUES

As you can guess from its title, 'All Blues' is related to the blues – a generally sad type of music once sung by black-American slaves of the 18th and early-19th centuries as they toiled in the fields, although some of its features can be traced back even further to origins in Africa. The blues reached a wider audience in the 1920s, through records and radio, and later transformed into a more up-tempo style known as rhythm and blues that influenced many styles of pop music from rock and roll onwards.

Traditionally, jazz musicians based their improvisations on chord patterns. One of the most popular was formed from the harmonies of the blues which, by the 1920s, had started to settle into a fairly standard 12-bar format based on three chords. In the key of G major, the chords are typically:

G	G	G	G	C	C	G	G	D	C	G	G
I	I	I	I	IV	IV	I	I	V	IV	I	I

Sometimes a few of the chords may differ, and any (or all) might include a 7th, but the important thing is that while the chords are the same three primary triads found in classical harmony, they are used in a totally different way. In particular, chord IV appears more frequently than chord V, and the key-defining perfect cadence (V–I) is missing. Also, instead of pairs of balanced phrases, the blues **progression** consists of *three* four-bar phrases.

> The term progression means a chord pattern.

Blues melodies are often made more expressive by lowering the pitch of the third and seventh degrees of the scale, and sometimes the fifth as well. These **blue notes** are often performed just a little flatter than normal, although they are shown as a full semitone lower in notation. 'All Blues' is in the key of G, but the seventh degree of the scale is almost always treated as a blue note:

MODAL JAZZ

A **mode** is simply a scale. We could describe a piece that uses major scales as being in the major mode, but the term mode is usually reserved for certain scales that are neither major nor minor. Try playing the white notes on a keyboard from G to the G an octave higher. This is called the **Mixolydian mode**: it differs from G major because its seventh degree is F♮, not F♯. And even though it has the same notes as C major, it doesn't sound the same because its home note is G, not C.

The Mixolydian mode uses the same notes as the scale we identified above – G major with a blue seventh.

'All Blues' is often described as modal jazz. Look at bars 9–12 in GAM and you will see a key signature of G major and a chord of G (with G in the bass) at the start of every bar. There is no doubt that G is the key note, and yet every F is F♮: this is the Mixolydian mode.

However, while it is true that Davis frequently used modes in the late 1950s, scholars are divided on whether a work such as this should be described as modal. The difficulty is that the F♮s are, as we saw in the previous section, simply blue notes – the flattened sevenths of G major. We'll return to this tricky point later.

Following the score

As we learnt earlier, there was no score for the tracks on 'All Blues'. Davis just made a few outline sketches and gave verbal instructions to his players. As is the case for many pop and jazz pieces, the score has been made later by writing down what was played in the recording – a type of score known as a **transcription**.

Because there is often more than one way to notate a particular passage, you may see other transcriptions of 'All Blues' in which the notation looks different. For example, in GAM it has been transcribed in $\frac{6}{4}$ time, so that each main section (labelled 'head' in the score) matches the 12-bar length of a blues progression. However, because the piece is a fast jazz **waltz** you may see other transcriptions that notate the music in $\frac{3}{4}$ time, spreading the chord progression out over 24 bars instead of 12 bars.

A **waltz** is a formal ballroom dance in $\frac{3}{4}$ time that first became popular in the early 19th century.

The first bar of the score is marked **swing quavers**. This is a rhythmic device that is common in much jazz, and refers to playing pairs of quavers unevenly, making the first slightly longer than the second.

© Viames Marino

Although the trumpet and saxophones are transposing instruments, they are notated at sounding pitch in the score. The bass part is for double bass and sounds an octave lower than printed. It is played pizzicato throughout. The drum part is notated on a five-line stave with a percussion clef, which indicates that the lines and spaces are for different instruments in the kit, rather than for notes of different pitch. The snare drum is played with wire brushes at the start – the word 'sweep' indicates that a brush is dragged across the drumhead.

Playing a snare drum with wire brushes

To save space, parts for accompanying instruments are not always shown in sections where they continue to play patterns they have played before, and the solos in bars 93–220 are not notated. The long rests with a figure 3 above indicate three bars that have not been notated in the transcription.

Structure

'All Blues' uses the most common of all structures in jazz, known as a **head arrangement**. It consists of a chord progression that is called the head because it is memorised (kept in the head) by all the players. In 'All Blues', the head is the 12-bar blues chord progression.

Some people believe that the term head refers to the fact that it comes at the start (the 'head') of the music. However, many jazz pieces (including this one) begin with an introduction before the head.

Each repetition of the blues progression is known as a chorus, and each of the improvised solos is based on four choruses, except the piano solo, which has two. Like many jazz works, we could regard the piece as a set of variations on the head. The choruses are framed by an introduction at the start and a **coda** (which is also based on the blues progression) at the end. In addition, each of the main sections is introduced by a four-bar **riff**. The following table of the structure is a simplified version of the one in GAM:

00:00	Bar 1	4-bar introduction (rhythm section)
00:11	Bar 5	4-bar riff (saxophones and rhythm section) followed by 12-bar head (muted trumpet added)
00:53	Bar 21	Riff and head repeated
01:35	Bar 37	Riff followed by four 12-bar choruses for trumpet (un-muted)
03:51	Bar 89	Riff (on piano) followed by four 12-bar choruses for alto sax
06:04	Bar 141	Riff (on piano) followed by four 12-bar choruses for tenor sax
08:17	Bar 193	Riff (on piano) followed by two 12-bar choruses for piano
09:28	Bar 221	Riff (with saxes) followed by 12-bar head (played by all, with trumpet now muted)
10:09	Bar 237	Riff and head repeated
10:51	Bar 253	Riff and coda (muted trumpet solo)

LISTENING GUIDE

Jazz musicians rarely use the term 'chord progression' – they describe the pattern of harmonies on which they improvise as the changes, because it consists of a set of changing chords.

Listen to the complete recording and make sure that you can identify the sections above. Did you think that the work sounded a little like *Electric Counterpoint*? That is because the many riffs (which include the constantly repeating figures in the accompaniment as well as the ones listed in the table above) are similar in effect to the ostinatos of Reich's composition, although they are far less complicated. Although we wouldn't describe 'All Blues' as a Minimalist work, Miles Davis' style in the 1950s was a rejection of the complexities of bebop, just as in the 1960s and 70s Minimalism would become a reaction to the complexities of Modernism.

As mentioned earlier, the precise chords in a blues progression can vary. In the next diagram we compare the blues progression we saw earlier with the one used in this piece. Minor 7ths above the bass are frequently added in the blues, as they are by Davis, but the more significant differences are marked by grey shading:

G	G	G	G	C	C	G	G	D	C	G	G
I	I	I	I	IV	IV	I	I	V	IV	I	I

12-bar blues in G

G^7	G^7	G^7	G^7	$Gm^{(7)}$	$Gm^{(7)}$	G^7	G^7	D^7	$E\flat^7$ D^7	F G	F G^6
I^7	I^7	I^7	I^7	$i^{(7)}$	$i^{(7)}$	I^7	I^7	V^7	$\flat VI^7$ V^7	$\flat VII$ I	$\flat VII$ I^6

'All Blues'

For the start of the second phrase, Davis prefers the minor version of the tonic chord to chord IV: G minor includes B♭, the 'blue third' of G major. The final phrase features chromatic chords (slightly simplified in this chart) and it ends on G⁶. This is a chord of G major plus a 6th above the root, resulting in the notes G, B, D and E. Known as an **added 6th chord**, it is one of the characteristic sounds in jazz of this period.

The repeated cadence in the final bars (F–G, F–G) is significant. The progression ♭VII–I is not a standard cadence, but it is common in modal music and is therefore known as a **modal cadence**. Even though we can explain F♮ as a blue note, blue notes seldom figure in the bass, so this modal cadence lends strength to the view that we should regard 'All Blues' as modal jazz.

Introduction (bars 1–4)

The waltz style is established by the rhythm section. Each player has a distinctive pattern that is repeated as a riff:

- The bass has a six-beat pattern with the tonic (G) on the first beat and the blue seventh of G (F♮) on the fourth beat
- The drums have a three-beat waltz rhythm, played quietly with wire brushes
- The piano has a tremolo-like figure that converges on G and F♮ – pianist Bill Evans recalled this as a 'little fluttering' that he just threw in on the day.

> This tremolo could be described as a pair of written-out **trills**.

Riff (bars 5–8)

Saxes in 3rds add a swaying figure to the rhythm section's accompaniment. It moves stepwise through a very narrow range, up to the blue seventh of G and back.

Head (bars 9–20)

We hear the blues progression for the first time in these bars, above which bandleader Miles Davis enters with a mid-range legato solo. His trumpet tone is produced with the aid of a Harmon mute with its stem removed – a sound so liked by Davis that it became his trademark. A Harmon mute is often used for the 'wah-wah' effect in music for cartoons when something unfortunate happens to a character, but Davis' preference for taking out the removable stem produces a very different, delicate and distinctive sound.

His melody is characterised by rising 6ths from D to B, mirroring the falling leaps in the bass part, but otherwise has a narrow range of a 5th, which suits the intimate atmosphere of 'All Blues' and is totally unlike the exhaustingly fast and high trumpet lines in the bebop style of Miles Davis' early years. Beneath the solo, the rest of the sextet continue much as before, adapting their parts to the changing harmonies.

Riff and head 2 (bars 21–36)

This section is a repeat of bars 5–20, with the small differences that are to be expected in an improvised performance.

Riff and trumpet solo (bars 37–88)

At bar 37, drummer Jimmy Cobb begins adding splashes of cymbal tone, and the return of the introductory riff gives Davis the opportunity to remove the mute for his main solo. He gradually increases the range of his playing to encompass just over two octaves, although much of his improvisation remains in the middle of the trumpet's range. The most noticeable difference in this section is the more rhythmic style of its short motifs, complemented by the pianist's change from a fluttering tremolo to crisp accompaniment rhythms. Notice how Jimmy Cobb has switched from brushes to sticks, and from bar 41 **keeps time** with a simple pulse played on the ride cymbal.

The dynamic range also increases in this section, there's more use of syncopation, and Davis adds a number of **grace notes** (printed in small type and played very quickly). Blue notes (B♭ and F♮) appear more frequently. The notes with X-heads (for instance in bars 41 and 43) are known as **ghost notes** and are produced with only a very faint tone. Another special effect used by Davis in this solo is the **fall off** – a short downward glissando at the end of a note (marked by a diagonal line in bars 52, 64 and 67). In his final chorus (starting in bar 77), Davis reverts to longer melodic lines, although in a higher (and wider) range than those he used in the head.

Riff and alto-sax solo (bars 89–140)

Miles Davis' last two notes in bar 89 overlap with the return of the introductory riff. This is now played only by the rhythm section, in order not to detract from the saxophone solos that follow.

© Horatiu Bota/www.shutterstock.com

A Harmon mute – the stem is the central part at the top that can be adjusted or removed

In jazz drumming, keeping time means playing a simple rhythm (usually on the ride cymbal) as a guide part around which other members of the band can play more complex, syncopated rhythms.

Whereas Davis' choruses were cool and restrained, Cannonball Adderley's alto-sax solo starts with terse rhythmic motifs that soon explode into a riot of scales and arpeggios in semiquavers and triplets. There are few rests or longer notes, and much of Adderley's improvisation is in the upper part of the range.

Riff and tenor-sax solo (bars 141–192)

After the return of the rhythm section's version of the introductory riff, John Coltrane's tenor-sax solo gradually introduces the intense 'sheets of sound' for which he had already become famous – fast scales and arpeggios played across the range of the instrument. These often involve intricate rhythms, such as triplets within triplets, and Coltrane frequently plays 'away from the chord', meaning that many of his notes clash with the underlying harmonies.

Riff and piano solo (bars 193–220)

The next appearance of the introductory riff leads into two choruses from pianist Bill Evans. The style is immediately much calmer, with long melody notes in the first chorus, accompanied by an elaboration of the chords from the introductory riff. His second chorus features **parallel chords** – strings of triads, 7th-chords and 9th-chords, sometimes with the left hand in contrary motion.

Riff and head (bars 221–252)

The original version of the introductory riff returns at bar 221, with Bill Evans resuming his tremolo four bars later. Meanwhile, Miles Davis reinserts his Harmon mute for the third head, which starts in bar 225. This section, along with the final head that follows, is so similar to the first two heads that we have to assume that this was composed (or at least pre-planned) material rather than improvisation.

Riff and coda (bars 253–268)

The introductory riff is heard for a last time in bars 253–256, at the end of which Davis enters with the coda. This is based on the blues changes, but melodically it has the simplest treatment of all. Davis uses only two notes (dominant and tonic) throughout its first two phrases, and then brings the work to its conclusion with the same simple, legato phrase he played at the end of the head.

Perhaps the most extraordinary fact about this long and famous recording is that it was recorded in a single take. Despite the reported last-minute preparation by Davis, the sketchiness of the materials he gave to his players and the lack of rehearsal, he gave his instructions to the band and, after a false start on the first take, 'All Blues' was recorded from start to finish in one go – no improvement was needed. Miles Davis was, of course, working with five of the most talented jazz musicians of his day.

Test yourself

1. What is the correct term for an ensemble of six musicians?
2. How does the mixolydian mode on G differ from a scale of G major?
3. What type of trumpet mute did Miles Davis prefer?
4. Davis sometimes plays ghost notes. What are ghost notes?
5. What do jazz musicians mean by **(a)** 'keeping time' and **(b)** the 'changes'?
6. How many blues choruses are there in 'All Blues'?
7. Much of 'All Blues' is based on riffs. What is a riff?
8. The piece ends with a coda. What does coda mean?
9. What is the meaning of 'swing quavers' printed at the head of the score?
10. Why was it surprising in 1959 that *Kind of Blue* was issued as a stereo recording?

Further listening

To broaden your knowledge of Miles Davis's style and other related music, here are some more works that you might enjoy:

- An excerpt from **Four** by Miles Davis appears in the Edexcel *A-level Anthology of Music*. Although the recording dates from 1964, the piece was written in 1954 when Davis was working in a style that is sometimes described as 'hard bop'. It reflects something of the fast pace and dissonant harmonies of the earlier bebop era.

- Other well-known tracks by Davis include **'So What'** (from the *Kind of Blue* album) and **'Milestones'**, part of an album of the same name recorded a year before *Kind of Blue*, in which the modal jazz style is more evident than in 'All Blues'.

- For something rather different, look out for Davis' 1958 album **Porgy and Bess** – an attractive set of arrangements from Gershwin's blues-based opera of the same name. For a glimpse of one of the routes jazz was to take over the next 15 years, try to listen to **Weather Report** (1971) by the group of the same name. Several of its members had earlier been associated with Miles Davis, but this album was one of the first to blend jazz with rock music in a style that became known as jazz fusion.

- Two very different blues-based songs were included in the first (2002) edition of GAM: one from 1936 and the other from 2001.

- For a thorough introduction to a wide range of jazz, look out for **Jazz Styles: History and Analysis** by Mark C. Gridley (published by Prentice Hall): www.jazzstyles.com. The full version comes with a CD that demonstrates 171 jazz techniques and another that includes 38 jazz classics, each analysed in the book.

Composing ideas

While studying 'All Blues' we have come across a number of techniques that could be used in your own compositions. Unless you are an experienced jazz player, writing a piece of jazz may not be a good idea, but a blues-based song or instrumental piece might be a possibility. If you choose a song, remember that blues lyrics normally consist of three lines per verse, the first two of which are usually identical or very similar. Study the blues changes carefully, remembering that chords can be altered or added to, providing the main outlines of its three four-bar phrases remain clear. Repetitions of the 12-bar chord pattern can be separated by contrasting interludes (like Davis' introductory riffs), and the whole work framed by an introduction at the start and a coda at the end. Because the harmonies in a blues tend to be repetitive, pay particular attention to getting variety in the melody and remember to make expressive use of blue notes.

Sample questions for Section A

Listen to the first 43 seconds of CD 2 Track 1 three times, with short pauses between each playing, as you answer the following questions. Don't consult the score or any other information before writing your answers.

1. The bass part starts with eight repetitions of a one-bar pattern. What is the correct musical term for a continually repeating pattern?

.... (1)

2. Complete the rhythm of this bass part on the line below. The first three beats are given. (3)

3. Briefly explain how the snare drum is played during this passage.

.... (1)

4. Write X in the box next to the musical term that describes the part played by the pianist in this music.

arco ☒   continuo ☒   rondo ☒
rubato ☒   tremolo ☒ (1)

5. The next instruments to join in are the saxophones. They play the same notes in parallel intervals. What is that interval: 3rds, 5ths, 6ths or octaves?

.... (1)

6. Complete the blanks in the following sentence:

The last instrument to enter is a ...., with its tone

modified by the use of a .... (2)

7. This piece is notated in G major. Name the pitch of the blue seventh in this key.

.... (1)

(Total 10 marks)

Sample questions for Section B

Before tackling this section read the information on writing extended answers, on page 167. Then complete your answers without consulting any notes or the score, and without listening to the recording.

The following questions are about 'All Blues' from *Kind of Blue* by Miles Davis.

(a) In which year did Miles Davis record this track? Put a cross in the correct box.

1939 ☒   1949 ☒   1959 ☒   1969 ☒   1979 ☒   (1)

(b) How many musicians play in 'All Blues'? .... (1)

(c) Comment on how Davis uses the following musical elements in this piece:

Structure
Harmony
Melody
Rhythm
Use of instruments   (10)

Use correct musical vocabulary where appropriate and remember that the quality of your writing, including spelling, punctuation and grammar, will be taken into account in this question. Write your answer on a separate sheet of paper.

(Total 12 marks)

SET WORK 8: 'GRACE' FROM THE ALBUM *GRACE* BY JEFF BUCKLEY

In the introduction to this area of study we learnt how traditional elements of Black-American music were a driving force in 20th-century jazz and popular music. However, during the same period local traditions of folk music in many parts of the world were disappearing fast. Before a large body of music was lost forever, music scholars began writing down (and later recording) traditional folk music in remote areas.

This was to spark a folk revival in the 1950s which became very commercial during the 1960s, when folk music would sometimes rub shoulders with the latest rock music in the charts. Some songs had traditional roots (such as the centuries-old *Scarborough Fair*), while others were newly-composed pieces that used a folk-like style (such as Bob Dylan's *Blowin' in the Wind* and Ralph McTell's *Streets of London*). Although the arrangements generally sounded modern, many of these songs had a direct link with the past in using lyrics that expressed popular thought about issues of the day, addressed in a simple and direct musical style.

Rather like jazz, the impact of folk on popular music has varied over the years. Some musicians have preferred to stay close to traditional styles of performance, but others (such as the Pogues in the 1980s) combined folk with the most extreme forms of rock of their day, and in the next area of study we shall see how a traditional Scottish folksong was to be reinterpreted in the year 2000.

Jeff Buckley's 1994 album *Grace* is often described as **folk rock** or alternative folk, but in reality it is a work that defies labels. It includes Buckley's interpretations of *Lilac Wine* (a song from 1950), Leonard Cohen's *Hallelujah* (written in 1984 and a 2008 hit for Buckley, following the revival of Cohen's song on *The X-Factor* TV show), and Benjamin Britten's 1933 setting of the *Corpus Christi Carol*, the words of which are well over 500 years old. Buckley's own compositions are just as diverse, with influences ranging from jazz to heavy metal. However, much of his music retains the folk tradition of using song as a vehicle for story-telling.

JEFF BUCKLEY (1966–1997)

Jeff Buckley was born in California to teenage parents who separated before his birth. His mother had learnt the cello and piano at school, while his father (the singer Tim Buckley) was about to release the first of several albums in the folk-rock style that was becoming increasingly popular in the 1960s. Tim Buckley was a powerful and versatile singer, later recording jazz- and soul-based songs before dying from a drugs overdose at the age of 29.

© Michel Linssen/Redferns/Getty Images

Although Jeff Buckley only met his father once or twice, there is little doubt that he inherited an extraordinary vocal ability, which Buckley recalled had extended back for many generations in his father's family. He also shared his father's wide-ranging musical tastes, amplified by the Spanish songs he learnt from his maternal grandmother and by the latest hits of Led Zeppelin and Jimi Hendrix, introduced to Buckley in the 1970s by his stepfather.

Buckley started learning the guitar at the age of five and later played electric guitar in his high school's jazz band. After leaving school at 18, Buckley spent a year at music college in Hollywood studying popular music – an experience he remembered largely for learning about harmony, from 20th-century art music to jazz. As we shall see, Buckley's own work was later to be characterised by its unusual harmonies and imaginative chord progressions.

After some years working as a guitarist, Jeff Buckley made a demo (demonstration) recording of his own songs in 1990, but more influential to his career was his decision to sing at a memorial concert for his father in 1991, where he performed two of his father's songs as well as some of his own material.

Jeff Buckley in 1994

The audience was spellbound – it was as if Tim Buckley's famous voice had returned but with even greater emotional depth and flexibility.

Jeff Buckley was accompanied in that concert by the guitarist Gary Lucas, and later in 1991 the two of them co-wrote two songs (including 'Grace') that would eventually appear on Buckley's only album – Lucas' contribution was mainly in writing the guitar riffs for the songs. Buckley broadened his repertorie and began performing as a singer, accompanying himself on guitar, in the cafés and clubs of New York, where he quickly came to the attention of the major record companies. In 1992 Columbia offered him a lucrative deal for three albums, the first of which was *Grace*. The Danish bassist Mick Grøndahl was engaged to play bass guitar and the American Matt Johnson was signed as the drummer. Gary Lucas was invited to play guitar on the two tracks he had co-written, and the jazz composer Karl Berger assisted with string arrangements for some of the songs.

Most of the album was recorded in late 1993, and it was released in August 1994. Although sales were slow at first, it was quickly recognised by fellow musicians and critics as a work of major importance. Buckley spent much of the next two years touring, both to promote *Grace* and to try out new material. He began working on his next album, provisionally called *My Sweetheart, The Drunk* in 1996 but, although several recording sessions for it took place, Buckley was unhappy with the results. On 29 May 1997, shortly before another session was due to take place, Jeff Buckley drowned in a swimming accident. He was 30 years old – a life only one year longer than that of his father, who's career Jeff's own had so often unwillingly echoed.

For more on Jeff Buckley, see www.jeffbuckley.com.

Thus, *Grace* was Jeff Buckley's only completed album. Unfinished material for the second album was issued under the title *Sketches for My Sweetheart, the Drunk* in the year after his death, and some of his other work (such as demo tapes and recordings made at live concerts) has also been issued. Inevitably, Buckley's tragically early death has led to him being described as rock's last great romantic.

'GRACE'

The title song of Buckley's album is a **rock ballad** – a song in a fairly slow tempo, usually about love, accompanied by a rock band. Many of Buckley's songs express a bleak outlook on love and here the lyrics also eerily seem to anticipate his own death by drowning. However, Buckley himself regarded 'Grace' to be a song about the way that true love can make it easier for people to accept their own mortality.

The song is in **verse-and-chorus** form, with an introduction before each of the three verses, and a bridge after the second chorus. The final verse breaks off halfway through and is followed by a coda which is based on the chorus.

The second half of each verse is different in character from the first half. Some people might describe the second half as a **pre-chorus** – a section that prepares for the chorus. This is the section that is omitted in verse 3.

Following the score

Tab is an abbreviation of 'tablature', a word that refers to its table-like appearance. It is a type of notation that dates back to medieval times, and for several centuries it was used for writing music for plucked-string instruments such as the lute. It reappeared (in a slightly different form) in the 20th century as a way to notate guitar music.

Although the harmonies look complicated, many are parallel chords formed by simply moving the same finger shape up and down the fingerboard, as shown by the guitar tab in bars 8–13 (where the 0 indicates an open string, creating an inner pedal note on G throughout this passage).

Notice that the lowest string of the guitar (normally E) has to be tuned down to D to reach the lowest pitches required. The guitar part is printed in both stave notation and guitar **tab**. This is a way of notating pitches by showing finger positions on the instrument, and is often accompanied by an indication of the rhythm shown as headless notes above the stave, although that is not done here.

The horizontal lines represent the six strings of the guitar, normally (from bass upwards) E, A, D, G, B and E, although in this piece the bottom string is D. The numbers on each line show which frets the fingers must be placed on to make the required notes. Each fret raises the pitch of the string by a semitone. The very first fingering is 3 on the D string. Three semitones above D is F, and you can see that this is the first note printed on the guitar stave above the tab. The second fingering is 1 on the G string. One semitone above G is A♭, and that is the second note on the guitar stave.

Like 'All Blues', the score has been made by transcribing the music from the recording. In GAM it is printed in $\frac{12}{8}$ time – four dotted-crotchet beats per bar – although you may come across other transcriptions that use $\frac{6}{8}$ time, which has two dotted-crotchet beats per bar (and therefore the song will have twice as many bars as the version in GAM).

After the start, the score shows just the main material in the song rather than giving every part in detail. The harmonies, which are quite complicated, are printed as chord symbols above the stave. Diagonal lines, such as the one in the vocal part of bar 10, indicate a glissando between notes.

LISTENING GUIDE

Introduction (bars 1–7: 0:00)

The song is in E minor but the introduction gives little hint of this, starting a semitone higher on a chord of Fm. The tonic chord of Em arrives in bar 3, where drums and bass enter, but the rest of this section is based on the two main chords of D major (D and A⁷), leaving the sense of tonality very ambiguous.

Verse 1 (bars 8–19: 0:27)

The tonal ambiguity continues into the first half of the verse, where the harmony is chromatic, with the bass moving in semitones (E–F♮–E–E♭ and then F♮–E–E♭–E♮). The melody is low in Buckley's range, and moves mainly by step, with slides between the few descending leaps, establishing the rather gloomy mood of the song. Notice the flexibility of Buckley's rhythms in which many of the shorter notes are syncopated for expressive effect.

In the second half of the verse (the pre-chorus), Buckley ironically moves to a higher register for 'my fading voice'. There are more leaps in the melody –

although the most prominent ones are still descending, and the phrases continue to have a falling profile. Here the use of the three **primary triads** of E minor at last clarifies the tonality of the song. Buckley illustrates the word 'love' with a falling **melisma** and the bass depicts 'the clicking of time' with **cross rhythms** in bars 14 and 17, effectively playing eight notes in $\frac{4}{4}$ time while Buckley's melody continues in $\frac{12}{8}$.

Chorus 1 (bars 20–24: 1:12)

The chorus is very minimal (just four syllables of text) and doesn't contrast strongly with the verse. The harmony is essentially the same chromatic progression heard in the first half of the verse (minus its opening chord), with the two top strings of the guitar (B and E) providing some grating dissonances where they clash with the rest of the chord. The melodic lines still fall, and Buckley illustrates the last word ('fire') with another long melisma.

Introduction repeated (bars 25–31: 1:31)

Listen carefully for the sound of the Em chord at the end of the chorus rising to the Fm chord at the start of this section. Apart from a few small changes, these seven bars are a repeat of the first seven bars of the song.

Verse 2 (bars 32–43: 1:57)

This is a repeat of verse 1 with adaptations in the vocal line to fit the new words, as well as some new material in the accompaniment (such as the eerie synthesiser effects after the word 'sorrow'). There is a more substantial change in bars 36–37 where the word 'love' prompts Buckley to rise to a high E and project the music on towards the second half of the verse – compare this with verse 1 (bars 12–13), where he sank to a low E on 'die' and then had a clean break before the next phrase. In bar 39 Buckley reaches a top A earlier than in verse 1, and in bar 43 he again projects the music onwards with a link into the chorus, reaching the highest note so far (a top B).

Chorus 2 (bars 44–48: 2:42)

This is a repeat of chorus 1.

Bridge (bars 49–59: 3:01)

The first four bars are based on sustained parallel triads, rising from E♭ to G and then falling back chromatically to Em. Above this the **vocalisation** (a passage of wordless singing) is in two parts, thickened up to sound almost like a choir in places. The chords recall the chromatic harmonies of the first part of the verses, without being identical.

In the rest of the bridge (from bar 53 onwards), the chords are taken from the second half of the verses (the pre-chorus section), although they have been rearranged and extended. Buckley's vocalisation sweeps ecstatically higher, seamlessly merging into **falsetto** for the highest notes. In the last three bars of the bridge, the lyrics and chords are the same as those at the end of verse 2 ('It reminds me …'), but the words 'pain' and 'leave' inspire Buckley to reach ever higher in his anguished solo.

Introduction repeated (bars 60–66: 3:42)

In another example of word-painting, the suggestion of time urgently ticking past is added, using the sound of strings being repeatedly tapped with the back of the bow, an effect known as *col legno* – 'with the wood' (of the bow).

Verse 3 (bars 67–72: 4:08)

As the song builds towards the coda, Buckley sings the first six bars of the verse an octave higher than before, avoiding falsetto in order to create a sense of strained anguish. The words 'go so slow' are illustrated with longer notes, mostly on the same pitch, after which the second half of this final verse is omitted.

Coda (bar 73 to the end: 4:31)

Flange is an electronic effect that gives the guitar a thick metallic sound.

This is the climax of the song and is based on repetitions of the falling chromatic chord pattern from the start of the chorus (F–Em–E♭maj⁷). A thick texture builds up as the performers improvise above this riff. Listen for the wailing lyrics of the chorus almost drowning under the weight of the **flanged** guitar sounds and cymbal splashes – another piece of word painting, referring back to 'drown my name' in verse 3.

Test yourself

1. Who assisted Jeff Buckley in the composition of this song?
2. For what, apart from composing, is Jeff Buckley most remembered?
3. How many beats per bar are there in $\frac{12}{8}$ time?
4. Give a musical term to describe the tempo of this song.
5. What is meant by the bridge in a pop song?
6. Which other set work that we have studied is a song that includes a bridge?
7. What musical term best describes the harmony in the first half of the verses and in the choruses?
8. Name **two** ways, not including the words, in which the last verse differs from the first two verses.
9. Give **two** different examples of word painting that can be heard on this track.
10. This track was first released in 1994 but when did Buckley actually compose the song?

Further listening

To broaden your knowledge of Jeff Buckley's style and other related music, here are some more works that you might enjoy:

- Try to listen to some of the other tracks on the *Grace* album. **'Last Goodbye'** was one of Buckley's commercially most successful songs and is closer to a standard pop song than most of his other work – although the simple chords soon become decorated with jazz-like dissonances. Listen for the quality of his vocal work in the songs by others on the album – the beautifully controlled upper notes in Britten's **Corpus Christi Carol**, the free rhythms and emotional delivery of Shelton's **Lilac Wine**, and his classic performance of Cohen's **Hallelujah**. A book of simple transcriptions of the entire album (including some songs that were added for later releases) is available from Music Sales Ltd. Also look out for **So Real: Songs From Jeff Buckley**, an album of some of Buckley's best songs.
- For a fascinating comparison of Jeff's voice with that of his father, try to hear some of the tracks on Tim Buckley's **Greetings From L.A.** (recorded in 1972). In his early days as a singer, Jeff Buckley performed cover versions of a number of folk-rock ballads by singers such as Van Morrison – his **Tupelo Honey** (dating from 1971) is included in the Edexcel *A-level Anthology of Music*. For something more recent, listen to Coldplay's early hit **Shiver** (2000) – a song that they admitted owed more than a little to the legacy of Jeff Buckley.

Composing ideas

While studying 'Grace' we have come across a number of techniques that could be used in your own compositions. The verse-and-chorus structure is widely used for songs in a range of styles. Generally, the chorus is more substantial than the one in 'Grace', and it usually forms a stronger contrast with the verses.

Most songs in this form tend to set each verse of the lyrics to the same music (with the melody slightly adapted to fit different words if necessary), while in the choruses both the lyrics *and* the music tend to be the same. Because this can sound very repetitive it is a good idea to include other sections, as Buckley did, such as an introduction at the start, a bridge in the middle and a coda at the end. Another idea is to have one of the verses played by a solo instrument rather than sung – this is known as an 'instrumental' and it also offers the benefit of giving the singer a breather. One more way to prevent such a song sounding too predictable is to make some changes in the later repeats of a section. We saw that Buckley reduced his final verse to just the first half – conversely, you could extend a final chorus to make a more impressive finish.

If you enjoy harmony you could experiment with chord progressions that are a bit out of the ordinary, such as parallel chords that circle chromatically around the same few pitches. If you are a guitarist writing for your own instrument, study Gary Lucas's riffs in 'Grace', as they provide an interesting model for good rhythm-guitar parts.

Sample questions for Section A

Listen to the first 48 seconds of CD 2 Track 2 three times, with short pauses between each playing, as you answer the following questions. Don't consult the score or any other information before writing your answers.

1. Complete the sentence below by using **two** terms from the following list.

    compound   simple   triple   quadruple

    This song is in .... metre.   (2)

2. At the point where the drums and bass enter, the chord is Em. Name the **two** chords that alternate during the rest of the introduction.

    .... and ....   (2)

3. The singer enters on an anacrusis. What is an anacrusis?

    ....   (1)

4. Write X in the box next to the correct description of the bass part below the singer's first phrase.

    circle of 5ths   ☒   falling chromatic scale ☒

    falling major scale   ☒   falling minor scale   ☒   (1)

5. How does the singer decorate the falling interval at the end of each of his two phrases?

    ....   (1)

6. Write X in the box next to the interval that shows the total range of the vocal part in this extract.

    3rd ☒   5th ☒   octave ☒   12th (1½ octaves) ☒   (1)

7. Give **two** *musical* reasons why you like or dislike this song.   (2)

    (a) ....

    (b) ....

                          (Total 10 marks)

Sample questions for Section B

Before tackling this section read the information on writing extended answers, on page 167. Then complete your answers without consulting any notes or the score, and without listening to the recording.

The following questions are about 'Grace' from the album *Grace* by Jeff Buckley.

(a) Name the guitarist who co-wrote this song with Jeff Buckley.

....   (1)

(b) What is the style of this song? ....   (1)

(c) Comment on how the following musical elements are used in this piece:

Structure
Metre and tempo
Rhythm
Harmony
Word setting   (10)

Use correct musical vocabulary where appropriate and remember that the quality of your writing, including spelling, punctuation and grammar, will be taken into account in this question. Write your answer on a separate sheet of paper.

(Total 12 marks)

SET WORK 9: 'WHY DOES MY HEART FEEL SO BAD?' FROM THE ALBUM *PLAY* BY MOBY

Technology has played an increasingly important role in popular music ever since electric microphones were first used for broadcasting and recording in the 1920s. The first electric guitars and electric organs appeared in the 1930s, while tape recording became a viable proposition in the 1940s. The miniaturisation of components led to the manufacture of a range of electronic instruments and effects units in the 1960s and 70s, but it was not until digital technology became widely available in the 1980s that such equipment became cheap and flexible enough to be used on a wide scale.

Richard Hall, who performs under the stage name of Moby, plays a number of instruments and has written in a variety of styles, but he made his reputation in the field of techno, the electronic dance music that first became popular in the late 1980s.

Play was Moby's sixth album and the first to become successful with a wider audience, not least due to the way that it introduces a range of more traditional musical elements into a modern electronic style.

RICHARD MELVILLE HALL (BORN 1965)

Moby in 2004

Hall grew up in America and claims to be distantly related to Herman Melville, the author of *Moby Dick* – hence his chosen stage name (as a composer he writes under his real name). He studied classical guitar and later learned to play keyboard, electric and bass guitar, and drums. Hall started playing in various bands while still at school, and later turned to DJing, but he struggled to get a recording contract until signed by a small company, who released his first singles. The second of these (called *Go*) just managed to make the UK top ten in October 1991.

Moby completed a number of albums over the next five years: *Everything is Wrong* (1995) was well received but reviews of the others were often less favourable. At the same time he was starting to build a reputation as a composer of film music, writing scores for *Heat* (1995, starring Robert De Niro) and *The Beach* (2000, starring Leonardo DiCaprio).

Moby spent most of 1998 working on the album *Play*, which was released the following year. Although initial reviews were mixed, appreciation of the work has grown over the years and it is now his best-known work, having sold more than nine million copies.

> For more about Moby, visit his website: www.moby.com.

Later albums in 2002, 2005 and 2008 have not been quite so successful, although they have been appreciated by Moby's fans. His latest album, *Wait For Me*, was released in June 2009.

On top of his busy studio work, Moby undertakes a heavy schedule of live performances and does much charity work, particularly in support of music therapy. He is a vegan (a person who avoids consuming anything produced by or from animals) and a campaigner against animal cruelty (his 1996 album was entitled *Animal Rights*). He has also produced a website (www.mobygratis.com) on which he has made many of his unpublished pieces freely available to film students and producers of not-for-profit films who require music to use in their work.

> A **sample** is a short segment taken from an existing recording to include in a new composition. Using a computer it can be manipulated in various ways, changing features such as its length and/or pitch. Samples are usually repeated a number of times – a process known as **looping**. Although sampling is common in pop music, it has given rise to a number of court cases for infringement of someone else's copyright.

PLAY

The album includes 18 tracks, of which 'Why Does My Heart Feel So Bad?' is the fourth and one of the longest, although this song, like many of the others, has very few lyrics.

A number of the tracks are based on **samples**, taken from vintage recordings of blues and gospel singers made in the 1950s, although Moby himself sings on some of the later tracks on the album. Apart from the samples, Moby wrote, played, engineered and mixed the album himself in his own home studio.

Nine of the tracks on *Play* were also issued as singles between 1998 and 2002: 'Why Does My Heart Feel So Bad?' reached No. 16 in the UK charts in 1999 and a remix version (featuring the American singer Kelis) reached No. 17 the following year.

The style of the album is usually described as techno dance music, although 'Why Does My Heart Feel So Bad?' is perhaps better described as 'downtempo' – a more relaxed style, often used in chill-out rooms or as background music.

An unusual aspect of *Play*, and one that brought Moby to the attention of a much wider audience, was the decision to make all of the tracks available on commercial license for other uses from the outset. The minimal lyrics and repetitive nature of many of the songs made it easy to isolate extracts to use in television advertisements and that is exactly what happened, with extracts appearing in commercials as varied as Bailey's Irish Cream to American Express. In the case of 'Why Does My Heart Feel So Bad?', the track has been licensed for use in an advert for Super-Bock beer, a trailer for the 2001 film *Black Hawk Down*, a central role in the 2004 animal-rights documentary *Peaceable Kingdom* – and, of course, for use in your GCSE anthology!

EQUIPMENT AND STRUCTURE

Like all of the works in Areas of Study 3 and 4, the score of 'Why Does My Heart Feel So Bad?' in GAM is a transcription from the recording. The work consists of loops built up in layers and the score shows how the main ideas are put together. For that reason, we'll confine ourselves here to some additional information.

The track is based on two samples taken from a song called *King Jesus Will Roll All Burdens Away*, written in 1947 by Kenneth Morris, an American composer and publisher of gospel music. It has been recorded many times, but the version used by Moby is thought to come from a 1953 record by the Shining Light Gospel Choir. The samples have an authentic 'vintage' quality because Moby doesn't remove the surface noise found on most gramophone records of that period – although his music is electronically based, he is keen that it should not sound sterile.

The first sample (labelled **A** in the score) features a male voice, with remnants of the backing singers still audible. It comes from the start of the first verse of the 1953 recording and, as the following table shows, Moby manipulates the sample in order to completely reverse the meaning of its words. By changing 'glad' to 'bad' the lyrics become an expression of hurt rather happiness.

The second sample (labelled **B** in the score) features a female voice and comes from the middle of the chorus in the original recording. Although the words don't exactly match Morris's song, it hasn't been manipulated in the same way as sample A – this is simply the sort of improvised response that is common in gospel singing.

Sample	Original lyrics	Moby's sample
A (male)	When I should feel so sad, why does my soul feel so glad? Why does my heart feel so happy and gay?	Why does my heart feel so bad? Why does my soul feel so bad?
B (female)	When I pray He opens doors for me, Doors I'm unable to see.	These open doors.

A Roland TR-909 drum machine

Moby's working method is to start with his chosen vocal samples, add new chords and rhythms to them, and then build up the track in a series of layers, using Steinberg Cubase software running on an Apple Mac computer. Moby recalled that the piano chords were generated on an Emu Proformance, a unit that first appeared in 1990. It uses samples of individual piano notes to produce its sounds and is played from a separate keyboard or from a sequencing program such as Cubase.

Moby then added the drum part using a Roland TR-909 drum machine, a piece of equipment that dates back to 1984 and the beginnings of techno music. He overlaid this with a sampled and looped breakbeat (a drum solo) from an unnamed hip-hop track, adjusting its tempo to fit the new composition. In the score, notice how the snare drum accents the **backbeats** (the second and fourth beats in each bar) – a very common device in many styles of pop music. The word clave (pronounced 'clah-vay') refers to the percussive sound of two hardwood sticks tapped together, which here play entirely off the beat.

The string parts (and additional piano sounds) were produced on Yamaha synthesisers, and Moby added reverb (short for reverberation) to enhance the piano and vocal tracks. Finally, Moby underpinned the work with a low bass line, starting at **A3** in the score. He describes it as a **sub-bass** because its pitches lie below the bass stave, although since it is sustained across each two-bar unit, it doesn't have the physically throbbing character of the type of sub-bass part usually heard in techno dance music.

An article about the equipment and methods used by Moby to create this track can be found at www.soundonsound.com/sos/feb00/articles/tracks.htm.

Both samples are harmonised very simply, using a new chord every two bars. For the first sample, Moby uses a falling **harmonic sequence** (in other words, the chords and bass in the first four bars are repeated a step lower in the next four bars):

The second sample has two different harmonisations, again with each chord lasting for two bars. The first (identified as **Bx** in the score) simply alternates chords of C and Am, while the second (**By**) alternates chords of F and C.

The music is printed without a key signature and we can see that the chord of Am figures prominently in the piece. However, it is not in the key of A minor – every G is natural and in the A sections every F is sharpened by an **accidental**. This is the **Dorian mode** (which you can find by playing the white notes on a keyboard from D to D an octave higher), transposed to start on A:

Dorian mode on D

Dorian mode on A

The change to a chord of C at the start of **Bx** *feels* like a change of tonality, but it is not until the chord of F introduces F♮ at the start of **By** that it becomes clear we have left the Dorian mode. Essentially, the **B** sections are in C major, although without its leading note (B) there is no real sense of modulating to a new key. Because the C-major sections use only six of the seven pitches in C major, we can describe them as **hexatonic**. The music is entirely **diatonic** in either the Dorian mode on A, or in C major.

The rather melancholy mood of the track comes not only from the lyrics but also from:

- The use of the Dorian mode for the main sections
- The two minor chords (Am and Em) at the start of these sections
- The narrow range and falling profile of most of the melodic ideas
- The thin, static nature of its ending.

The structure of the song is described in the score, but we can summarise the use of the two samples in the following diagram (in which each box represents eight bars):

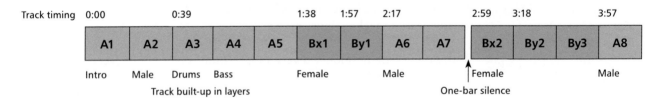

Track timing	0:00		0:39			1:38	1:57	2:17		2:59	3:18		3:57
	A1	A2	A3	A4	A5	Bx1	By1	A6	A7	Bx2	By2	By3	A8

Intro   Male   Drums   Bass   Female   Male   Female   Male

Track built-up in layers   One-bar silence

Moby regards this as a **verse-and-chorus** structure, in which the A sections are the verse and the B sections form the chorus. The chorus is differentiated by the use of the female voice with a new melodic idea, the change in chord pattern, and the move from the Dorian mode to the key of C major. Notice how the regularity of Moby's eight-bar sections strongly contrasts with the irregular bar lengths in Jeff Buckley's 'Grace'.

■ **A1**: An introduction in which the harmonies for sample **A** are played mainly as **broken chords** on the piano, without a clear sense of pulse (we could describe this as being played in **free time**).

■ **A2**: Sampled male voice added and the beat becomes clearer. Note the 'electronic ghostings' marked in the score – these remnants of the backing singers in the original sample are noticeably clipped at the end of the seventh bar.

■ **A3**: The addition of drums and other percussion now makes the beat crystal clear. Moby also adds a sequential **countermelody** for synth-strings and piano (later this is played only by piano).

■ **A4**: The texture is thickened with chords for synth-strings and a bass line.

■ **A5**: A more rhythmic, syncopated version of the main chord pattern appears in the piano part with a little decoration of some chords.

■ **Bx1**: The two-bar female sample is played four times above chords of C and Am.

■ **By1**: The female sample is re-harmonised with chords of F and C. It again appear four times, but now the sample is sometimes re-triggered to provide an echo effect that sounds like a **canon**. Notice the gospel-like shouts of praise in the sample.

■ **A6**: The same as **A5**, but with ghostly echoes of the voice created by **digital delay**. The echoes are produced by a heavily processed version of the sample, in which the lower frequencies have been removed by passing the signal through a **high-pass filter** (sounding a bit like listening on a telephone).

■ **A7**: A repeat of **A6**. It is followed by a one-bar silence in which we just hear fading echoes.

■ **Bx2**: The female voice is now more distant, the chords are static and the piano and drums drop out.

■ **By2**: Similar to **By1** (voice returns to the foreground, and piano and drums come back in).

■ **By3**: Repeat of **By2**.

■ **A8**: The male voice, accompanied only by static chords, returns to form a coda (or outro). Piano and drums have now completely dropped out.

> In techno dance music a silence (often punctuated by sound effects) is called a **breakdown** because the arrangement momentarily seems to break down.

Test yourself

1. From what style of music are the vocal samples in this piece taken?
2. Many of the samples are looped. What does looped mean?
3. The track starts with broken chords. In which other set work have we encountered broken chords played on a piano?
4. Are the opening sections of this piece in the dorian mode or the mixolydian mode?
5. Explain the difference between the dorian mode and the mixolydian mode.
6. What are backbeats and which instrument emphasises them in this piece?
7. What is a countermelody?
8. Apart from the difference in voice, how does Moby differentiate the chorus from the verse in this work?
9. List **three** ways, not including the lyrics, in which Moby makes this music feel sad.

Further listening

To broaden your knowledge of Moby's style and other related music, here are some more works that you might enjoy:

- Listen to some of the other tracks on *Play*. **'Natural Blues'** and **'Honey'** include samples of traditional blues singers in the south of the USA, recorded many years ago by the great folk-music expert Alan Lomax. **'South Side'**, one of Moby's most successful singles, is rock-influenced, while in contrast **'Porcelain'** consists largely of ambient textures. A simple transcription of the entire album is available from International Music Publications. Also look out for Moby's earlier album, ***Everything is Wrong*** (1995).
- There are two examples of club-dance remix in the original (2002) edition of GAM, one of which includes a track presented in three alternative mixes. The 2006 edition of GAM contains four examples of modern dance music, including a 2005 track by the **Chemical Brothers**.

Composing ideas

While studying 'Why Does My Heart Feel So Bad?' we have come across a number of techniques that could be used in your own compositions. We have already seen how Reich constructed a contrapuntal piece in layers, using overlapping riffs, but Moby's looped samples are used in a simpler way, to create an essentially homophonic texture. To provide variety, he uses a different sample for the chorus section as well as different chord patterns, moving from dorian modality to C-major tonality in the process. Notice how even when the same chord pattern is repeated, Moby makes it more interesting with features such as the countermelody and changes in the layout of the harmonies (sometimes syncopated, sometimes sustained and sometimes presented as broken chords). Similarly, the samples are processed and arranged to create different effects such as the canon-like echoes, and Moby throws in that silent bar towards the end, just at the point when the regularity of the eight-bar patterns is becoming rather predictable.

If you decide to compose a piece based on samples, note that you should identify the source of all material that you haven't composed yourself.

Remember that although your compositions must be related to the areas of study, you don't *have* to base them on ideas from the set works. In the case of this area of study, it is enough for your work to be related to any typical aspect(s) of Popular Music in Context.

Sample questions for Section A

Listen to CD 2 Track 3, from 0:39 to 1:37 three times, with short pauses between each playing, as you answer the following questions. Don't consult the score or any other information before writing your answers.

1. This extract is based on a repeating pattern of four chords. The first two are Am and Em. What are the third and fourth chords?

.... and .... (2)

2. Name a percussion sound used on this track that is *not* an instrument normally found in a drum kit.

.... (1)

3. Give the correct musical term for the part played by string and piano sounds above the voice in this extract.

.... (1)

4. Which of the following is the correct rhythm of the repeated idea in this high part? Put a cross in the correct box. (1)

$\frac{4}{4}$ 𝅗𝅥 ♩ ♩ ☒ $\frac{4}{4}$ 𝅘𝅥. 𝅘𝅥𝅮𝅘𝅥𝅮 ♩ ☒

$\frac{4}{4}$ ♩ 𝅗𝅥 ♩ ☒ $\frac{4}{4}$ 𝅗𝅥 𝅘𝅥𝅮♩ 𝅘𝅥𝅮 ☒

5. How does the piano part change in the final section of this extract?

.... (1)

6. Write X in the box next to the musical term that describes the tonality of this entire extract.

atonal ☒   chromatic ☒   minor ☒   modal ☒   (1)

7. Briefly explain **three** different ways in which music technology has been used in 'Why Does My Heart Feel So Bad?'

(a) ....

(b) ....

(c) .... (3)

(Total 10 marks)

Top Tips

Look out for questions such as number 7 that refer to the whole work rather than just the extract. Here you can write about the use of music technology in any part of the set work, rather than just the section played in the exam.

Sample questions for Section B

Before tackling this section read the information on writing extended answers, on page 167. Then complete your answers without consulting any notes or the score, and without listening to the recording.

The following questions are about 'Why Does My Heart Feel So Bad?' from *Play* by Moby.

(a) In which year did Moby record this track? Put a cross in the correct box.

    1959 ⊠   1969 ⊠   1979 ⊠   1989 ⊠   1999 ⊠   (1)

(b) What is the style of this music? ....   (1)

(c) Comment on how Moby uses the following musical elements in this piece:

Structure
Melody
Rhythm
Harmony and tonality
Music technology   (10)

Use correct musical vocabulary where appropriate and remember that the quality of your writing, including spelling, punctuation and grammar, will be taken into account in this question. Write your answer on a separate sheet of paper.

(Total 12 marks)

Today, the term 'world music' is used to refer to the traditional (or folk) music of any country, including our own. It also includes crossover or fusion styles that result from outside influences, such as jazz or western pop music, blending with local traditions.

Few people had heard the traditional music of other countries until steamships and railways made long-distance travel easier in the 19th century. Even then, with no means of recording sound, people back home had no way of knowing what such music sounded like unless they attended one of the great international exhibitions of the age, when performers from distant lands would sometimes be invited to represent their country's culture. For example, the Universal Exposition held in Paris in 1889 included a traditional gamelan ensemble from Java in South-East Asia as well as a gypsy band from Spain.

By the early 20th century, musicians and scholars were starting to realise that there was a vast amount of music in the world that was almost unknown outside the region in which it was performed, and that it was in danger of disappearing in the modern world. They therefore started to study and record it, using the simple recording equipment of the day. Later in the century, plane travel and portable tape recorders made it practical for **ethnomusicologists** (scholars who specialise in world music) to explore cultural traditions all over the world – a task so enormous that it continues today.

During the 19th century some composers would occasionally include features of their own country's traditional music in their works – Chopin was one of the first, using Polish dance styles such as the mazurka and polonaise. However, it was not until the 20th century that composers really began to investigate music from further afield. Gamelan music influenced some of the works of Debussy, John Cage and Benjamin Britten, and you may recall that Reich composed *Drumming* after his visit to Ghana to study African drumming. You will also hopefully remember that Afro-Cuban music (an important influence on the bebop style of jazz) and the rhythms of Latin-American music had both been strong influences on the music of Leonard Bernstein.

A wider awareness of world music started to develop in the 1960s, when migration from former colonies brought many people and their music to the west, and increasing prosperity took more westerners abroad. This was the decade in which the Beatles included Indian instruments in some of their songs and music from the Caribbean first appeared in the UK Top 10. An appetite for new types of music quickly developed, and charts in the 1970s included tracks ranging from an Arab-pop fusion song by Led Zeppelin to traditional Romanian panpipe music and choral folksongs from Bulgaria. In France, musicians from former French colonies in north Africa introduced the sounds of Algerian and Moroccan music to Paris, and it was there that the first annual World Music Day was held in 1982. In the same year, the first World of Music, Arts and Dance festival was held in Britain to introduce the public to music from other cultures – the WOMAD movement has now spread to more than 20 other countries. It was also in the 1980s that recordings of world music started to become widely available from major music retailers, rather than just specialist record shops, the Real World Records label was created to promote world music and a special category for world music was established in the charts.

The three set works in this area of study are highly contrasted, musically and geographically. The first is a modern arrangement of a traditional Scottish folksong, the second and third are examples of traditional music from north India and west Africa. We haven't included a time line for this final area of study as it is almost impossible to date most types of traditional music.

SET WORK 10: *SKYE WAULKING SONG*, PERFORMED BY CAPERCAILLIE

Although we have come to know about most world music only fairly recently, the situation is different with the music of the British Isles. In England, collections of folk music started to appear in print as early as the 17th century. When the industrial revolution resulted in large population movements from the countryside to the cities, further efforts were made in the 1830s and 40s to collect and publish what became known as 'national songs'.

The foundation of the Folksong Society in 1898 prompted another round of collecting, but the music and words in these early publications were often modified to suit contemporary taste, with modal tunes being rewritten in major keys, songs with unusual rhythms being squeezed into regular time signatures and everything being underpinned with tasteful piano accompaniments. This was the form in which generations of schoolchildren learned to sing folksongs from the government-recommended *National Song Book* of 1905.

Meanwhile, folk traditions were continuing to disappear. Several musicians (including the composer Vaughan Williams) made more accurate attempts to write down English rural folksong from local singers, but English collectors were hampered by their preference for pencil and paper, which couldn't capture every performance detail in the way that the recording machines preferred by American scholars could. And the English collectors focused on music from the countryside, ignoring the large amount of industrial folksongs, particularly work songs to enliven boringly repetitive tasks, which had developed when people moved off the land during the industrial revolution.

All of this meant that when a new folksong revival began in the 1950s and 60s, based on treating the music as a living art rather than a preserved relic, it proved refreshingly popular. Folk music started to adopt some of the features of pop music, with the use of amplified voices and guitar accompaniments. Folk clubs, many of which still operate today, opened to promote the performance of traditional songs as well as new works in which folk-like material is given a contemporary treatment.

Although much of the above also applies to Scotland, Ireland and Wales, folk music in those countries never disappeared to the same extent, especially in the remote regions, and it continues to play an important role in fostering national identity. Although there are links between the folk music of Scotland and Ireland, that is not the case with the music of Wales. However, for marketing purposes the traditional music of all three countries is today described as 'Celtic folk music'.

As in England, Scottish folk music went through a revival in the 1960s. Modern adaptations of traditional music soon started to appear, resulting in **Celtic fusion**, the style of this set work (although you may also see it described in more general terms as **folk rock**).

Capercaillie

The Scottish folk band Capercaillie (pronounced *Cap–ir–kay–lee*) was formed in 1983 when its founding members were still students at Oban High School in the West Highlands. They came together to play for local dances, known as cèilidhs (pronounced *kay-lees*). If you pronounce both words correctly, you will spot that Capercaillie is a pun (a word-play) on cèilidh. In normal use Capercaillie refers to the largest member of the grouse family – a bird that became extinct in Scotland in the 18th century, was reintroduced in 1837 but has since again become an endangered species in the region.

Capercaillie recorded their debut album in 1984 and by 2008 had produced 14 studio albums. Many of the tracks on these are sung in Gaelic, the traditional language of the Highlands. Their recording of *Coisich, A Rùin* became the first ever song in Scots Gaelic to enter the UK Top 40 after being used as the theme tune for a TV documentary featuring Prince Charles. Capercaillie has recorded music for several other television programmes and for the Hollywood film *Rob Roy* (in which their lead singer also appeared as a character). The set work is the first track on Capercaillie's album *Nàdurra* (Naturally), released in September 2000.

The album features a mix of folk and modern instruments that is typical of Celtic fusion. The traditional instruments include:

- ◼ The fiddle (the folk musician's preferred name for the violin).
- ◼ The **accordion**. Moving the bellows in and out causes air to vibrate metal reeds, controlled by the keyboard and the buttons (the latter supply bass notes and chords).
- ◼ The uilleann pipes. Their tone is softer and sweeter than the more famous Great Highland bagpipes, although produced in a similar way, by air passing through a double reed. However, the air supply comes from elbow-operated bellows rather than by blowing. Musically they have more flexibility than the Highland bagpipes and, although they have drones to produce continuous pedal notes, these are not always used in performance.

The modern instruments in *Skye Waulking Song* are the synthesiser, bass guitar and drum kit. The track also features a Wurlitzer piano, a predecessor of the electric piano, introduced in the 1950s. Unlike a normal piano, the hammers strike small steel rods, the vibrations from which are picked up and amplified. It was originally produced for home and school use, although it is sometimes heard in American country music.

At the start of the track you can hear the Wurlitzer piano sharing the melody with a plucked-string instrument called a **bouzouki**. This member of the lute family is usually associated with the music of Greece, but it has been adopted by a number of Celtic folk musicians in recent decades.

© Richard Bartz

A capercaillie

Gaelic is spoken by more than 50,000 people in Scotland and is the main language in the Western Isles, although the total number of speakers has been declining for many years.

The singer on CD 2 Track 4 is Karen Matheson, who was one of the founding members of Capercaillie along with accordionist Donald Shaw (who is now Karen's husband). For more about Capercaillie, visit their website at www.capercaillie.co.uk – you can hear other examples of their work if you click your way through to the 'audio and video' section of the 'releases' menu.

The uilleann pipe

A piano accordion. Some folk musicians prefer a button accordion, which has buttons on both sides of the instrument.

A bouzouki

WAULKING

Until the early 20th century, many Highland families produced tweed cloth for their own use and to sell to supplement their small incomes. Once the cloth was woven, it had to be softened and made more airtight against the harsh climate. This was done by soaking the tweed in human urine (the ammonia in which also intensified the dyes) and laying it out on a large board. A group of women would then pound the cloth against the wood, moving and turning it at intervals.

It is thought that waulking could be the origin of the common Scottish family name Walker. In England, a similar but more mechanised process was known as fulling, the origin of the surname Fuller. For more about waulking, see www.thistleandbroom.com/scotland/waulking.htm.

An 18th-century engraving of Scotswomen singing as they waulk cloth

This process, which took many hours, was known as waulking (a Scottish spelling of the English word walking) because it was sometimes done with step-like movements of the feet, although more often the women used their hands. To help

In a song, a refrain is a phrase that returns at the end of each line or verse of the text.

synchronise their movements they would sing rhythmic waulking songs, usually in a **call-and-response** style, with one person singing a solo phrase and everyone replying with a short **refrain** sung to nonsense syllables. Waulking songs were thus a type of work song, intended to help coordinate and enliven repetitive tasks. Not surprisingly, a day of waulking was often followed by a cèilidh in the evening when the men returned home!

Capercaillie has recorded arrangements of a number of the many traditional waulking songs from the Highlands and islands of Scotland. In addition to the set work, their Gaelic hit mentioned earlier, *Coisich, A Rùin*, is a waulking song, and they even recorded an album with the punning title of *Sidewaulk*, which includes a waulking song from the island of Barra.

SKYE WAULKING SONG

'Chuir m'athair mise dha'n taigh charraideach' (My father sent me to the house of sorrow) is a small excerpt taken by Capercaillie from a long lament called *Seathan, Mac Righ Èireann* (John, Son of the King of Ireland), which it is estimated would take more than an hour to perform from beginning to end. Traditionally, it would have been sung unaccompanied by a solo female voice, with the other women joining in a refrain at the end of each line.

You can read an English translation of the full text of *Seathan, Mac Righ Èireann* at www.parametermagazine.org/seathan.htm.

The song is the lament of a woman for her dead husband, son of an Irish chieftain, with whom she had been forced to wander the world. The text was collected in the late 19th century but the style of its language suggests that it was then already some 200 years old and the origins of the tale probably go back centuries earlier. Because traditional sagas of this type were passed from one generation to the next orally (that is, by word of mouth) the language and details often changed over the years, and several alternative versions of the text exist.

Following the score

The score is a transcription from the recording and shows only the main details of the music. It is another piece in compound quadruple metre ($\frac{12}{8}$ time).

Soloist Karen Matheson has a beautiful and very low alto voice which is similar in range to a tenor. Notice that her part in the score is notated in the vocal tenor clef, in which the small 8 below the clef indicates that the music sounds an octave lower than it would if printed with a normal treble clef.

The rapidly repeated notes in the violin part are written as dotted semibreves with **tremolo** beams (bars 2 and 3). The abbreviation N.C. in bar 24 stands for 'no chord' – in fact, the entire accompaniment stops in this bar.

A translation of the lyrics is printed in GAM. Remember that the refrains are sung to nonsense syllables, sometimes referred to as vocables.

© Lieve Boussauw

Karen Matheson of Capercaillie

Like many folksongs, the melody is **pentatonic** – in other words, it uses a five-note scale. You can find the major pentatonic scale by playing just the black notes on a keyboard, starting on F♯. This tune uses the same scale, but one semitone higher, starting on G:

Major pentatonic on G

Although the vocal line is pentatonic, the accompaniment is not because it uses all of the notes of G major, including C and F♯. Although the song is entirely **diatonic** in the key of G major, it has a modal feel because the dominant chord (D) is avoided – the main chords are G, Em and C.

The vocal line is based on a pair of phrases, each followed by its own refrain. The following pitch outline shows how phrase 1 starts on the upper dominant (D) and is followed by a refrain that falls to the tonic (G). Phrase 2 starts on the lower dominant (D) and is followed by a refrain that ends on the upper dominant.

Phrases 1 and 2 are, when sung complete, both harmonised with a chord of G, except in bar 46 (where the chord of Em⁹ in any case includes all three notes of a chord of G), or where there is no chord. The refrains are contrasted by being harmonised with chords of C and/or Em, except in bar 45 (where the chord of Am⁹ includes the notes of both these chords).

When performed traditionally, in unaccompanied call-and-response style, the refrains would usually be sung by everyone, forming the response to the soloist's calls. In Capercaillie's arrangement, the refrains are sung solo until bar 25, where the backing singers join in. In some parts of the song, each line of text is sung twice, first to one phrase (followed by its refrain) and then to the other (followed by its refrain).

Let's see how these paired phrases alternate in the mainly **syllabic** setting of the text.

Section	Bars	Call		Response
Introduction and preliminary line of text	1–9	Eight-bar instrumental introduction followed by refrain 2		
	10–11	Chuir m'athair mise dha'n taigh charraideach	Phrase 1	Refrain 1
	12–15	Vocal echo of end of refrain 1 and instrumental		
	16–17	Chuir m'athair mise dha'n taigh charraideach	Phrase 2	Refrain 2
Verse 1	18–19	'N oidhche sin a rinn e bhanais dhomh	Phrase 1	Refrain 1
	20–21	'N oidhche sin a rinn e bhanais dhomh	Phrase 2	Refrain 2
	22–23	Gur truagh a Righ nach b'e m'fhalairidh	Phrase 1	Refrain 1
	24–25	Gur truagh a Righ nach b'e m'fhalairidh	Phrase 2	Refrain 2*
	26–27	M'an do bhrist mo làmh an t-aran dhomh	Phrase 1	Refrain 1
	28–29	M'an do bhrist mo làmh an t-aran dhomh	Phrase 2	Refrain 2
	30–31	M'an d'rinn mo sgian biadh a ghearradh dhomh	Phrase 1	Refrain 1
	32–33	M'an d'rinn mo sgian biadh a ghearradh dhomh	Phrase 2	Refrain 2*
Verse 2	34–35	Sheathain chridhe nan sul socair	Phrase 1	Refrain 1
	36–43	Vocal echo of end of refrain 1 and instrumental based on refrain 2*		
	44–45	Tha do bhàta 'nochd 's na portaibh	Phrase 2	Refrain 2
	46–47	Och, ma tha, chaneil i socair	Phrase 1	Refrain 1
	48–49	Och, ma tha, chaneil i socair	Phrase 2	Refrain 2*
	50–51	O nach robh thu, ghaoil, na toiseach.	Phrase 1	Refrain 1
Coda	52–56	Vocal echoes of end of refrain 1		
	57–65	Refrain 2* twice more (bars 57 and 59) and fade-out instrumental		

The asterisk (*) indicates a variant of refrain 2 that rises to a top G on its second syllable.

At first sight, this may appear complicated, but your ears should tell you that all that happens is that two phrases (each followed by their respective refrain) alternate throughout the piece, except in sections where the focus is mainly on the instruments. In a traditional performance, the solo singer would add vocal ornaments to the melody to give the variety that is provided by the instrumental sections in this version. Here the vocal line is sung simply, although there are echoes of the end of refrain 1 in the instrumental sections and a variant of refrain 2 (marked * in the table) that rises to a top G on its second syllable.

A **cluster chord** is a group of adjacent pitches, here E, F♯, G, A and B.

We now need to look at the instrumental sections. The arrangement immediately declares its modernity by starting with a **cluster chord** based on Em, played on a synthesiser. The words 'with modulation' above this part mean that the pitch slightly fluctuates, like **vibrato** on a string instrument. The violin's tremolo on D above this chord makes it clear that the key is not E minor (which requires D♯), and when the bass enters in bar 3 it begins to establish the key of G major with brief dominant–tonic patterns (D to G) across the barlines in bars 3–4 and 7–8. Nevertheless, because the main chords in the introduction are Em and G, both decorated with diatonic dissonances in the melody (shared in **dialogue** by Wurlitzer piano and bouzouki), the overall effect sounds modal and 'new age' (a term coined in the 1980s for meditative, folk-like music).

The term **dialogue** describes a texture in which phrases pass from one instrument to another.

Notice the gentle **cross rhythms** in the drummer's hi-hat pattern, which cut across the normal divisions of the beat in $\frac{12}{8}$ time:

The instrumentalists base many of their motifs on the vocal phrases. For example, the first three notes of vocal phrase 2 (D–E–D) are heard at the starts of bars 4, 6, 8, 10 and so on.

Notice the contrast between bar 24 (sung unaccompanied) and bar 25, where the full band enters. This climactic moment is emphasised by the first appearance of the varied version of refrain 2 (rising to a top G in the vocals), strumming from the bouzouki, and by the first use of a chord of C. The drummer underlines this moment by changing to a new pattern in which the $\frac{12}{8}$ rhythm becomes much clearer and backing singers join in the refrains.

A **plagal cadence** consists of chord IV followed by chord I. In the key of G major, that is a chord of C followed by a chord of G.

The melody in the main instrumental section (starting at bar 37) is based on this varied version of refrain 2, and is extended to reach a second climax in bar 42. Notice the improvised counterpoint in this passage.

The coda consists of accompaniment patterns set to alternate chords of C and G, giving the effect of repeated **plagal cadences** as the music fades away, never having settled on a dominant chord at any point in the entire song.

Test yourself

1. Work out the lowest and highest notes in the vocal melody and then state its total range (e.g. a 7th).
2. Explain what is meant by a cluster chord.
3. How can you tell that the instrumental parts are not pentatonic?
4. Listen carefully to bar 25, and then explain how the backing singers relate to the vocal melody in this bar.
5. How do the uilleann pipes differ from the usual type of bagpipe associated with Scottish music?
6. Name two instruments, apart from the uilleann pipes, used in this recording that are often heard in folk music.
7. Name three instruments in this recording that would not be heard in a traditional performance of folk music.
8. What musical term would you use to indicate that there are no chromatic notes in this piece?
9. The refrains are sung to vocables. What is meant in music by (a) a refrain and (b) vocables?
10. Briefly explain how singing a work song such as this would help with the job of waulking fabric.

Further listening

To broaden your knowledge of folk music, here are some more works that you might enjoy:

- A traditional performance of **Seathan, Mac Righ Èireann** is given by the Scottish singer Flora MacNeil on her album *Orain Floraidh* (Songs of Flora), Temple Records COMD2081. It is sung unaccompanied, with an ornamented vocal line. Flora MacNeil recalls learning the song from her mother's cousin, who regarded it more as a sad lament than a waulking song. As often happens with folk music, many of the melodic details differ from Capercaillie's version. Another version of the *Seathan* story can be heard on the album *Chi Mi'n Geamhradh* (I See Winter), sung by Catherine-Ann MacPhee (Greentrax CDTRAX038).
- Greentrax also produces the CDs **Waulking Songs from Barra** (CDTRAX9003) featuring various singers from the Western Isles, and **Waulking Songs** (CDTRAX099) which features the Glasgow-based vocal group Bannal. Their CD of **Music from the Western Isles** (CDTRAX9002) makes a good introduction to a range of Scottish folk music in Gaelic.
- Macmeanmna Records (www.gaelicmusic.com) produce a CD with DVD of waulking songs called **Bho Dhòrn Gu Dòrn** (From Hand to Hand) sung by Bannal. The DVD contains a 30-minute documentary on waulking (SKYECD 32).
- Look out for the performance of *Skye Waulking Song* that Capercaillie recorded for BBC4 – you may be able to find it on www.youtube.com. It will give you the chance to see the group at work and to hear an arrangement that differs in a number of ways from the one in GAM.
- In addition to Capercaillie's other tracks on *Nàdurra*, try to listen to the Scottish electric folk music of **Runrig**, the innovative use of Highland bagpipes in the folk-rock style of **Wolfstone**, and the Celtic-fusion tracks of **Shooglenifty**. For a more general understanding of how modern folk styles developed, look out for recordings by groups such as **Fairport Convention** and **Steeleye Span**, plus **Jethro Tull's** three folk-rock albums from the late 1970s.

Waulking songs are just one of many different types of work song, traditionally sung to help co-ordinate repetitive tasks and make them less boring. Look out for (and try singing) other types, including industrial folksongs, work songs sung by slaves in the fields or by labourers building American railroads, and sea shanties sung by sailors when hauling ropes and raising the anchor. There's a large collection of shanties at www.gutenberg.org/files/20774/20774-h/20774-h.htm, but note that they would originally have been sung unaccompanied or perhaps supported by a simple accompaniment played on a button accordion.

Composing ideas

While studying the *Skye Waulking Song* we have come across a number of techniques that could be used in your own compositions.

You could try writing a piece to accompany an advertisement for the Scottish Tourist Board or the Scottish Wool Centre, featuring music in a Celtic-fusion style. If you are choosing to submit an arrangement for the composing unit you could base it on an existing Scottish folk tune – there are many in published collections, and traditional song and dance melodies are available on a number of web sites.

If you decide to write your own tune, keeping to the notes of a pentatonic or hexatonic scale will help create a folksy feel, or you could base the melody on a mode, such as one of those we discussed earlier in this book. The accompaniment doesn't need to be limited to the notes you have used in the tune, but the harmonies in folk music are often quite simple and diatonic. Remember how Capercaillie created a folk-like feel by avoiding the dominant chord of G major and instead used mainly chords I, IV and VI (sometimes with added notes).

You could use a verse-and-chorus form, or base your work on the structure of *Skye Waulking Song*, using a call-and-response style with alternating refrains at the end of each line. Both can be rather repetitive, so think carefully about ways to introduce variety, such as decorating the melodic line, occasionally changing the harmonisation and including instrumental sections.

The same ideas would work with folk styles from other parts of the British Isles, or you could try writing your own modern-day work song. If you prefer to compose purely instrumental music, you could write or arrange a folk dance suitable to play at a cèilidh. Two popular ones are:

- ◼ The strathspey, which is in a fairly slow $\frac{4}{4}$ time and features a rhythm known as the Scotch snap that reverses the normal order of notes in a dotted rhythm: ♪♩.
- ◼ The reel, which is a fast dance often in $\frac{2}{4}$ time, with plenty of semiquaver movement.

To be effective as dance music, the piece would need to be composed in regular 8- or 16-bar sections, perhaps using a pattern of phrases such as AABBCCAA.

Sample questions for Section A

Listen to CD 2 Track 4, from 1:42 to 2:15 five times, with short pauses between each playing, as you answer the following questions. Don't consult the score or any other information before writing your answers.

Here are the words of the extract, with each line numbered for reference. An English translation is given for the even-numbered lines (the odd-numbered lines are nonsense syllables).

1. *Hi ri huraibhi o ho*
2. *M'an do bhrist mo lamh an t-aran dhomh*
   Before my hand broke the bread for me
3. *O hi a bho ro hu o ho*
4. *M'an do bhrist mo lamh an t-aran dhomh*
   Before my hand broke the bread for me
5. *Hi ri huraibhi o ho*
6. *M'an d'rinn mo sgian biadh a ghearradh dhomh*
   Before my knife cut the food for me
7. *O hi a bho ro hu o ho*
8. *M'an d'rinn mo sgian biadh a ghearradh dhomh*
   Before my knife cut the food for me

1. Name the language in which this song is performed. .... (1)

2. Write X in the box next to the type of scale on which the vocal melody is based. (1)

    chromatic ☒   hexatonic ☒   minor ☒   pentatonic ☒

3. How does the melody of line 5 differ from the melody of line 1?

.... (1)

4. Complete the melody heard in line 8. The rhythm is given above the stave. (5)

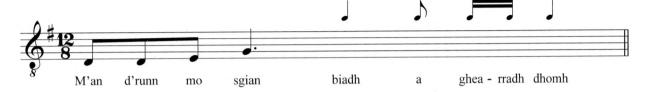

5. This extract uses three chords. The first one is given below.
Complete the other two, using stave notation. (2)

(Total 10 marks)

 Top Tips

In question 5, the chord's name tells you its lowest note.

Sample questions for Section B

Before tackling this section read the information on writing extended answers, on page 167. Then complete your answers without consulting any notes or the score, and without listening to the recording.

The following questions are about the *Skye Waulking Song*, as performed by Capercaillie.

(a) Identify the style of this music. .... (1)

(b) Name one way in which the performance by Capercaillie differs from a traditional performance of this song.

.... (1)

(c) Comment on how the following musical elements are used in this piece:

Tonality and harmony
Melody
Rhythm
Structure
Word setting (10)

Use correct musical vocabulary where appropriate and remember that the quality of your writing, including spelling, punctuation and grammar, will be taken into account in this question. Write your answer on a separate sheet of paper.

(Total 12 marks)

SET WORK 11: *RAG DESH* (NORTH INDIAN)

The classical music of north India is traditionally presented by a few highly skilled performers to a small and attentive audience. The music is improvised but it keeps to an outline that is well understood by the listeners who, like the performers, often sit on a carpeted floor. They may silently tap along to the music, respond to feats of technical and artistic skill with anything from a murmur of approval to a huge round of applause, or even request their favourite pieces.

Improvisations can last from just a few minutes to several hours and concerts don't normally have a fixed programme. There are usually at least three performers, each with a specific role in the music:

- A soloist (either a singer or a player of a melodic instrument)
- A percussionist, who normally plays the tabla (a pair of drums struck with the hand)
- A musician who plays a repetitive or drone-like accompaniment.

Indian musicians learn their skills during a long apprenticeship with a respected teacher (sometimes a family member) during which they listen, imitate and memorise. Notation is sometimes used when learning, but performances are always given from memory. Indian classical music is based on melody and rhythm (sometimes supported by a drone) rather than on keys and chords.

Much of the information for this set work is given in GAM, so here we will just emphasise the important points.

Rag

Improvisation is based on the notes of a **rag** (pronounced *rahg*). Although this looks a little like a scale, it is more complicated because some of the notes in the ascending version of the rag frequently differ from those in the descending version. Also, performers are expected to emphasise or avoid certain pitches, and to use various combinations of notes that help identify the rag. There are about 100 rags in use today, most of which are associated with a particular time of day and/or season. All three recordings in GAM are based on *rag desh*, which is traditionally performed in the late evening and is associated with the monsoon season of heavy rain in India. The pitches don't exactly correspond with the notes of western scales, but their closest equivalents when starting on C are:

The technical terms in Indian music come from the Hindi language, which doesn't use the western alphabet. You may see different forms of the words given here (such as raga or ragam instead of rag), sometimes with special accent signs over some of the letters. Examiners will understand what you mean if you use the simple spellings given here.

Tal

Rhythm in Indian classical music is based on a pattern of beats called a **tal** (pronounced *tahl*). Five examples are shown in GAM. As in western music, the tempo can vary, and the beats may be filled with a variety of rhythm patterns, as seen in the example of *rupak tal* on page 103 of GAM. A tal is therefore like a bar in western music, although usually longer – for instance, the first piece ends in *tintal*, which has 16 beats, similar to four bars of $\frac{4}{4}$ time. The first beat of a tal is called **sam**, and acts as a reference point to help keep the improvisation together.

Structure

A traditional instrumental performance of a rag generally progresses from a slow introduction to a fast and exciting conclusion. There can be many sections, but most performances include the following three parts:

- The **alap** is a slow introductory section in free time, in which a soloist introduces the notes of the rag, accompanied only by a drone. The soloist gradually moves upwards by an octave or more from the home note and then slowly makes their way back to it, introducing characteristic motifs associated with the rag. The entire section is improvised, and it may be followed by further, faster sections.
- A clearer sense of pulse appears in the **gat**, which introduces the tal and the accompanying tabla (small drums). The gat itself is a short, pre-composed idea on which the soloist then improvises, this time fitting the rhythm to the tal. Variations on the gat melody alternate with freely improvised material, and the tabla player will often improvise patterns to fit the tal. A second, faster gat is often included as the music starts to get more exciting.
- The term **jhalla** is often used for the final section, in which the rhythmic activity becomes more intense. Jhalla means 'a shower' and it refers to the cascades of **tans** (scales) and lively strumming of strings often used to provide a climactic end to the improvisation.

RAG DESH PERFORMED BY ANOUSHKA SHANKAR

CD 2 Track 5 is a recording of a live performance by the sitar player Anoushka Shankar. She is the half-sister of the singer-songwriter Norah Jones and daughter of Ravi Shankar, one of the most famous of all Indian musicians, who worked with the Beatles and the classical violinist Yehudi Menuhin in the 1960s. The recording was made at a concert given in New York's Carnegie Hall on 23 October 2001, where Anoushka shared the platform with her famous father (who was her teacher and who wrote the composed material in *Rag Desh*).

The track features the **sitar**, a plucked-string instrument with a long neck, and a resonator at the lower end that is made from a hollowed-out, dried gourd (a plant of the pumpkin family). There are typically 20 steel strings on a sitar, although the number can vary. The seven main strings are plucked with a metal plectrum worn on the index finger of the right hand. Three of these (known as **chikari**) are played

© Frank Micelotta/Getty Images

Anoushka Shankar

only as open strings, to punctuate the rhythm or to create drone effects. The other four are used to play melodic lines, the player using the index and middle fingers of the left hand to stop the string against any of up to 19 large metal frets in order to produce different pitches. The frets are moveable to assist tuning.

The characteristic shimmering sound of the sitar comes partly from the effect of a metal plectrum on steel strings but also from the sound of some 13 extra resonating strings that run below the main strings, passing beneath the upward-curved frets. The player doesn't touch these but they vibrate in sympathy when the main strings are plucked and are often described as sympathetic strings.

The steel strings are very flexible and an important aspect of sitar playing, especially in slower passages, is a technique called **meend** in which the left hand pulls the string being plucked to create expressive changes of pitch (a little like a pitch bend). This can be clearly heard in the opening section of Shankar's performance. These ornaments can be less than a semitone (intervals known as **microtones**), although a much wider range is possible. Unlike guitar playing, the fingers of the left hand are not normally raised from the string, except when moving to another string, so there tends to be a good deal of sliding between notes.

© Manoj Valappil/www.shutterstock.com

Tabla

Anoushka Shankar is accompanied by a pair of Indian drums known as **tabla**. They are played with various combinations of finger and hand strokes, and the tone varies according to where and how hard the drums are struck. Each head is mounted with a patch made from a paste of iron filings and rice flour which gives further opportunity to vary the sound.

The smaller of the two drums is made of hollowed-out wood and is played with the fingertips of the right hand – thus it is known as the **dayan**, which means 'right'. The drum head is held tightly in place by straps, and it can be tuned to a specific pitch by moving cylindrical blocks of wood wedged between the straps and the drum shell, which change the tension of the head. The dayan is usually tuned to the note Sa (the home note of the rag).

The larger drum of the pair, unsurprisingly called the **bayan** ('left'), is made of copper and has a deeper tone of indeterminate pitch.

In traditional rag performances such as this, the tabla enters after the introductory section(s) and then accompanies the soloist, sometimes improvising short solos in alternation with the main instrument in a call-and-response style.

A listening guide to this track, with CD timings, is given in GAM. Take special note of the following three points:

See page 156 for an explanation of the tihai mentioned in the notes in GAM on this section.

■ The alap is played only by the sitar. It outlines the notes and characteristic phrases of *rag desh*, and establishes the mood of the piece.
■ The slow gat begins at 0:55, followed a few seconds later by the entry of the tabla in jhaptal. At 9:27 the tabla player breaks into tintal for the fast gat.
■ The lively rhythmic effects of the jhalla begin at 10:10, signalling the final section of the performance.

For more on Anoushka Shankar, visit www.anoushkashankar.com where you can hear samples of her other work. Shankar's first few albums consist of music in the traditional style of her father, but more recently she has started to record sitar music in a much more contemporary style.

'MHARA JANAM MARAN' IN *RAG DESH*, SUNG BY CHIRANJI LAL TANWAR

The performance of *Rag Desh* on CD 2 Track 6 takes the form of a bhajan, a Hindu devotional song. The words, which are nearly 500 years old, were written by Mira Bai (1498–1547), a princess, poet and singer who was born in Rajasthan (a state in north-west India that shares a border with modern Pakistan). She was devoted to Lord Krishna, a deity worshipped by many Hindus, and composed many poems in his praise.

This recording is taken from the album *Mewar Ree Mira* (Mira of Mewar), a collection of eight bhajans by Mira Bai, released in 2004. The soloist is Chiranji Lal Tanwar (known as Chiranji Lalji), a singer of light Indian classical music from the state of Rajasthan, who often performs on Indian television and radio.

He is accompanied by two string and three percussion instruments. The sarod is a plucked-string instrument with main and sympathetic strings like the sitar, but it is shorter and has no frets. The lack of frets results in the characteristic meend (slide) between notes.

The sarangi is a bowed string instrument, often used to accompany singers because it is thought to resemble the sound of the human voice. It has three main strings that are stopped with the fingernails of the left hand, and it is played with a heavy bow held in the right hand. There are also up to 35 additional strings that vibrate in sympathy with the bowed notes. The player sits cross-legged and the instrument is held in an upright position against the chest, with its base resting on the player's feet.

© Norbert Klippstein/India Instruments

Sarod

© Norbert Klippstein/India Instruments

Sarangi

The three percussion instruments are the tabla, a small pair of Indian cymbals and a **pakhawaj**. The pakhawaj is a long cylindrical drum with a small head at one end and a larger head at the other end. It is laid on a cushion in front of the seated drummer, who plays lower notes with the left hand on the larger end, and higher notes with the right hand on the smaller end.

Like an instrumental rag, the song starts with an alap, in which the notes of *Rag Desh* unfold, first in the sarangi part and then in the vocal part. The first few bars of the vocal line are printed in GAM and you can see that Chiranji Lalji begins with the first nine pitches of the rag, touching a brief ornamental B♭ on the ascent. These are the same pitches as those shown on page 151 of this book, except that they are all a semitone higher. Singers and solo instrumentalists choose the pitch at which they wish to perform the rag, and then everyone tunes to this pitch.

In the next section, we will see that the third performance of *Rag Desh* is a semitone higher still.

The song is also similar to an instrumental performance in the way that the tabla joins in after the alap, here playing in *keherwa tal*. However, after this the song follows the structure outlined in GAM, with verses that end with a refrain (formed from the first line of the song). The verses are separated with short instrumental interludes featuring the plucked sarod answered by the bowed sarangi. There is therefore no real build-up of excitement as you would expect in an instrumental rag, although Lalji decorates important words with expressive ornaments, long **melismas** and occasional rapid tans.

RAG DESH PERFORMED BY STEVE GORN AND BENJY WERTHEIMER

A **shruti box** was originally a mechanical device with accordion-like reeds and small bellows, designed to produce a continuous drone. In recent years, electronic versions have become popular, not least because they save the tedious task (once assigned to trainee Indian musicians) of playing very long drones on string instruments.

This third improvisation on *Rag Desh* comes from the album *Priyagitah: The Nightingale*, released in 2004. It features two American musicians who have become expert performers on traditional Indian instruments. Steve Gorn plays the **bansuri**, a large bamboo flute with fingerholes but no keys. He shares the alap with Benjy Wertheimer, who plays the **esraj**, a bowed string instrument with frets, four main strings, and a number of sympathetic and drone strings.

After the alap, Wertheimer switches to tabla for the rest of the piece. The performance is underpinned by a drone on the notes Sa and Pa, which appears to be produced by an electronic **shruti box**, and in the background it's possible to hear a **swarmandel** – a harp-like plucked string instrument with up to 36 strings laid out over a flat sounding board, similar to a European zither.

This final improvisation on *Rag Desh* is split over three tracks. CD 2 Track 7 contains the alap, in which the notes of the rag slowly unfold over the drone. They are introduced first by the bansuri and then the esraj. As the phrases become shorter, Gort and Wertheimer exchange ideas in **dialogue**, echoing and responding to each other's improvisations.

Bansuri

Make sure that you can hear the difference between the two different forms of the note Ni, which in this performance are C♯ when rising and C♮ when falling. The distinctive C♮ is particularly prominent at 0:39 in the bansuri solo and at 1:31 in the esraj solo.

CD 2 Track 8 contains the slow gat, which starts with a bansuri solo over the drone. This gives Wertheimer the chance to switch to the tabla, which enters in *rupak tal* at 0:31. Listen carefully to his very crisp finger-style on the smaller drum of the tabla. The actual gat starts at 0:43 and it then becomes the subject of the flute improvisation. From 3:06 to 3:32 the focus switches to the tabla's improvisation on the tal, which is accompanied by simple repetitions of the gat in the flute part.

Esraj

The end of this section is signaled by a rhythmic device called a **tihai** (pronounced *tee-high*) that is heard in all three versions of *Rag Desh*. It consists of three repetitions of a short pattern (which can sometimes include rests) that cut across the normal accents of the tal, creating cross rhythms. The third of these patterns normally ends on the sam. For example, in eight-beat *keherwa tal*, a tihai might cut across the alternately strong and weak accents with a three-beat pattern like this:

For more about the two soloists in this piece, see their websites at www.stevegorn.com and www.benjymusic.com.

CD 2 Track 9 contains the final section of the piece, which is based on a fast gat in 12-beat *ektal*. The fast tans help it to sound like a jhalla, and the improvisation ends with the special *chakradar tihai* (three tihais in succession), that is a bit like a cadenza in western music – a final opportunity for the soloist to show off their skill.

> ### Test yourself
>
> 1. Name the elements (e.g. 'harmony' or 'texture') that are important in the classical music of north India.
> 2. Briefly explain the purpose of each of the three types of strings on a sitar.
> 3. The sitar is a plucked string instrument. Name another Indian plucked string instrument and explain how it differs from the sitar.
> 4. Name two different bowed string instruments heard in the performances of *Rag Desh*.
> 5. How, apart from size and pitch, do the two drums in a tabla differ?
> 6. North Indian music often includes microtones. What is a microtone?
> 7. Chiranji Lalji's vocal performance of *Rag Desh* includes melismas. What is a melisma?
> 8. List three main sections of a typical rag performance in their correct order.
> 9. What is the name for a pre-composed melody that is included in the performance of a rag?
> 10. Explain the difference between a *meend*, a *tan* and a *tihai*.

Further listening

To broaden your knowledge of Indian classical music, here are some more works that you might enjoy:

- On **Steve Gorn's** website (www.stevegorn.com/video.php) there are video clips of a different improvisation on *Rag Desh*, and several other pieces. You can also listen to audio samples from *Priyagitah* and his other albums in the 'recordings' section of the website. There are MP3 samples of **Anoushka Shankar's** work in the media section of www.anoushkashankar.com.

- The original (2002) edition of GAM includes a vocal performance of *Rag Durga* (with tabla accompaniment) and *Rag Brindabani Sarang* (for sarod and tabla). It also contains an example of bhangra – the fusion of traditional music from the Punjab with western disco. The 2006 edition of GAM includes a recording of *Dhun in Devgiri Bilavel* performed on the sitar by Ravi Shankar, Anoushka's father, and a tabla solo in 16-beat tintal. It also contains a song (*Tujhe Dekha To*) written for the famous Bollywood film industry, that combines elements of both Indian and western music.

- A recording and score of *Rag Bhairav*, featuring a sarangi as the main instrument, are included in the Edexcel *A-level Anthology of Music*.

- For a simple introduction to some of the main types of world music, including the music of India and (for our next set work) Africa, look out for the book 'Music Worldwide' by Elizabeth Sharma, in the series *Cambridge Assignments in Music* (ISBN-13: 9780521376228). The book itself is short and modestly priced, but the useful CD of music examples to go with it is rather expensive (available separately as ISBN-13: 9780521374811).

- Finally, look out for the album *West Meets East*, recorded in 1967 but now available on CD, which brought Indian music to the attention of many western ears through its innovative combination of Ravi Shankar, the great Indian sitarist, and Yehudi Menuhin, the great classical violinist.

Composing ideas

While studying the three versions of *Rag Desh* we have come across a number of techniques that could be used in your own compositions.

You could try writing a piece based on the main principles of a traditional rag performance – a melody instrument, a drone and a small pair of hand drums. You might also choose to use the structural features of a rag, starting with free rhythms in the alap, then establishing a clear pulse when the drums enter, and aiming for a really exciting conclusion. Although it is not really possible to achieve the shimmering quality and microtonal pitch variation of Indian music on most western instruments, you may be able to find a sitar (or similar) sound on a synthesiser to play the drone and give the right sort of background atmosphere.

The piece could be based on the notes of an actual Indian rag, or you could make up your own set of notes. Remember that the rising and falling versions of a rag are often different: some notes may be flat (although never Sa, Ma or Pa), but the only sharp used in traditional Indian music is on the note Ma.

Don't forget the importance of ornamenting the melodic line. If you have an instrument, such as the violin, on which it is possible to slide between notes and produce a wide vibrato, you may be able to capture the right style. If not, the frequent use of short, neat ornaments to decorate the melody should work well.

Sample questions for Section A

Listen to the first 62 seconds of CD 2 Track 8 three times, with short pauses between each playing, as you answer the following questions. Don't consult the score or any other information before writing your answers.

1. Name the wind instrument heard in this excerpt. .... (1)

2. What is heard beneath this wind instrument at the start of the excerpt?

.... (1)

3. What is the correct name for the drums that enter halfway through the excerpt?

.... (1)

4. The drums establish a repeating cycle of beats known as a *tal*. Show the type of tal used in this extract by writing a cross in the correct box below.

7-beat rupak tal ☒   8-beat keherwa tal ☒
12-beat ektal ☒   16-beat tintal ☒   (1)

5. Shortly after the drums enter, a *gat* is heard. Briefly explain what is meant by a gat.

.... (1)

6. This excerpt is based on a version of *rag desh* in which the home note corresponds to the pitch D, as shown below. Complete the rag by adding one missing note at each place marked * **and** write the correct accidental in front of the only note that needs one. (3)

7. Name the section of the rag heard *before this extract begins*.

.... (1)

8. The section before this extract includes an instrument called an esraj. Show what type of instrument this is by crossing the correct box below.

bowed string ☒   brass ☒   percussion ☒
plucked string ☒   woodwind ☒   (1)

(Total 10 marks)

Top Tips

This set work has introduced a number of new and probably unfamiliar technical terms. It is likely that you will be expected to recognise and use the correct words in the exam, at least for the names of instruments and for the main features of a rag, so try not to rush your study of *Rag Desh*, especially if you are tackling it quite late in the course.

Sample questions for Section B

Before tackling this section read the information on writing extended answers, on page 167. Then complete your answers without consulting any notes or the score, and without listening to the recording.

The following questions are about the versions of *Rag Desh* that you have studied.

(a) Name the region **and** the country (e.g. 'west Australia') on which the musical style of all three performances is based.

.... (2)

(b) Choose **two** of the performances and then *compare* how each uses the following musical elements:

Instruments (including voice)
Structure
The ways in which the notes of *rag desh* have been used
The type(s) of tal used
Any other interesting aspects of improvisation. (10)

Use correct musical vocabulary where appropriate and remember that the quality of your writing, including spelling, punctuation and grammar, will be taken into account in this question. Write your answer on a separate sheet of paper.

(Total 12 marks)

SET WORK 12: *YIRI* PERFORMED BY KOKO

Our final set work comes from west Africa, a region with a rich musical heritage that has had a major impact on the rest of the world because many of its features spread via the slave trade to the Caribbean and the USA, from where it had a direct influence on the jazz, rock and blues styles of today.

Much of the traditional music of Africa, like that of north India, was (and still is) performed by professional musicians, so it is not always appropriate to refer to it as folk music. Families of griots (praise singers) were attached to the households of tribal chiefs and would sing songs at important events such as births, weddings and funerals.

Drums have special significance in Africa as symbols of political or religious power, and they too are often associated with tribal chiefs and royal families. African musicians do not refer to playing their instruments, but to teaching them to speak – they do not like playing drums from areas outside their own region because these don't speak the same language. This link between language and music is important. The relative pitch of spoken words affects their meaning in most African languages and these inflexions can be imitated by the talking drum to communicate messages, as explained below.

Two of the most important types of melodic instrument in west Africa are the harp-like **kora** and the **balafon**, a tuned percussion instrument (similar to the xylophone) that has an important role in our set work.

KOKO

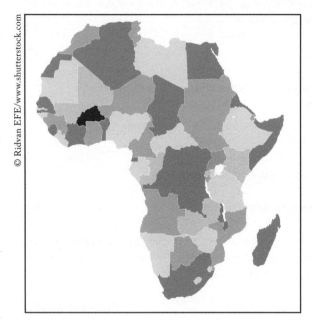

Burkina Faso in Africa

Koko is a group of six musicians, led by the singer and balafon player Madou Koné, from the land-locked country of Burkina Faso in west Africa. Although it has an area larger than that of the United Kingdom, its population is less than twice that of Greater London. Burkina Faso was a French colony from 1898 until 1960, and French is still its main official language.

'Yiri' is the fourth track on Koko's album *Burkina Faso: Balafons et Tambours d'Afrique* (Balafons and African Drums), released in 2002. 'Yiri' is the local dialect word for wood, and its use as the title of this track probably refers to the importance of wood in the making of drums and instruments such as the balafon.

Koko includes two balafons (or balaphones). This percussion instrument consists of up to 21 tuned wooden bars, hung in a frame and played with two padded beaters. Bottle-shaped gourds of carefully selected sizes are fixed below the bars, making the sound a little more resonant than that of the western xylophone. However, it is not possible to sustain long notes and so, as with the xylophone, both beaters are used to create a tremolo, as heard in the opening bars of *Yiri*.

Balafons sometimes have only four or five notes in each octave, depending on the region from which they come, but those in *Yiri* use a heptatonic (seven-note) scale that is roughly similar to the major scale in western music.

A demonstration of balafon tuning and playing is available on video in the section headed Sambla Community Konkolikan at www.musicvideos. the-real-africa.com/ burkinafaso – it includes pictures of several performers playing a single balafon.

Balafon showing the resonators made from bottle gourds

The members of Koko play several types of drum.

The **djembe** is the most well-known of all African drums. It is shaped like a large goblet and has a head of goatskin, held under high tension by ropes. It is played with both hands, and a variety of tones is possible depending on how and where the player strikes the head of the drum.

The **dunun** (or dundun) is a bass drum, similar to the djembe, but with a more cylindrical shape.

The **bara** is a small drum, made from a gourd, with a head of thin goatskin held under relatively light pressure. It has a warm tone and is often used to accompany the balafon in Burkina Faso.

Djembe

The term **talking drum** is not one that African musicians would use because they regard most instruments as being able to 'speak'. It has many local names and forms, but almost always has an hour-glass shape with a waistline that is narrower than its ends.

The talking drum is usually hung from the left shoulder, held steady under the arm, so that the left hand can press on a tensioning thong to alter the pitch of the sound as it is being played. Notes are played by the right hand, usually with a hooked beater that has a flattened head, although it can also be played directly with the hand or fingertips.

Talking drum

Its English name arises from the wide range of tonal effects that are possible by striking the head in different places, by altering the tension of the skin while a note is sounding to produce a gliding effect, and by using the left hand to dampen notes. All of this helps the player to mimic the rise and fall of the languages used in the region.

Following the score

The score in GAM is a transcription from the recording – the performers would have played from memory and not from notation. The key signature of six flats looks alarming, but it simply reflects the balafon tuning. The musicians would not have thought of playing in the key of Gb major. The score includes two terms more usually found in jazz and rock scores. The word 'fill' in bar 18 refers to the djembe player occasionally decorating the basic rhythm to move the music forward. The word 'break' in bar 34 and elsewhere marks the start of passages in which the balafon features as a soloist. Later in the piece the music is sometimes not written out if it continues in the same style for some bars. For instance, the figure 12 in bar 83 indicates that the passage continues for 12 bars in a similar style.

LISTENING GUIDE

0:00	An **introduction** in free time. The texture is monophonic and the balafon outlines all seven pitches of the scale, with a tremolo on every note, apart from those printed in small type. In western music these small notes are known as acciaccaturas (pronounced *at-chak-ka-too-rahs*) and, as here, are played as quickly as possible.
0:18	A clear pulse in quadruple metre begins with a two-bar phrase that is immediately repeated in parallel octaves when the second balafon player joins in. Bar 12 is in parallel 5ths, but octaves return in the next bar.
0:34	Drums enter, playing a simple pattern split between instruments. Notice how the lower balafon part in bars 17–20 uses the falling idea (Db–Cb–Ab) from bar 8, but in a different rhythm, and repeats it as a short ostinato. Rhythms start to become more complex from bar 21 onwards, with syncopation in every bar, a triplet pattern and a temporary change to triple metre in bar 27.
1:09	**Chorus A**, sung by unison voices. Notice how the ends of the short falling phrases are echoed by the balafon in bars 28–30. The opening phrases end on Db, while the final ones finish on Gb.
1:25	**Balafon solo** with drum accompaniment. Every bar is syncopated and most phrases follow the pattern of the chorus by ending on Db and then, at the end, on Gb. Again, most phrases fall from high to low.
1:44	A repeat of **chorus A**, with some differences in the balafon accompaniment.
2:01	**Balafon solo** (in a low register) with a strong emphasis on Gb as a home note.
2:10	**Vocal solo**, starting with a long note but continuing with short falling phrases. The singer is accompanied by simple ostinati played by one balafon and then by both. The choir echoes the final phrase in call-and-response style.
2:45	The **vocal solo** continues, and the balafon introduces lively cross rhythms (the accented groups of three semiquavers in bars 68–69, where you would normally expect semiquavers to be played in groups of four). There's another interjection from the choir in bar 77, just before the end of the solo.

3:28	**Balafon solo** (in a high register). Notice how the entry of the next chorus is signalled by a single bar of $\frac{3}{4}$ time, just as it was in bar 27 (before the first appearance of chorus A) and in bar 41 (before the second appearance of chorus A).
4:00	**Chorus B**. Although this is identified with a different letter in GAM, the melody has essentially the same falling outline as chorus A, and similar interjections from the balafon. Following a short instrumental interlude, the chorus is repeated at 4:31.
4:45	**Balafon solo**, again emphasising G♭ as the home note and featuring fast, *virtuoso* rhythms. From bar 122 the soloist plays a variation on chorus A, anticipating the return of the singers at bar 128.
5:20	**Chorus A** is sung for the third time (still in unison).
5:36	A final **balafon solo**.
6:24	The **coda** is based on a new idea for both balafons that is repeated and extended to form a two-bar unit. These two bars are repeated (starting on the last quaver of bar 155). A further repeat, beginning on the last quaver of bar 157, is interrupted by the ting of a small bell, marking the end of the piece. Notice how the ending is indicated by a new melodic idea, and not by any slowing down or pause in the tempo.

In bars 154–158 the second balafon plays an outline version of the first balafon part. Performing two different versions of the same tune at the same time creates a *heterophonic* texture – a feature common in many types of world music, although this example is very simple.

We can see from this table that the structure of the piece is a series of choruses, each followed by a solo for one of the two balofon players, with a central vocal solo that includes choral responses. The whole performance begins with an instrumental introduction and ends with an instrumental coda.

Like many traditional pieces, the music is almost entirely **hexatonic** – the note F appears in the introduction (and F♭ in bar 12), but is otherwise mainly avoided. The absence of F (the leading note of G♭ major) tends to make the music sound modal rather than major in tonality, although the prominent use of D♭ and (especially) G♭ gives it a strong sense of being in G♭ major.

Most of the phrases fall from high to low, and many of the melodic ideas are based on small cells of notes (such as G♭–E♭–D♭). Each of the three main elements in the piece (balofons, drums and voices) have clearly defined roles that are maintained throughout and which are combined to form the overall layered texture. There is no variation in tempo, and little contrast in dynamics.

Test yourself

1. In which part of Africa is Burkina Faso?
2. Traditional African music is not normally written down. How do the musicians learn specific pieces?
3. Which major key is represented by a key signature of six flats?
4. Why does this piece sound modal?
5. What type of instrument is a balafon?
6. The resonators on a balafon are made from gourds. Name another instrument that can be made from a gourd.
7. What is the most well-known type of African drum?
8. What is the difference between tremolo and an acciaccatura, both of which are heard in the introduction?
9. Would you describe the vocal parts in this piece as syllabic or melismatic?
10. What is the meaning of 'yiri'?

Further listening

To broaden your knowledge of African music, here are some more works that you might enjoy:

■ Try to listen to some of the other tracks by Koko on their album ***Burkina Faso: Balafons et Tambours d'Afrique*** (Air Mail Music, SA141076). You may have to search for a specialist world-music shop if you want to obtain the CD, but short samples are available on several websites, including www.sternsmusic.com/disk_info/SA141076.

■ The original (2002) edition of GAM includes two pieces of African drumming: ***Kundum*** (recorded by the Drummers of Ghana) and ***Nzekele*** (recorded by Les Percussions de Guinée). There are three pieces of African music in the 2006 edition of GAM: ***Ashanti Ntumpani*** is played on a pair of talking drums from Ghana, ***Yamfa*** is a duet for two players of the kora (a plucked-string instrument), and ***Inkanyezi Nezazi*** is a piece of unaccompanied music for male-voice choir that comes from South Africa. It also includes ***Igede***, an example of an African pop style called highlife, which is a blend of western harmonies with African rhythms, played by a combination of instruments from both traditions.

■ Mustapha Tettey Addy, the master drummer who plays ***Ashanti Ntumpani*** in the 2006 edition of GAM, also features in the Edexcel *A-level Anthology of Music*. There he plays ***Agbekor***, a traditional dance from Ghana, on a type of talking drum known as the *atsimevu*.

■ One of the most famous names from Burkina Faso is *Farafina*, which is both a training school for musicians and an eight-piece performing group with a similar line-up to that of Koko. Look out for their CDs ***Bolomakote*** (Intuition Records, INT2026) and ***Faso Denou*** (Real World, CAROL23280), and visit www.culturebase.net/artist.php?308.

Composing ideas

While studying *Yiri* we have come across a number of techniques that could be used in your own compositions.

Drums play an important role in west African music, although they have fairly simple parts in *Yiri*. If you write a piece for drums alone, there will be no melody or harmony, so you would need to think carefully about how to make the work sufficiently interesting. You could perhaps use changes of time signature, cross rhythms, and a good range of different drum sounds. Consider special effects such as playing on the rim of a drum, damping the drum head in different ways, and using different types of sticks and beaters.

Writing a piece for tuned percussion with drums offers much greater potential. For an African type of sound consider including different sizes of xylophone and, if you have access to one, a marimba (a large xylophone with tubular resonators under the bars). African music often includes shakers, rattles and claves (two pieces of hard wood tapped together). It also commonly features rhythms played on the type of bell heard at the very end of *Yiri* – this type of sound can be mimicked by a cowbell from a drum kit tapped with a drumstick. You may also be able to include synthesiser sounds such as 'kalimba' (based on an African instrument in which the notes are produced by twanging metal strips fixed to a wooden resonator).

Simple melodic cells formed from notes of a hexatonic scale (as in *Yiri*) would work well. Try to develop them into interlocking ostinato patterns, like those in bars 59–63 of *Yiri*, and vary them as the work progresses. Include some sections in call-and-response style, and have some solo passages (possibly improvised) for the main instruments. Adding voices might enhance the mood of the piece, even if they just contribute occasional joyous shouts such as the cries of 'Yiri' in the set work. It's often a good idea to build up pieces of this type in layers – drums, then ostinato patterns and finally the main melodic ideas – but make sure that you vary the texture, perhaps by having several instruments drop out in some sections.

Remember that although your compositions must be related to the areas of study, you don't have to base them on ideas from the set works. In the case of this area of study, it is enough for your work to be related to any typical aspect(s) of World Music.

Sample questions for Section A

Listen to the first 48 seconds of CD 2 Track 10 four times, with short pauses between each playing, as you answer the following questions. Don't consult the score or any other information before writing your answers.

1. Name the instrument **and** the texture heard in the slow introduction.

Instrument ....

Texture .... (2)

2. Complete the following sentence by adding the correct musical term.

The performer decorates each of the opening notes with a

.... (1)

3. After the slow introduction the following melody is heard twice in succession. Complete the four missing notes (the rhythm is printed above the stave). (4)

4. Write a cross in the box below to show how this melody is harmonised on its second appearance.

with chords ☒   with a drone ☒
in parallel 5ths ☒   in parallel octaves ☒   (1)

5. Name **two** different types of drums that play in the last part of the extract.

.... and ....   (2)

(Total 10 marks)

Sample questions for Section B

Before tackling this section read the information on writing extended answers, on page 167. Then complete your answers without consulting any notes or the score, and without listening to the recording.

The following questions are about *Yiri*, performed by Koko.

(a) Name the country from which this music comes.

....   (1)

(b) In which part of Africa is this country?...   (1)

(c) Comment on how the following musical elements are used in this piece:

Metre
Rhythm
Melody
Texture
Instruments and voices   (10)

Use correct musical vocabulary where appropriate and remember that the quality of your writing, including spelling, punctuation and grammar, will be taken into account in this question. Write your answer on a separate sheet of paper.

(Total 12 marks)

The final question in Section B of the Unit 3 exam will ask you to write in detail about one or more of the set works. You are likely to have to put the work in context, for instance by giving its date and style, or by stating where you might expect to hear it performed. You may have the opportunity to give (and justify) your opinions about the set work and to mention related works that you know. However, most of the marks are likely to be awarded for writing about how the elements of music, such as rhythm, melody and harmony, are used in the set work.

The quality of your written communication will be marked and you will be expected to use technical terms correctly. For a good mark you not only have to write accurately about the music, but you also need to convey your ideas logically, with correct spelling, punctuation and grammar.

Top Tips

If you find writing difficult, use short sentences. Make sure that each one starts with a capital letter and ends with a full stop. Use a separate paragraph for each element of music that you discuss.

In order to write a logical answer, deal fully with each point in turn. Your answer will not seem logical if, in the middle of writing about structure, you suddenly add something about melody that you had previously forgotten.

Top Tips

It is well worth spending a few minutes in the exam making rough notes of the points you will include under each heading. This will help you to write a much more logical answer.

In an exam it is easy to waste time by repeating a point in different words, for example by stating that the word setting is syllabic and then later pointing out that there are no melismas. Making the same point twice gets no extra marks and could be seen to reflect poorly on the quality of your written communication.

Top Tips

If you can only think of one point to write about a feature, don't waffle on about it. Write it down concisely and then move on – there will almost certainly be several points you can make about other features, providing you don't waste time.

One of the most useful tips for Section B of the paper is to get plenty of practice in writing answers on each set work under exam conditions, perhaps using the sample questions given in this book.

THE ELEMENTS OF MUSIC

The next part of this chapter gathers together the information on the elements of music that have been introduced earlier in this book. Use it, and the glossary of technical terms that follows, as part of your revision. Most people find it very helpful to work out a revision timetable, setting aside regular times to go over each set work in turn. Remember that while books can be useful, ears are of even more help to a musician. Technical terms such as sequence or blue notes are of little use if you cannot hear their musical effect.

> **Top Tips**
>
> If you can illustrate a technical term by giving an accurate demonstration of it on your instrument or with your voice, it is likely that you have understood what it means.

Above all, remember that your best resource is your teacher. If you don't understand something, then *ask*. But don't leave it until the end of the course, when he or she will be preoccupied with administering coursework – try to keep up to date with all your work throughout the course.

Although you are likely to be asked to comment on specific musical elements in the exam, these are not always totally independent. For instance, if a piece includes balanced phrases of regular length, this could be mentioned under melody or structure. However, you should make sure that you comment on all of the elements that are listed in the question, even if you have more to say about some than others.

Metre

Metre refers to the pattern of beats in a passage of music. In duple metre there are two main beats per bar, in triple metre there are three, and in quadruple metre there are four.

- If the upper figure of the time signature is 2, 3 or 4 the metre is called **simple**: each beat can be split into two shorter notes of identical length
- If the upper figure of the time signature is 6, 9 or 12 the metre is called **compound**: each beat can be split into three shorter notes of identical length.

In a lot of music the metre is regular – in other words, the time signature doesn't change. Regular metres are described with two words – the first is either simple or compound, the second is duple, triple or quadruple:

2 beats per bar	$\frac{2}{4}$ simple duple metre	$\frac{6}{8}$ compound duple metre
3 beats per bar	$\frac{3}{4}$ simple triple metre	$\frac{9}{8}$ compound triple metre
4 beats per bar	$\frac{4}{4}$ simple quadruple metre	$\frac{12}{8}$ compound quadruple metre

If there is no clear beat, as at the start of Anoushka Shankar's performance of *Rag Desh*, we say that there is no regular metre. Later in this piece the metre is based on the tal, as it is in the other performances of the rag.

Mention if the metre changes during a piece, or if the music contains any unusual use of metre, such as the combination of simple triple ($\frac{3}{2}$) and compound quadruple ($\frac{12}{8}$) in the later parts of Reich's *Electric Counterpoint*.

Tempo

Tempo is the speed of the beat, which may be indicated by an Italian word, such as Allegro (fast) or may be shown more precisely by a metronome mark. For example, the tempo of 'Something's Coming' is given as ♩ = 176, which means 176 crotchet beats a minute. That's almost three crotchets a second – a very fast tempo.

Mention any changes in tempo, including ritardando (slowing up) near the end of a section, and any temporary fluctuations in tempo caused by the use of rubato or pauses. If the speed doesn't vary, don't ignore the obvious – say that the tempo is unchanging.

Rhythm

Rhythm refers to the patterns made by notes and rests. If you are asked to write about rhythm, concentrate on the most distinctive features, such as the insistent quaver–quaver–crotchet patterns in the first subject of the first movement of Mozart's Symphony No. 40. Mention important contrasts, such as those between dotted rhythms, even quavers and long notes in 'And the Glory of the Lord'.

Remember to draw attention to any specific rhythmic devices, such as the use of syncopation, hemiola or triplets. Also mention any particular rhythmic effects, such as cross rhythms or swung rhythms, or phrases that begin with an anacrusis. There is some overlap between rhythm and metre, so you might also want to mention the use of pauses or rubato under the heading of rhythm.

Melody

As with rhythm, concentrate on just the main features. Are the melodies diatonic, chromatic, pentatonic or hexatonic? Are there blue notes? Are the melodies based on the pitches of an Indian rag? Do they move mainly by step, mainly by leap, or a combination of both? Are they smooth or angular in outline? Do they have a narrow range or a wide range? Are they high or low in the instrument's or voice's range? Do they transfer from one instrument or voice to another? Are the melodies decorated with lots of ornamental notes, or are they plain and simple?

How is the melody constructed? Is it formed from motifs that are repeated or used in sequence, or does it unfold as a continuous line? Does the melody include scale patterns or arpeggios? Is it lyrical or fragmented? Does it have an overall shape – rising, falling or arch-like? Does it fall into a series of regular phrases that sound like questions and answers? Are the main melodies in the work contrasted or similar?

As you can see, you should have plenty to write about if you are asked to comment on the use of melody in a set work.

Top Tips

Think carefully before using the word 'sequence' as a verb. 'Handel sequenced the motif' means that he played into a sequencer, a piece of equipment not invented at the time! You need to use sequence as a noun: 'Handel used the motif in sequence'.

If you use letters to identify a melodic idea, such as 'motif A', you must first explain what part of the music you mean by motif A.

Harmony

Harmony refers to the chords used – it isn't an invitation to write in general about the accompaniment. Comment on whether the harmony is mainly consonant or mainly dissonant. Write about the types of chords used – are they mostly diatonic triads, or are they complex chords, perhaps containing chromatic notes? Mention any chord progressions that play an important role in the music and try to comment on the **harmonic rhythm** – that is, the rate at which the chords change. For example, the harmonic pace is slow in Moby's 'Why Does My Heart Feel So Bad?', where every chord lasts for two bars, whereas in Handel's 'And the Glory of the Lord' there are often two or three different chords per bar.

A discussion of harmony might also include the use of any pedals in the music, and the role of cadences. If there are frequent perfect and imperfect cadences to define keys, we say that the harmony is functional. Point out any prominent cadences in the work, such as the plagal cadence with which Handel ends 'And the Glory of the Lord', or the modal cadences that occur in 'All Blues'.

Tonality

Remember that tonality is nothing to do with the tone of the music. It refers to the use of major and/or minor keys in a work and, for exam purposes, it also includes the terms modal and atonal. Mention if the tonality is defined by cadences and if the composer uses different keys as a structural device – such as the contrast between G minor and B♭ major for the two main subjects in the first movement of Mozart's Symphony No. 40, or the change from tonic major to tonic minor for the middle section of Chopin's Prelude No. 15.

You may also want to point out if parts of the music are based on certain sets of notes such as a pentatonic or hexatonic scale, or on the notes of an Indian rag, and whether the tonality is coloured by chromatic writing.

Texture

This is another word that is often misunderstood, leading to lost marks in exams. Texture refers to the way that the various simultaneous lines in a piece relate to one another. The main terms that you are expected to use are:

Monophonic	An unaccompanied melodic line
Homophonic	A tune with accompaniment
Contrapuntal (or **polyphonic**)	Two or more simultaneous melodies

If the music is monophonic, is it performed by one person or by several playing or singing in either octaves or in unison?

If the music is homophonic, is the melody supported by block chords or by an accompaniment of broken chords or rhythmic figures of some kind? Is there anything else of interest in the texture, such as a countermelody or dialogue?

If the music is contrapuntal, do the parts imitate one another? Are there any canons? How many independent lines are there in the counterpoint? If you can't remember, at least give an indication. For example, *Electric Counterpoint* builds to a dense contrapuntal texture, while bars 84–87 of 'And the Glory of the Lord' contain an example of a thin contrapuntal texture.

Point out if contrasts in texture contribute towards the structure of the music, such as the alternation of homophonic and contrapuntal textures in 'And the Glory of the Lord' or the use of counterpoint in the development section of the set work by Mozart.

Structure

Structure can refer to the overall form of the piece and to the phrase structure of individual sections. In some set works the overall form can be labelled (for example, sonata form or ternary form) but in other cases it may need to be explained. Try to show the purpose of the various sections – for instance, the exposition in sonata form introduces the main keys and themes, the coda is a concluding section to confirm the tonic key, and an instrumental interlude in a song adds variety and also gives the singer a break.

Mention any devices that contribute to the structure, such as Mozart's use of dominant preparation to signal the imminent return of the tonic key, or the use of ostinato or riff as a unifying device within a section.

It's not practical to comment on the phrase structure throughout a whole set work, but draw attention to any important aspects, such as Mozart's use of balanced phrases, the way in which the sections of 'All Blues' are determined by the 12-bar structure of the blues progression, or how the phrases in *Yiri* are formed from short motifs and are often of irregular lengths.

Resources

You may be asked about how instruments and voices are used in a set work. As well as the names of individual instruments and voices, it will sometimes be convenient to write in terms of families (the strings, the woodwind and so on). Examiners will be more interested in seeing if you know how the resources are used, rather than just listing their names. Which instruments have solos, which accompany, which are used in various combinations? Do the instruments mainly double the voices (as in much of the movement by Handel), or are they more independent (as in the guitar parts of 'Grace')?

You should *briefly* explain any important unusual instruments, particularly in the world-music works, stating the contribution they make to the overall effect. Also mention any prominent special effects, such as the use of tremolo in the introduction to *Yiri*, the contrast between pizzicato and arco strings in 'Peripetie', Miles Davis' use of a Harmon mute, or the slides and ornaments in the various settings of *Rag Desh*.

In the case of vocal music, this is the place to mention the word setting – is it syllabic or melismatic, and is there any use of word painting? Also indicate the roles of the singers, either as soloist, choir or backing group to a soloist.

If a question includes the word timbre, remember that it means tone colour – it is another term that often causes confusion in exams. For example, the main instrumental timbre in 'And the Glory of the Lord' is that of bowed strings. The timbres in Mozart's symphony are more varied, and include prominent solos for various types of woodwind instrument, often used in combination. 'Peripetie' includes a huge range of orchestral timbres (pizzicato and arco strings, muted brass and so on) while Miles Davis, in 'All Blues', modifies the timbre of his trumpet with a Harmon mute. Even works written for a solo instrument (such as Chopin's Prelude) or a group of similar instruments (such as the guitars in *Electric Counterpoint*) reveal a range of timbres, resulting from how (and where in its range) the instrument is played.

Dynamics

As with the other elements, examiners won't want a list – they will hope to see if you understand how dynamics contribute to the work as a whole. For example,

Handel expected his performers to use terraced dynamics even though not many are marked in the score. Chopin's dynamics are more subtly graded, with many crescendos and diminuendos between different dynamic levels. Schoenberg's dynamics are dramatic and extreme, with heavily accented notes and violent contrasts between *pp* and *fff*. However, if there's little dynamic contrast, as in *Yiri*, then say so!

Other questions

In works where technology plays an important part in the production of the music, such as the pre-recorded tracks of *Electric Counterpoint* or the samples in the song by Moby, you could be asked to describe how the technology has been used.

The exam specification mentions that you could be asked to make comparisons between two set works. Earlier in the book we gave an example of this type of question, by asking for a comparison of two different versions of *Rag Desh*. However, the two works could come from different areas of study. In general, this type of question can be easier because you will have twice as much to write about, but a good answer will need careful organisation. It is best to make direct comparisons about each of the specified elements in turn, rather than writing about one work and then the other.

It is also possible that you might be asked to express your opinion about a work. Again, we gave an example of this (as a Section A question) at the end of our work on 'Peripetie'. As we said there, examiners will not care whether you like the piece or not – what they want to see are the musical reasons you give to justify your opinion.

The specification indicates that students should know how the set works relate to similar works written around the same time. The sample paper provided by Edexcel gives no example of this type of question, but this is where your further listening could come in useful, as you might be asked a simple question that goes a little beyond just the set work itself. It is certainly possible that, either in Section A or Section B, you could be asked to name some typical features of the style represented by the set work. You might be asked to comment on the original purpose of the music you have studied (music for the concert hall, the theatre, the home, for work or social gatherings, and so on) and you could be asked to state where you might hear it being performed today.

EXAMPLE ANSWERS

Remember that there will be two questions in Section B, of which you have to answer only one. Spend a minute or two in the exam thinking about the best choice, as there is nothing worse than getting halfway through an answer before realising that the alternative question would have been a better option.

For a good mark, you need to present plenty of accurate and relevant information in a clear way, with the correct use of musical terms and few (if any) mistakes in spelling, punctuation or grammar. However, you are not expected to produce a long essay. If you write with real focus, it is perfectly possible to get full marks for an answer that will occupy less than a page.

Here, to end with, are three (imaginary) answers to the same question, with some comments on the type of mark they could receive.

Comment on how Chopin uses the following musical elements in his Prelude No. 15 in D♭ major:

Structure
Tonality
Texture
Melody
Writing for the piano

Remember to use correct musical vocabulary where appropriate.

(10 marks)

1.

> raindrop starts up with an intro and then choppin jumps into ABA
> form where he has pedals several times a bar that sound like rain
> thundering down on a tin roof but then he spoils it by going to the
> wrong key in the middle 4 the boring bit (u can see I don't rate it as
> high as Moby) but the tonality is very sweet on the outside where
> the texture is major
>
> the melody is decorated with lots of enharmonics but raindrop needs
> some chords to play it on the gitar I can reccomend a much better
> peace which is not old-fashioned I called it rainstorm and its in my
> composition folder

Although the lack of a sentence structure make this very short answer difficult to read, there are a few reasonably accurate observations. The piece can correctly be described as ABA form, although the technical term (ternary) is missing and there is no introduction in this piece. The outer sections have been correctly described as major, although the terms texture and tonality have been misunderstood. There is some awareness that decoration of the melody is important, although the grace notes have been misidentified as 'enharmonics'.

The small amount of remaining factual material is either incorrect or irrelevant. The pedalling indications for the pianist have been confused with pedal as a harmonic device, and the comment about 'rain thundering down on a tin roof' would leave the examiner wondering if the candidate had actually heard the music. Describing the middle section as in 'the wrong key' is an unwanted value judgment – the key was obviously right for Chopin, and it makes sense to modern ears because it is simply the minor version of the tonic key (albeit written with a different key signature). The comment about the lack of chords seems puzzling – perhaps 'chords' means 'chord symbols'. The final point about work for Unit 2 is irrelevant to the question.

The quality of written communication is very poor. In addition to the absence of punctuation and capital letters, misspelling the composer's name gives a poor impression (especially as it is given in the question), and there are several other incorrect spellings. Also, it isn't acceptable to use texting abbreviations (such as u for 'you' and 4 instead of 'for') in the type of formal writing expected in an exam.

Overall, an answer such as this would be unlikely to achieve much more than about two of the available ten marks.

2.

> The prelude by Chopin is in ternary form and hard to play. The dynamics are changing all the time with crescendos and diminuendos to make the music expressive, and it gets very loud in the middle. The tonality is very beautiful and would have been enjoyed by young ladies playing the piece on their salon pianos. Chopin was born in Poland, but he worked in Paris and wrote his piano preludes on an island in the Mediterranean. He died in 1849 after he had become very famous. The texture is quite thin but it gets thicker and minor in the middle section. The main melody has long phrases and groups of ornamental notes. In the middle section the melody is more like chords in the bass and is rather angry, as if the raindrops had become a storm. A new tune appears near the end, but Chopin doesn't do anything with it. The piece is well written for piano, with lots of pedaling, but Chopin could have chosen an easier key.

This answer includes points about all five elements listed in the question, although none are explored in depth. The form has been correctly described as ternary, but there is no detail about how the final section differs from the first section and there is no identification of the coda. The second sentence (about dynamics) is true, but will not add anything to the mark because the question doesn't ask about dynamics. Similarly, the points about Chopin's life take time to write out but add nothing that answers the question that has been set.

Stating that the tonality is 'very beautiful' is merely an opinion that will leave the examiner wondering if the writer understands the meaning of tonality. Later it is correctly mentioned that the middle section is in a minor key, but it would have been better to make this point in the sentence about tonality, and to name the key, showing how it relates to the major key of the rest of the piece.

Similarly, the statement about the texture is rather vague although it gets amplified later (again, out of order) where it is correctly stated that the melody is in the bass in the middle section. There is no reference to the texture being homophonic throughout.

The main melody is correctly described as having long phrases and ornamental notes, but there is no mention of the shape of the melody or the way that it has a ternary phrase structure within the overall ternary form of the piece (a point that could alternatively have been made under structure). There is little about the piano writing, apart from a mention of pedalling – saying that it is 'well written for the piano' is merely an opinion unless some examples are given.

This is a competent answer in several respects and is written in clear sentences. However, few of the points are dealt with in depth and there are significant omissions (including a failure to mention the repeated pedal notes that give the work its nickname, no mention of the enharmonic shift to the tonic minor for the middle section, or the abbreviated repeat of the first section that is followed by a coda). The answer is not well organised because some points are dealt with out of order and there are digressions about dynamics and Chopin's life. There are also value judgments about the difficulty of the music – which may be hard for a novice pianist, but in the overall context of Chopin's piano music (other examples of which should be known) it is not especially technically demanding. The comment about choosing an easier key for the music suggests that the writer is unaware that Chopin's Op. 28 is a cycle of preludes in all 24 keys – the keys are not chosen randomly.

Overall, an answer such as this would be likely to achieve around half of the available ten marks.

3.

The Raindrop prelude is in ternary form, with a middle section in the tonic minor key. The first section itself has a ternary phrase structure. The middle section consists of 16 bars that are repeated, followed by a new idea. When the first section returns it is shortened and followed by a coda.

The music is in D♭ major, with modulations to related keys in the first section. An enharmonic modulation leads to the middle section, where the tonality changes to the tonic minor (C♯ minor), and there is a return to D♭ major for the ending.

The texture is homophonic, with a right-hand melody in the outer sections, and left-hand motifs in the central part. Repeated pedal notes, mainly on the dominant (A♭ or G♯), are an important part of the texture and their constant quaver rhythm is the reason why the prelude is thought to sound like raindrops.

The opening melody descends through the notes of the tonic triad and then rises in an arch shape. It is repeated and it continues in long, smooth phrases that are often decorated with groups of grace notes. The melody in the middle section is totally different, being low in the bass with a plain rhythm. Chopin introduces a new melody in the coda but it is not developed and seems more like a taster of a new piece.

Chopin exploits the piano's melodic qualities in the first section, with a singing melody and harmonies sustained by the use of the pedal. In the middle section he uses the low bass range and the resonant power of thick chords in the very loud section. He was famous for his early Romantic works for piano.

This is a much more substantial answer, with several good points on each of the five specified elements. Setting out the answer in paragraphs, one for each element, and using mainly short sentences makes it clear to read. The standard of spelling, punctuation and grammar is high, and a number of technical terms have been used correctly. Although there is more that could be said, work of this kind is likely to receive credit in the highest category, with nine or possibly all ten available marks being awarded.

Aim for a clear, concise and informative answer of this kind, and you will deserve to do well. Good luck in your studies!

GLOSSARY

Accent. A note given special emphasis, either because of its prominent position or because it is marked with a symbol (such as >) to indicate that it should stand out.

Acciaccatura (pronounced *at-chak-ka-too-rah*). An **ornament**, printed as a small note with a slash through its tail, which is played as quickly as possible before the main note that follows it.

Accidental. A sharp, flat or natural sign used during the course of a composition, rather than as part of a key signature. Accidentals apply to all notes of the same pitch that occur later in the same bar, unless cancelled by another accidental. The effect of an accidental continues beyond the end of the bar if the note concerned has a tie which links it to a note in the next bar.

Accordion. An instrument with hand-operated bellows that force air to vibrate metal reeds. The sound is controlled from small buttons on both sides of the bellows, although piano accordions have a small vertical keyboard instead of buttons on the right-hand side. The instrument is often used in folk music.

Added 6th chord. A chord formed from a **triad** plus a 6th above the root (e.g. C–E–G–A).

Alap. The slow introductory section in a performance of a north Indian **rag**. The soloist introduces the notes of the rag in **free time**, accompanied by a **drone**.

Alto. A low female voice. Alto parts can also be performed by men singing **falsetto**.

Alto clef. A **clef** which indicates that middle C is on the middle line of a **stave**, used for viola parts.

Anacrusis. One or more weak-beat notes before the first strong beat of a phrase. Often called a 'pick up' in jazz and pop music.

Arco. An instruction for a string player to use the bow, usually after playing **pizzicato**.

Arpeggio. A chord played as successive rather than simultaneous notes.

Articulation. The precise way in which notes are performed, such as **legato** (smoothly), **staccato** (detached) or **accented**.

Atonal. Western music that is not in a **key** or a **mode** and that is often dissonant.

Augmentation. A proportionate increase in the note lengths of a melody, e.g. when two quavers and a crotchet are augmented they become two crotchets and a minim. The opposite of augmentation is **diminution**.

Augmented chord. A chord consisting of two major 3rds stacked above each other (such as C–E–G♯).

Backbeat. A term used in pop music to describe accenting the normally weak second and fourth beats in ₄ time.

Backing vocals. Sung parts that accompany the main singer in a pop song. Sometimes labelled in scores as *bvox*.

Balafon. A west-African **xylophone** with wooden bars and resonators made from bottle-shaped gourds.

Balanced phrasing. *See* **periodic phrasing**.

Bansuri. A large bamboo flute with finger holes but no keys. One of the oldest Indian instruments.

Bara. A small drum from west Africa, made from a gourd, with a head of thin goatskin.

Baroque. The period between about 1600 and 1750, and its music.

Bass. 1. A low male voice. **2.** The lowest-sounding part of a composition, whether for voices or instruments.

Bayan. The larger of the two drums in Indian **tabla**.

Bhajan. A Hindu devotional song from north India.

Bhangra. A **fusion** of western pop styles with traditional Indian music from the Punjab region.

Blue note. *See* **Blues scale**.

Blues. A musical **genre** which evolved in the USA, drawing on west-African traditions that arrived via the slave trade. Typical features include **blue notes**, **call-and-response** patterns and the use of the **twelve-bar blues** progression. The words of a blues are often (but not invariably) melancholy, dealing with the problems and trials of life. The blues has been a major influence on many types of popular music and jazz.

Blues scale. A scale in which some degrees, typically the third and seventh, are up to a semitone lower than their pitch in a major scale. These are known as blue notes.

Bouzouki. A plucked string instrument of the lute family usually associated with the music of Greece, but used by a number of Celtic folk musicians in recent decades.

BPM. Abbreviation of beats per minute. A precise indication of **tempo**.

Break. In pop and jazz, an instrumental solo (usually improvised).

Bridge. 1. A contrasting passage in a pop song. **2.** The structure on stringed instruments that supports the strings and carries their vibrations to the body of the instrument.

Broken chord. A chord in which the notes are sounded individually in patterns, rather than together. An **arpeggio** is a type of broken chord.

Cadence. A point of repose at the end of a phrase, often harmonised by two chords. *See* **imperfect cadence**, **modal cadence**, **perfect cadence** and **plagal cadence**.

Call-and-response. A performing technique in which a soloist sings or plays a phrase to which a larger group responds with an answering phrase.

Canon. A **contrapuntal** device in which a melody in one part is later repeated note for note in another part, while the melody in the first part continues to unfold.

Cantabile. Italian for singable. A term sometimes used to describe an instrumental melody that is, or should be performed, like a song.

Cell. Another term for a **motif**. It most often refers to a small group of notes or a short rhythm in some 20th-century modernist styles.

Celtic fusion. A blend of traditional styles from Celtic areas (such as Scotland, Ireland or Wales) with features of modern pop music.

Chakradar tihai. Three **tihais** in succession in north Indian music.

Chamber orchestra. A small orchestra.

Changes. A term used in jazz for a chord **progression**.

Chikari. The drone strings on a **sitar**.

Choir. A group of singers performing together, whether in **unison** or in parts.

Chord. Three or more pitches sounded simultaneously, although just two notes can often imply a chord by their context. In a **broken chord** or **arpeggio**, the notes are sounded separately but in close proximity to each other.

Chord progression. *See* **progression**.

Chordal texture. A **homophonic** texture that consists mainly of block chords.

Chorus. 1. A body of singers who perform together. **2.** The section of music that follows the verse in **verse-and-chorus** form.

Chromatic. Notes that don't belong to the current **key**. The opposite of **diatonic**.

Circle of 5ths. A series of chords whose **roots** are each a 5th lower than the previous chord (e.g. E–A–D–G–C). In practice the bass usually alternates between falling a 5th and rising a 4th, which produces a less angular line from the same set of pitches.

Classical. 1. Music written between roughly 1750 and 1825. **2.** In a wider sense, any music that is related to specific historic traditions, such as Indian classical music. **3.** In a still broader sense, any type of music that is regarded as 'art music' rather than pop, folk or jazz – so styles as varied as Baroque, Romantic, Expressionist and Postmodernist can all be described in a very general way as 'classical'.

Clef. A symbol defining the pitches of the notes on a **stave**.

Closing section. The final part of the **exposition** or **recapitulation** in **sonata form**.

Cluster chord. A chord made from a group of adjacent pitches, such as E, F♯, G, A and B.

Coda. A closing section at the end of a movement, song or other piece.

Codetta. A short **coda**, used to conclude a section within a longer movement.

Col legno. An instruction for a string player to use the wood, rather than the hair, of the bow.

Compound time. A **metre** in which each beat can be divided into three shorter notes of equal length. The opposite of **simple time**.

Concord. *See* **Consonance and dissonance**.

Consonance and dissonance. The relative stability (consonance) or instability (dissonance) of two or more notes sounded together. Consonant intervals and chords are called concords. Dissonant intervals and chords are called discords.

Continuo. A bass part in **Baroque** music from which accompanying chords (often indicated by figures) are improvised on a harmony instrument, such as a **harpsichord**, organ or lute. The part is also usually played on one of more bass instruments, such as cello, bassoon or double bass.

Contrapuntal. A texture that uses **counterpoint**.

Contrary motion. Simultaneous melodic lines whose pitches move in opposite directions.

Countermelody. A new melody that occurs simultaneously with a melody that has been heard before.

Counterpoint. Two or more different melodies sounding together.

Crescendo. A gradual increase in loudness, often abbreviated to *cresc*. The opposite of **diminuendo**.

Cross rhythm. A rhythm that conflicts with the regular pattern of beats, or the combination of two conflicting rhythms within a single beat (e.g. a **triplet** of quavers against two normal quavers).

Dayan. The smaller of the two drums in Indian **tabla**.

Degree. The name or number of a particular note in a scale in relation to its home note (which is described as the tonic or first degree).

Development. The central section of **sonata form**. The term is also used more generally to describe the manipulation and transformation of motifs and themes in any sort of music.

Dialogue. A texture in which motifs are exchanged between different parts without the use of **imitation**.

Diatonic. Notes that belong to the current **key**. The opposite of **chromatic**.

Digital delay. An electronic effect in which a sound is replayed after a very short delay. Often it will be played back a number of times in quick succession, giving the effect of a repeating, decaying echo.

Diminished 7th. 1. An interval notated as a 7th that is one semitone smaller than a minor 7th, such as E to D♭. **2.** A chord based on this interval, and made up of superimposed minor 3rds (or their enharmonic equivalents), for example E–G–B♭–D♭.

Diminuendo. A gradual decrease in loudness, often abbreviated to *dim*. The opposite of **crescendo**.

Diminution. A proportionate reduction in the note-lengths of a melody, e.g. when two quavers and a crotchet are diminished they become two semiquavers and a quaver. The opposite of diminution is **augmentation**.

Discord. *See* **Consonance and dissonance**.

Dissonance. *See* **Consonance and dissonance**.

Djembe. A goblet-shaped west-African drum played with the hands.

Dominant. The fifth degree of a major or minor scale (e.g. D is the dominant in G major).

Dominant 7th chord. A **triad** on the dominant (the fifth degree of the scale) plus a diatonic 7th above its **root**. In C major the dominant chord consists of G, B and D. The dominant 7th chord is G, B, D and F.

Dominant preparation. A section, usually at the end of the **development** in a sonata-form movement, that prepares for the return of the home key by emphasising the **dominant** chord or dominant key.

Dorian mode. A scale that can be found by playing an octave of white notes on the piano from D to D. It can be transposed to start on any note. For example, a dorian scale on C is C–D–E♭–F–G–A–B♭–C.

Dotted rhythm. A two-note pattern consisting of a dotted note followed by a note one-third of its length. Several such patterns in succession create a distinctive, jerky rhythm. *See also* **Scotch snap**.

Double sharp. A sign (𝄪) that indicates a pitch two semitones above the natural note. For example, F𝄪 is the same pitch as G.

Doubling. The performance of the same melody, in **unison** or in **octaves**, by two or more musicians at the same time.

Drone. A bass note that sounds throughout a passage of music, similar to a continuous **pedal**. Drone strings on instruments such as the sitar can only sound single notes and are used for playing drones.

Dunun. A west-African bass drum, similar to the **djembe**, but with a more cylindrical shape.

Dynamics. The varying levels of loudness or softness in music.

Enharmonic equivalents. Two notes or keys which sound the same but are notated differently, such as C♯ and D♭.

Ensemble (pronounced *on-som-b'l*). A group of performers.

Episode. A distinct section within a **movement**.

Esraj. A bowed string instrument from north India with **frets**, four main strings, and a number of **sympathetic** and **drone** strings.

Ethnomusicologist. A scholar who specialises in the study of musical traditions, particularly those outside the influence of western music.

Exposition. The first section in **sonata form**, during which the main ideas are presented.

Expressionism. An early 20th-century style characterised by the expression of inner fears and obsessions, often through distorted or violent artistic ideas.

Fall off. In jazz and pop music, a short downward slide at the end of a note.

Falsetto. A technique of singing notes higher than the normal top register.

Fiddle. A common name for the violin in folk music.

Fill. In pop music and jazz, a brief improvised flourish (often on drums) to fill the gap between the end of one phrase and the beginning of another.

First subject. The main theme in a **sonata-form** movement.

Flanging. An electronic effect, sometimes used with electric guitars, that creates a distinctive sweeping sound. Originally it was produced by slowing down one tape recorder in relation to another by pressing on the flange of the tape spool.

Flat. 1. A sign (♭) which lowers the pitch of a note by a semitone. One or more flat signs at the beginning of a stave make a **key signature**. Each flat in a key signature lowers notes with the same letter name by a semitone throughout the rest of the stave. A flat inserted immediately in front of a note is an **accidental**, and its effect only lasts until the end of the bar. **2.** An adjective describing a note that is sung or played at a lower pitch than it should be.

Folk-rock. A **fusion** of rock music with elements of traditional folk music.

Forte. An instruction to play loudly. Usually shown by the symbol *f*.

Fortissimo. An instruction to play very loudly. Usually shown by the symbol *ff*.

Free time. Music without a regular beat.

Frets. Raised strips running at right angles across the fingerboard of instruments such as the guitar, lute and sitar, used to locate the required pitches on each string.

Fusion. Music in which two or more styles are blended together, such as **bhangra**.

Gat. In north Indian music, a pre-composed idea that the soloist announces and then improvises upon during the performance of a **rag**.

General pause. A total silence in a piece for a number of performers.

Genre (pronounced *jon-ruh*). A category of compositions, such as symphonies or gospels songs.

Ghost notes. In jazz and rock music, notes that are played extremely quietly and with very little tone.

Glissando. A slide from one pitch to another.

Grace note. An ornamental note printed in small type near to a principal melody note.

Harmon mute. A trumpet mute commonly used for producing 'wah-wah' effects. Miles Davis often used a Harmon mute with its stem removed, producing a rounder and very characteristic tone.

Harmonic. On string instruments (including the harp and guitar), a very high and pure sound produced by placing a finger on a string very lightly before plucking or bowing.

Harmonic progression. *See* **progression**.

Harmonic rhythm. The rate at which chords change. Also known as the harmonic pace. This could be on every beat, every other beat, every bar, every two bars – there are many possibilities and often the harmonic rhythm varies throughout a piece.

Harmonic sequence. A chord **progression** that is immediately repeated at a different pitch.

Harpsichord. A keyboard instrument on which strings are plucked when keys are pressed, used particularly in **Baroque** music.

Hauptstimme. German for 'principal part'.

Head arrangement. A jazz performance that consists of improvised variations on a memorised chord **progression**.

Hemiola. A rhythmic device in which two groups of three beats (*strong–weak–weak, strong–weak–weak*) are performed as three groups of two (*strong–weak, strong–weak, strong–weak*).

Heterophonic. A texture made up of a simple tune and a more elaborate version of it performed at the same time.

Hexachord. A set of six pitches (not necessarily a **scale**).

Hexatonic scale. A scale of six pitches.

High-pass filter. An electronic effect used to remove the lower frequencies of a signal.

Highlife. A west-African pop-music genre, created from a **fusion** of local drums and rhythms with western guitars and dance-band instruments.

Homophonic. A texture in which one part (usually the highest) has the melodic interest, which the other parts accompany.

Idiomatic. A style that is characteristic of (and feels natural for) the instruments and/or voices concerned.

Imitation. A **contrapuntal** device in which a melody in one part is copied a few notes later in a different part (and often at a different pitch) while the melody in the first part continues. Only the opening notes of the original melody need to be copied for this effect to be heard. If parts exchange ideas without any overlap, the texture is described as **dialogue**, not imitation. *See also* **canon**.

Imperfect cadence. Almost any chord followed by chord V (the **dominant** chord) at the end of a phrase.

Improvisation. A performance in which most or all of the music is made up on the spot.

Instrumental. 1. Music performed by instruments, without the use of voices. **2.** A section in a song that features instruments rather than singing.

Interlude. Music played between sections of a longer piece.

Interval. The distance between two pitches, including both of the pitches that form the interval. So, in the scale of C major, the interval between the first and second notes is a 2nd (C–D), the interval between the first and third notes is a 3rd (C–D–E), and so on.

Intro. Abbreviation of 'introduction' – a preparatory section before the main part of a composition.

Inversion. 1. The process of turning a melody upside down so that every interval of the original is maintained but moves in the opposite direction. **2.** A chord is inverted when a note other than the **root** is sounded in the bass. **3.** An interval is inverted when one of the two notes is placed in a different octave, so that instead of being below the other note it is above it (or vice versa).

Jhala. Lively rhythmic playing that marks the final section in the performance of a north Indian **rag**.

Keeping time. An expression used mainly in jazz drumming to mean playing a simple rhythm as a guide part, against which other musicians can improvise more complex, syncopated lines.

Key. The relationship between pitches in which one particular note called the **tonic** acts as the home or key note. Its pitch determines the key of the music. So a composition in which C is the tonic is in the key of C. It will be in C major if it uses the notes of the major scale on C, or C minor if it uses the notes of the minor scale.

Key signature. One or more flat signs, or one or more sharp signs, placed immediately after a clef at the beginning of a stave. The effect of each sign lasts throughout the stave and applies to all notes with the same letter name.

Kora. A long-necked harp used in west-African music.

Layering. The process of constructing a composition in layers (e.g. bass part first, then a melody, then individual accompaniment patterns), rather like a multi-track recording in which each track is completed before another is added.

Leap. An interval greater than a tone between consecutive notes of a melody. The opposite of a **step**.

Legato. Notes that are performed smoothly, without gaps between them. The opposite of **staccato**.

Looping. The process of repeating a **sample** a number of times. The term dates from the days of tape recorders, when a short piece of tape was made into a loop so that it could constantly repeat. These days, computer software is used.

Lute. A fretted plucked string instrument.

Lyrics. The words of a popular song or the words of the vocal items in musicals.

Major and minor. Greater and lesser. A major interval is greater than a minor interval by a **semitone**. The interval between the first and third degrees of a major scale is four semitones, one semitone greater than the interval between the same degrees in a minor scale.

Meend. A **glissando** between notes in north Indian music.

Melismatic. A vocal style in which several notes are sung to the same syllable. The opposite of **syllabic**.

Melody and accompaniment. A type of **homophonic** texture in which the accompaniment has some independence from the tune.

Metre. The repeating patterns of strong and weak beats that underpin the rhythms of many types of music.

Metrical displacement. The repetition of an idea in a different part of the bar, so that what were previously accented notes become unaccented, and vice versa. A technique used in some **Minimalist** music.

Mezzo. Italian for half. The instruction *mezzo forte*, usually shown by the symbol *mf*, means moderately loud, while *mezzo piano* (*mp*) means moderately soft.

Microtone. An interval smaller than a **semitone**.

MIDI. Musical Instrument Digital Interface: a system for exchanging music performance data between suitably equipped computers and/or electronic instruments.

Minimalism. A musical style of the late 20th century. It was a reaction against the complexities of Modernism and is characterised by the varied repetition of simple rhythmic, melodic and harmonic ideas.

Minor. *See* **Major and minor**.

Minuet. An elegant dance in ¾ time, found mainly in music of the Baroque and Classical periods.

Mixolydian mode. A scale that can be found by playing an octave of white notes on the piano from G to G. It can be transposed to start on any note. For example, a Mixolydian scale on C is C–D–E–F–G–A–B♭–C.

Modal. Music based on a **mode** rather than on a key.

Modal cadence. A cadence-like progression of two chords in modal music.

Mode. A scale of seven pitches. Major and minor scales are types of modes, but the term mode is usually reserved for other types of scales, such as the **Mixolydian mode** and the **Dorian mode**.

Modernism. A cultural movement of the early 20th century that rejected tradition in order to create new forms of expression that in music are often complex and dissonant. *See also* **Postmodernism**.

Modulation. The process of changing key.

Mono. *See* **Stereo**.

Monophonic. A texture consisting of a single unaccompanied melody, which may be performed by a soloist or by many people performing in unison or in octaves.

Motif. A short, distinctive melody or rhythm that is used in various ways to form much longer passages of music.

Movement. An independent section in a longer piece of music.

Multi-track recording. A recording technique whereby several tracks of sound are recorded independently but can be played back together.

Musical. A large-scale composition in a popular style, written for the theatre and involving staged drama sung to an instrumental accompaniment.

Natural. A sign (♮) which cancels a previous accidental or which cancels the effect of one of the sharps or flats in a key signature.

Natural horn. A horn without valves and thus limited to a certain selection of notes determined by the length of its tubing.

Nebenstimme. German for 'secondary melody'.

Ninth chord. A **triad** plus the notes that are a 7th and a 9th above the **root**.

Note addition. A process in **Minimalist** music in which notes are added in stages to build up a repeating idea.

Octave. The interval between the first and last degrees of an eight-note major or minor scale. The two notes forming this interval are 12 semitones apart and have the same letter name.

Octave displacement. The process of moving a note of a melody into a different octave, producing a very angular line.

On-beat and off-beat notes. Notes performed on strong and weak beats of the bar respectively.

Opera. A large-scale composition for the theatre, involving staged drama sung to an instrumental accompaniment.

Oral tradition. Music handed down from one generation to another by listening and memorising, rather than by reading notation. Note that oral refers to the mouth (implying that the tradition is handed down by spoken instructions) and is not the same as aural (which means by ear), even though aural might be considered a more appropriate term.

Oratorio. A large-scale composition for solo voices, choir and orchestra, usually on a Biblical subject, but intended for concert performance.

Orchestra. A large group of instrumentalists, usually including string players, and often woodwind, brass and percussion sections as well. A full size symphony orchestra usually has at least 60 players. Smaller groups are often called **chamber orchestras**. A string orchestra consists only of violins, violas, cellos and double basses.

Organ. **1.** A large, mechanically-blown wind instrument with sets of pipes controlled by one or more keyboards, often including a pedalboard played by the organist's feet. **2.** An electronic instrument, originally invented to imitate the sound of a pipe organ, but which now often includes a wide selection of other sounds and effects.

Ornaments. Notes, often indicated by special signs, which decorate the main notes of a melody. *See* **grace note** and **trill**.

Ostinato. A rhythmic, melodic or harmonic pattern repeated many times in succession. Often called a **riff** in pop music.

Pakhawaj. A long cylindrical drum used in north Indian music. It has skins at both ends and is played in a horizontal position with the palms and fingers.

Pan. A control that determines the position (from extreme left to extreme right) of a sound in a stereo field.

Parallel chords. A succession of identical (or very similar) chords that move in the same direction.

Parallel intervals. A succession of identical (or very similar) intervals that move in the same direction.

Parallel keys. Two keys that share the same **tonic**, for example, C major and C minor. They can also be described as the tonic major and tonic minor keys respectively.

Pause. An extension of a note or rest beyond its normal length, causing a temporary interruption of the beat.

Pedal. **1.** A sustained or repeated note sounded against changing harmony. **2.** A foot-operated lever on instruments such as the piano, organ and harp.

Pentatonic scale. A scale of five pitches.

Perfect cadence. Chord V (the **dominant** chord) followed by chord I (the **tonic** chord) at the end of phrase.

Periodic phrasing. Paired phrases of similar length that sound like a question followed by an answer. Sometimes called 'balanced phrasing', it is a typical feature of music in the Classical period.

Phrase. A section of a melody that makes a statement, although not necessarily a complete statement, and that often ends with a **cadence**.

Phrase structure. The length and pattern of melodic phrases that make up a section of music. For example, the verse of a song might have a structure of four four-bar phrases in the pattern ABAC.

Pianissimo. An instruction to play very softy, usually shown by the symbol *pp*.

Piano. **1.** A keyboard instrument in which strings are sounded by felt-covered hammers. **2.** An instruction to play softly, usually shown by the symbol *p*.

Pitch. The height or depth of a note or series of notes.

Pizzicato. An instruction for the player of a bowed string instrument to pluck the strings. *See also* **Arco**.

Plagal cadence. Chord IV (the **subdominant** chord) followed by chord I (the **tonic** chord) at the end of a phrase.

Polyphonic. A texture made up of two or more different melodies sounding together. Today the terms polyphony and counterpoint are used interchangeably, so a polyphonic texture is the same as a **contrapuntal** one.

Postmodernism. A late-20th century reaction to the complex, dissonant **modernism** of much music earlier in the century. Postmodernism is characterised by simple, but novel structures and a return to mainly diatonic harmony. One of the best known Postmodernist styles is **Minimalism**.

Pre-chorus. In a pop song, a **bridge** between the verse and chorus that prepares for the arrival of the chorus.

Primary triads. The **triads** on the first, fourth and fifth degrees of a scale.

Programme music. Music that is intended to tell a story or suggest a specific image.

Progression. A succession of chords, such as a **cadence**, a **circle of 5ths** or a **twelve-bar blues**. In jazz, a chord progression that forms the basis for improvised variations is known as the **changes**.

Pulse. The beat in a piece of music.

Rag (pronounced *rhag*). A pattern of ascending and descending notes used as the basis for melodic improvisation in Indian classical music. Also used as the name for an improvised performance based on these notes.

Range. The distance between the lowest and highest notes of a melody or composition, or the distance between the highest and lowest notes that can be played on an instrument or sung by a vocalist.

Recapitulation. The final section of **sonata form**.

Refrain. A phrase in a song that returns at the end of each line or verse of the text.

Register. A particular part of the range of a voice or instrument, such as a high register or a low register.

Related keys. Keys whose scales have most of their notes in common.

Relative major, Relative minor. Keys that share the same key signature, such as G major and E minor.

Rest. A silence within a musical line.

Resultant melody. A new melody that emerges when two or more different melodies are played at the same time.

Reverb. Abbreviation of reverberation. The complex series of reflections that occurs when sound is made in an enclosed space. Digitally produced reverb is often added to recordings.

Rhythm. The patterns produced by notes and rests of various lengths.

Riff. In jazz, pop and rock, a short melodic pattern repeated many times in succession. *See also* **Ostinato**.

Ritornello. An opening instrumental section in Baroque music, parts of which return in related keys during the rest of the movement.

Rock ballad. A song in a fairly slow tempo, usually about love, accompanied by a rock band.

Romantic. In music, the period between about 1825 and 1900.

Rondo form. A musical structure in which a main section alternates with contrasting sections, creating a pattern such as ABACA.

Root. The note that corresponds with the letter-name of a chord. For example, the root of a chord of C is always the note C, no matter which of its three pitches (C, E or G) is the bass note.

Rounded binary form. A musical structure in two main parts, in which material from the opening returns towards the end, transposed to the tonic key if necessary (ABA[1]). It differs from **ternary form** in having a B section that leads without a break into the abbreviated repeat of the opening material.

Rubato. Refers to creating an expressive rhythm by making some notes fractionally longer than notated, at the expense of others that are made fractionally shorter. A common performance technique in some types of Romantic music.

Sam. In north Indian music, the first beat of a **tal**.

Sample. A short segment taken from an existing recording to include in a new composition. It can be manipulated in various ways by computer software, changing features such as its length and/or pitch. Samples are usually repeated a number of times – a process known as **looping**.

Sarangi. In north Indian music, a fretless bowed instrument with three main strings and a range of other strings that vibrate in sympathy with them.

Sarod. A north-Indian plucked string instrument, like a **sitar** but shorter and without any frets.

Scale. A collection of pitches arranged in order from low to high. Melodies based on segments of scales are described as scalic.

Score. A document representing how a piece of music should be played or how it was played.

Scotch snap. A two-note pattern that reverses the normal order of a **dotted rhythm** because the short note comes before the longer dotted note, producing a distinctive snappy effect.

Second subject. The subsidiary theme in a **sonata-form** movement.

Second Viennese School. The name given to a group of 20th-century composers who worked in the Austrian city of Vienna for at least part of their lives.

Semitone. Half of a tone: the smallest interval in common use in western music.

Septuplet. Seven notes played in the time of four of the same value.

Sequence. 1. The immediate repetition of a motif or phrase in the same part but at a different pitch. A chord progression can be treated in the same way (*see* **Harmonic sequence**). **2.** Performance data stored by a **sequencer**.

Sequencer. Computer software (or a purpose-built electronic device) for the input, editing and playback of music performance data using **MIDI**.

Seventh chord. A **triad** plus a note a 7th above the **root**.

Sextet. A group of six performers and music written for such a group.

Sharp. 1. A sign (♯) that raises the pitch of a note by a semitone. One or more sharp signs at the beginning of a stave make a key signature. Each sharp in a key signature raises notes with the same letter name by a semitone throughout the rest of the stave. A sharp inserted immediately in front of a note is an accidental, and its effect only lasts until the end of the bar. **2.** An adjective describing a note that is sung or played at a higher pitch than it should be.

Shruti box. An originally mechanical but now electronic device that can be used to sound a drone in north Indian music.

Simple time. A **metre** in which each beat can be divided into two shorter notes of equal length. The opposite of **compound time**.

Sitar A north-Indian plucked string instrument with moveable frets, and a number of melody strings, **drone** strings (called **chikari**) and **sympathetic** strings.

Solo. 1. A performance by a single musician. **2.** A piece or passage of music written for a single musician.

Sonata form. The most common structure for the first movement (and often other movements) of sonatas, symphonies and other types of music in the Classical period and later. Ideas are presented in the first section, called the exposition, extended in a central section called the development, and return in a final section called the recapitulation.

Soprano. A high female or unbroken boy's voice.

Sounding pitch (also known as concert pitch). The note(s) actually sounded by an instrument whose part is written at some different pitch. For example, the bass guitar sounds an octave lower than written, so when the player plucks middle C, the sounding pitch is an octave below middle C.

Staccato. Notes that are performed shorter than printed so that each is detached from its neighbours. Often shown in notation by dots above or below the notes affected. The opposite of **legato**.

Stave. A set of parallel lines on which pitches are notated.

Step. An interval of a tone or semitone between adjacent notes in a melody. The opposite of a **leap**.

Stereo. Abbreviation of stereophonic. A system that captures and replays sound on two independent but synchronised channels. This mimics the effect of listening to live music, where slight differences between what we hear with each of our ears helps give depth and perspective to the sound. Before stereophony became widely available in the late 1950s, recordings were monaural (often described as 'mono') with all of the sound emerging from just one source such as a single loudspeaker.

Sub-bass. A very low bass part in electronic dance music and related styles, which is amplified so that it is felt more as a series of thuds than as specific pitches.

Subdominant. The fourth degree of a major or minor scale (for example C in the key of G major).

Subject. A theme that plays an important part in a composition.

Swarmandal. A harp-like plucked string instrument used in north Indian music. It can have up to 36 strings which are stretched over a flat sounding board.

Swing quavers, swung quavers. In jazz and some types of pop music, the division of the beat into pairs of notes in which the first is a little longer than the second.

Syllabic. A vocal style in which each syllable is set to its own note. The opposite of **melismatic**.

Sympathetic string. A string that is not played but that vibrates 'in sympathy' when similar notes are played on other strings.

Symphony. A large-scale orchestral work, most commonly in four movements.

Syncopation. The effect created when accented notes are sounded off the beat or on weak beats, often with rests on some of the strong beats.

Synthesiser. An electronic instrument that can produce and modify sound. It can be used to imitate other musical instruments and to produce non-musical sounds.

System. A group of **staves** in a score that are played simultaneously.

Tab. An abbreviation of tablature – a way of writing music, usually for guitar, as small diagrams that show finger positions on the instrument, sometimes accompanied by an indication of the rhythm to play.

Tabla. In Indian music, a pair of drums played with hands and fingers by a single performer. The smaller of the two drums is called the dayan, and the larger is the bayan.

Tan. The term for a fast scale-like passage in north-Indian music.

Tal (pronounced *tahl*). A recurring pattern of beats in Indian music that forms the rhythmic basis for **improvisation**.

Talking drum. An African drum with various local names and forms, although almost always an hour-glass shape with a waist that is narrower than its ends. It has considerable tonal variety depending on where it is struck and how the tension on the drum head is varied, making it possible to mimic the patterns of speech.

Techno. A style of 1980s sequencer-based electronic dance music, with few or no vocals. Its main emphasis is on intricate drum tracks, samples and effects, rather than on melodic material, chord changes or strong bass parts.

Tempo. The speed of the underlying beat.

Tenor. A male voice higher than a **bass**, but lower than an **alto**.

Ternary form. A three-part structure (ABA) in which the first and last sections are similar while the central section forms a contrast. *See also* **rounded binary form**.

Terraced dynamics. Clear contrasts, rather than gradual changes, between loud and soft sections. A feature often found in **Baroque** music.

Texture. The relationship between the various simultaneous lines in a piece of music. See page 181.

Theme. A musical idea (usually a melody) that plays an important role in a piece of music.

Tie. A curved line joining two or more consecutive notes of the same pitch. It indicates that they are to be performed as a single note lasting for the total length of all of the notes that are tied together.

Tihai. A short pattern in north Indian music that is played three times, often cutting across the normal accents of the **tal** but ending on the **sam**, played to mark the end of a section.

Timbre (pronounced *tam-bruh*). Tone colour. The clarinet has a different timbre to the trumpet, but the clarinet also has different timbres in various parts of its range. Timbre can also be affected by the way an instrument is played, for example by using a mute or plucking a string instead of using the bow.

Time signature. Two numbers, one on top of the other, on a stave. The upper number usually indicates the number of beats per bar and the lower number indicates the time value of the beat.

Tonality. The use of major and/or minor keys in music, and their relationship. For exam purposes, tonality also refers to the terms **modal** and **atonal**.

Tone. 1. An interval of two semitones, for example C–D. **2.** The **timbre** of a particular instrument or voice.

Tonic. The first degree of a major or minor scale.

Tonic major, tonic minor. Two keys that share the same tonic, for example C major and C minor. They can also be described as the parallel major and parallel minor keys.

Transcription. A score made from a recorded performance or from a different system of notation. The term is also used for a written adaptation of a piece for different performing resources.

Transformation. A compositional technique in which a melody, rhythm or chord progression is changed so that it takes on a new character, while still remaining recognisable. The process was used by a number of Romantic composers and is common in **Minimalist** music.

Transition. A passage linking two sections of a composition, such as the first and second subjects in **sonata form**. Usually called a **bridge** in jazz and pop music.

Transpose. The process of writing or performing music at a higher or lower pitch than the original.

Tremolo. The continuous, rapid repetition of either a single pitch or two alternating pitches.

Triad. A chord of three pitches consisting of a bass note and the notes a 3rd and a 5th above it.

Trill. An ornament (often shown as *tr*) consisting of the rapid alternation of two pitches a step apart.

Trio. 1. Music for three solo performers. **2.** Music for a single performer written throughout in three contrapuntal parts. **3.** The middle section of the minuet–trio–minuet (or scherzo–trio–sherzo) group that forms the third movement of many classical symphonies and string quartets.

Triplet. A group of three notes of equal length played in the time of two of the same time value.

Tritone. An interval of three whole tones, e.g. F–B.

Tutti. A passage in which all or most of the members of an ensemble are playing.

Twelve-bar blues. A chord progression that originated in blues songs, which has been widely adopted in jazz and pop music. It consists of three four-bar phrases and typically has one chord per bar in the pattern I–I–I–I, IV–IV–I–I, V–IV–I–I, although there are many variants, including adding 7ths to any of the basic triads.

Uilleann pipes. A type of Irish bagpipe, originally known as union pipes, now used in many kinds of folk music. The air supply comes from elbow-operated bellows. The range of notes is wider than the more familiar Great Highland bagpipes of Scotland, and the tone is sweeter.

Unison. The effect of two or more people performing the same note or melody. The result of everyone in a choir singing the same melody is often described as unison, even if the men are actually singing an octave below the women.

Variations. A musical structure in which a theme is repeated, each time with alterations to one or more of its original elements.

Verse and chorus. A standard form used in popular song in which the verses usually have similar music but different words. Each verse is followed by a contrasting chorus in which both the words and the music are usually the same on every appearance. There may also be an introduction at the start, a coda at the end, and instrumental sections in the middle to provide variety.

Vibrato. Small, rapid fluctuations in pitch used by singers and players of string and wind instruments to give warmth and expression to the tone.

Virtuoso. A performer of outstanding technical ability.

Vocalisation. Wordless singing, often to a vowel sound such as 'ah'.

Vocal tenor clef. A treble clef with a small figure 8 attached to its bottom loop, indicating that the music sounds an octave lower than it would if written in a normal treble clef.

Waltz. A ballroom dance in $\frac{3}{4}$ time that became widely popular in the 19th century.

Whole-tone scale. A scale in which every note is one whole-tone step above or below its neighbours.

Word painting. The illustration in music of the meaning (or suggestion) of particular words or phrases in a text. For example, the use of a rising interval for the word 'rejoice' or a discord for the word 'pain'.

Word setting. The way in which notes are allocated to the syllables of the text in vocal music. The style of setting may be **syllabic**, **melismatic** or a combination of both, and it may include examples of **word painting**.

World music. A term often (if rather generally) used to refer to any type of traditional or folk music, sometimes including fusion styles that result from a blend of local traditions with outside influences.

Xylophone. A percussion instrument in which beaters are used to strike a set of tuned wooden bars.